DATE DUE

Burt Franklin: Research & Source Works Series #180
(Essays in Literature & Criticism #7)

THE ENGLISH CHRONICLE PLAY

THE ENGLISH

CHRONICLE PLAY

A STUDY IN THE POPULAR HISTORICAL
LITERATURE ENVIRONING
SHAKESPEARE

BY

FELIX E. SCHELLING

Burt Franklin: Research & Source Works Series #180
(Essays in Literature & Criticism #7)

Burt Franklin
New York, N. Y.

Published By
BURT FRANKLIN
235 East 44th Street
New York, N.Y. 10017

ORIGINALLY PUBLISHED
New York 1902

Reprinted 1968

This work has been reprinted on
long-life paper

Printed in U.S.A.

PREFACE

In the following pages an attempt has been made to tell the history of one of the many and various strands which, twisted and interwoven, form the brilliant and heterogeneous Elizabethan Drama. There is always a danger in thus seeking to separate what in reality is part of an integral whole ; for not only was the English Chronicle Play deeply influenced by the wealth of literature in other forms which dealt with the general subject of English history, but it influenced and was in turn affected by many other varieties of drama that flourished simultaneously with it. None the less the Chronicle Play can be treated independently with greater justice than any other form of the drama ; for whatever the superficial influences upon it, it retained from first to last a character essentially national and English.

The most potent influences on the English drama when Marlowe, Shakespeare and Fletcher held the stage were the spirit of culture which centered in the court and emanated from Italy, and the spirit of learning, the seats of which were appropriately the Universities and the Inns of Court. The spirit of Italian culture was earliest typified in the drama by the court plays of Lyly the Euphuist, and later combined with

v

other influences in the great romantic drama of Marlowe and Shakespeare. The spirit of learning first became manifest in the regular drama in plays of the type
of *Gorboduc*, and was further exemplified in the tragedies and comedies of modified classical tone of Jonson,
Chapman, Daniel and others. Neither of these general
types was wholly unaffected by the other, especially in
the many forms which both later evolved. A third
master influence in the development of the English
drama has been by some unwisely denied. This is
the English national spirit, the spirit which, from the
days of the early sacred drama to the present time,
has animated those scenes which seek the simple dramatic representation of everyday life or strive to make
real the deeds of great historical personages of the
past. When all has been said for the effect of the
study of Seneca, the imitation of Plautus, pilferings
from Italy and the inspiration of romance, it is this
national fiber which remains the heart and soul of the
Elizabethan stage, whether displayed in overpowering
tragedy like *Arden of Feversham*, in hearty comedies
such as *The Merry Wives of Windsor*, or in the long
series of plays depicting the history of English kings
which for years disputed with the romantic drama the
supremacy of the stage. This is not the place in which
to trace these relations. It is sufficient here to affirm
that the impulse under which the English Chronicle
Play developed was distinctively national and little in-

fluenced by artistic selection of material or by scholarly avoidance of incongruity and anachronism. The past was frankly translated into the terms of the familiar present. The life of this drama was its ingenuous fidelity to the actualities of everyday life. In these qualities consisted largely its power to move the men of its day.

That Shakespeare should form the center of any phase of study of the age of Elizabeth needs neither justification nor excuse. Of the thirty-seven plays commonly included in editions of his works ten concern the lives and deeds of English sovereigns and events of their reigns, and three others—*King Lear*, *Macbeth* and *Cymbeline*—are set in legendary British times. It is thus apparent that more than a third of Shakespeare's activity as a dramatist was devoted to the Chronicle Play. Nowhere is his preeminence over all his contemporaries at once so striking and so complete. The only approach to his stately procession of English kings from John to Henry VIII. is a single play of Marlowe, another of Ford and a few disjointed scenes of Heywood. And yet nowhere is Shakespeare discerned to be so fully and so logically the product of his age; building on what he found, essaying no miracles, unerring master of every possibility of his art, yet contravening no natural law, reaching what had seemed the unattainable not by the cataclysm of irresistible genius and inspired haphazard, but by the orderly processes of growth.

The foundations of the following study are in the
plays themselves and in the several contemporary
records of the drama, chief among them Henslowe's
indispensable *Diary* and the registers of the Stationers'
Company. The author is not one of those that seek
to belittle the eminent services of our elder English
dramatic critics. Malone, Dyce and Gifford followed
with respect, Lamb and Coleridge with enthusiasm
and Collier at all times with circumspection are guides
whom none can afford to despise. Admirable too is
the assiduous industry and learning with which scholars
like Klein and Professor Ward have traversed large
sweeps of the drama or, like the many able German
writers of monographs, have illuminated specific parts
of the subject ; while with all his wanderings and
contradictions, in the mass of material which he has
unearthed and in the happy suggestiveness of many
of his surmises Mr. F. G. Fleay has done all students
of the English drama an inestimable service.

The Table of Extant Plays presents in epitome the
classification which has resulted from this study. In
the middle column will be found those plays which
strictly fulfil the conditions of the historical or biographical Chronicle Play. On either hand are grouped
the allied species which owe their method—but not
their subject-matter—to the earlier influence of Seneca
or which strayed into the fields of pseudo-history,
myth or romance. The List of Plays refers the reader

to the sources of information and may serve as a bib-
liography in outline.   The dates of first acting in both
lists must be regarded as approximate from frequent
want or conflict of evidence.   An edition later than
the first is mentioned only where the play has been
reprinted in a collection or journal, or separately published with a more or less authoritative text.   Titles,
after first mention in the text, are shortened and
normalized for convenience.   The passages from plays
quoted in the text are given as nearly as possible in
the typography of the original editions; not, it is
hoped, from any idolatrous worship of every "Elizabethan goose-print," as Lowell once put it, but from
a conviction that the form and the spirit of old literature are generally so indissolubly wedded that the
one is certain to be impaired by any tampering with
the other.

For the loan and use of books my thanks are especially due to Dr. Horace Howard Furness, to the
libraries of Harvard, Cornell and Columbia Universities and to the British Museum, the courtesies of
which, though extended to all, are none the less deserving of appreciative recognition.   To my friend
and colleague, Professor Clarence G. Child, I owe
grateful acknowledgment for much sympathy, for
many valuable suggestions and for the Index.

FELIX E. SCHELLING.

December, 1901.

CONTENTS.

THE ENGLISH CHRONICLE PLAY

I

FORERUNNERS OF THE CHRONICLE PLAY

It is the purpose of this book to relate the story of the English Chronicle Play, to treat of its origin, its flourishing in the age of Queen Elizabeth and of its decline in the two following reigns, and to touch so far as necessary its relation to other forms of contemporary drama and literature. Among the many and diverse forms which the English drama displayed in the latter part of the sixteenth century there is none which was at once so popular in its day and so distinctively English as that which drew its subject-matter from the historical lore of the national chronicles. For years this variety of drama disputed with Romantic comedy and tragedy the supremacy of the stage and only yielded to defeat with the subsidence of the national spirit of which it was born. The English Chronicle Play began with the tide of patriotism which united all England to repel the threatened invasion of Philip of Spain. It ebbed and lost its national character with the succession of James, an un-English prince, to the throne of Elizabeth. Within the period from 1586 to 1606 (counting in a few out-riders before and after) no less than a hundred and fifty plays of the general type of the chronicle history were written and performed, ranging in subject from the mythical coming of Brute to England, through the doings of legendary Britons, of more historical Roman, Saxon and Norman times, to events of which some of the auditors may have been recent witnesses or even participants. These plays spread on broad canvas and with equal facility the civil broils of king and feudal baron, the murderous intrigues of usurping tyranny or the glories of English arms abroad. There is no human passion from the dainty loves of Prince Edward and the fair maid of Fressingfield or the pathos of the repentance of erring Jane Shore to the infatuated criminality of Macbeth and the sublime ravings of King Lear which is not found in these re-markable plays; which, beside the work of a score of lesser playwrights, include some of the most con-summate dramatic work of Marlowe, Greene, Hey-wood, Fletcher and Ford and more than a third of the dramas which have given immortality to Shakespeare.

The Chronicle Play has been called distinctively English. Its growth was indigenous, its spirit national. Neither the schoolmaster, with his scraps of learning and covert didactic purpose, nor the University man with his Senecan ideals and apothegms had much to do with it : nor had the Italianate English courtier, whose conduct was guided by the nice rules of Castiglione's *Il Cortegiano* and whose parleyings were euphuistic. Or if either had, he sank the scholar and the courtier in the Englishman and responded to the mimic appeals to his patriotism as he had responded, irrespective of the ties of tradition and religion, to the actual call of his queen to repel the attack of a foreign invader. It is for this reason that the Chronicle Play discloses an independence in nature and growth above that of any other species of the contemporary drama. With little of the learning of the schools upon it and less of the exotic culture of Italy, the Chronicle Play may be considered in the development of the English Drama practically as a thing apart. Indeed its affiliation to the wealth of historic literature in verse and prose, which was springing up about it and to which our attention will be presently addressed, was closer than its relation to other varieties of the drama. In this aspect the Chronicle Play becomes the crown of a deeply rooted interest in historic tradition which has animated English literature from the earliest times, an interest which sought utterance in dramatic form in the reign of Elizabeth because the dramatic was the most potent mode of literary expression in that favored age.

The old sacred drama had been devoid of national feeling or character, and so it remained. It persisted

in collective and single mysteries, in the morality and
bible play, and came to an end when its original
design, the teaching of biblical story, was forgotten
and a specific didactic purpose had ceased to animate
it.   But this latter element was not lost.   It was
merely transferred, undiluted and unrestrained, to the
scholastic morality and interlude, whence it continued
in diminished rigor in the Senecan play and in the
college drama, and percolated even into the popular
stage, there to act, for the most part, as a regulative
and restraining force.   But didacticism had the power,
artistically speaking, of leading nowhither.   The
spark of dramatic life in the midst of all this mum-
ming, symbolism, allegory and preaching, lay in the
simple representations of the life of the Holy Family
and in the interpolated comedy scenes of both mystery
and morality, of which the interlude of Mak, the
Sheep-stealer, in the *Townley Mysteries* is an excellent,
if a stock, example.   This element of comedy is referable to man's love of home and familiar surroundings
and is ultimately the root of that form of the drama
which deals with the relations of everyday life and
whose instinctive creed is a rigid adherence to fact.
But there was another well-spring of secular drama
which lay beyond the domain of mystery and moral
play.   This is to be found in the sturdy undergrowth
of medieval balladry, in the rude but wholesome stories
of folk-lore in which the popular love of action and

the spirit of English nationality was preserved. The ultimate source of this element is in the sense of community, of feudal faith and loyalty, and in man's love of country. A play may disclose a ruling interest in the present: in the delineation of contemporary civic or rural life, domestic and family relations set in English scene and represented under English conditions, or in the travels and adventures of contemporary Englishmen abroad. Or a play may disclose a ruling interest in the past: in national history, biography of great personages, legend or folk-lore. Herein is the chief diversity of the two groups just distinguished and the line of their demarcation. The historical group and a large part of the dramas of domestic life are frankly realistic and concerned with the representation of deeds and the actors of them alone. But an important group of domestic plays give a satirical turn to their representations of life, thus handing down unbroken the traditions of the medieval stage. On the other hand, plays derived from folk-lore or treating of travel and adventure are frequently tempered with the spirit of romance. Though our present concern is wholly with that class of plays which rises out of an interest in the deeds of the past and is nourished by the spirit that makes a people a nation, the circumstance that this spirit often manifested itself in terms of the present makes an arbitrary line of demarcation impossible. Scenes portraying the relations of everyday Elizabethan life shall then claim our attention only in so far as they become an element in the presentation of what is more strictly the English historical drama.

The English Chronicle Play traced to its origin discloses one root in the old sacred drama, a second in the non-religious pageantry of the middle ages and in the popular folk-lore of old English balladry. From the first is derived the play of St. George, from the second that of Robin Hood and the few pageants commemorative of local historical events, such as the *Hock Tuesday Play* of Coventry. Medieval delight in processions and pageantry calls for no word here. Pageantry was universally employed in the presentation of the religious drama and allegorical and figurative devices from sacred and classic history were common on secular and political occasions, especially in the "riding" as the ceremonials attending a royal or other entry were called. Here we naturally look for the earliest examples of the representation of historical characters. In "a riding against Queen Margaret," as the phrase went, wife of Henry VI., at Coventry in 1455, St. Edward and King Arthur figured, the latter as one of the nine worthies. In 1511 another Margaret, the Scottish Queen, was welcomed to Aberdeen in a riding in which "the giant emperor Bruce" and "the Stewarts" offered addresses of welcome.[1] When

[1] Sharp, *Dissertation on Pageants*, 1825, p. 146, and *The Queen's Reception at Aberdeen*, *Works of Dunbar*, ed. 1863, p. 288.

Queen Elizabeth moved in procession through London to her coronation the first pageant which she met was that of a battlemented arch spanning the street from two towers, the one supporting the branches of a red rose-tree, the other a white. On successive stages rising to the middle were placed figures personated by children representing the princes of the houses of Lancaster and York and the parents of the queen, whilst an image of her majesty's self crowned the whole.[1]

But such pageants as these are rare and held but a small place beside the Virtues and Vices, the biblical and classical figures in which medieval pageantry abounds. English annals offer no analogue to the interesting *mystères patriotiques* which the misfortunes of the Hundred Years' War caused to flourish in France.[2] The germ of the national drama in England is none the less recognizable in several varieties of early dialogues, pageants and shows. There is record as early as 1416 of a pageant of St. George of Cappadocia acted before the Emperor Sigismund and Henry V. on the former's visit to Windsor.

[1] See *The Passage of our most drad Soveraigne Lady Quene Elizabeth*, 1558-9, reprinted by Nichols, *Progresses of Queen Elizabeth*, 1823, I. 38. This device of the union of the houses of Lancaster and York was repeated at Norwich in 1578.

[2] Cf. *Le Mystère du siège d' Orléans*, originally a procession, but repeated yearly with a representation of the events of the siege. *La Décomfiture de Talbot advenue en Bordelais*, 1453, and the allegorical *Le Léopard anglais* acted before Charles VIII. at Vienne in 1493. On this general topic see Bapst, *Essai sur l' Histoire du Théâtre*, 1890, p. 15.

This production was divided into three parts and exhibited first, "the armyng of Seint George and an
Angel doyng on his spores"; secondly, "Seint George
ridyng and fightyng with the dragon with his spere
in his hand"; and lastly, "a castel, and Seint George
and the Kynges daughter ledyng the lambe in at the
castel gates."[1] It is not clear from the description
whether this performance was a dumb show or a moral
play. The subject is certain, however, and we may
surmise that in the year succeeding the battle of
Agincourt and before a foreign prince who had come
to England expressly to mediate peace with a con-
quered foe, the spirit of English patriotism had at
least as much to do with the choice of theme as any
celebrity of the militant Cappadocian saint. Ten
Brink is of opinion that the play of St. George was
widely spread in England, and he adds: "in many
places this drama may have contained remnants of
a native tradition reaching far into the past."[2] That
this is more than mere surmise is proved by certain evidences, few but conclusive. In a letter bearing date
April 16, 1473, Sir John Paston complains: "I have
ben, and ame troblyd with myn over large and curteys
delyng with my servants." To instance which he
mentions one "W. Woode whyche promysed yow
and Dawbeney, God have hys sowle, at Castre, that

[1] Collier, *History of English Dramatic Poetry*, 1831, I. 20.
[2] *Geschichte der englischen Litteratur*, 1893, II. 305.

iff ye wolde take hym in to be ageyn with me, that
then he wold never goo ffro me, and ther uppon I
have kepyd hym thys iij yer to pleye Seynt Jorge
and Robyn Hod and the Shryff off Notyngham, and
now when I wolde have good horse, he is goon into
Bernysdale, and I withowt a keeper."[1] Here the
juxtaposition of "Seynt Jorge" and "Robyn Hod"
with the keeping of a man for the acting of such parts
in the household of a baron is highly suggestive and
indicates a complete transfer of George from the category of saints to the rôle of a popular hero. Mention of a later performance of a play on the subject
of St. George is that of Bassingbourne, in 1511.
This play was plainly of a religious cast and concerned "the holy martir Seynt George." It was
presented on St. Margaret's Day and several neighboring villages joined in defraying the expenses.
Still another play of St. George was "regularly acted
on All Souls' Day at a village a few miles from
Chester."[2] Two short specimens of plays of this
class have been preserved. They are *The Oxford-
shire St. George Play*, performed at various times and
places up to 1853, and *The Lutterworth Christmas
Play*, acted apparently for the last time a decade later.
Both are too conscious and full of modern and extraneous influences to be regarded as in any wise

[1] *The Paston Letters*, ed. Gairdner, III. 89.
[2] See Sharp, as above, p. 34, and Child, *English and Scottish
Popular Ballads*, 1898, V. 291.

actually typical of the remote past out of which it is not improbable that they have actually descended.

From the plays of St. George we turn to those on Robin Hood. The close connection of the two has already been suggested by the passage from the letter of Sir John Paston quoted above. The affiliations of the plays on Robin Hood are neither religious, ethical nor dramatic, but epic, in their relation to popular balladry, and national from the fact that this redoubtable hero of outlawry became in English folk-lore the typical figure of the yeoman's ideal of free England. This is not the place in which to discuss the dramatic qualities of old English ballads, especially as our present concern is wholly with those ballads in which the first growths of national feeling may be traced. In the typical ballad of Robin Hood we have the recital of the deeds of many personages and that recital frequently takes the form of dialogue, at times of the most animated nature, where the countenance and attitude of the reciter, his changes of voice and variety of gesture, must have counted for much. It was only a matter of time for the steps to be taken which transformed epic recital to dramatic presentation. That this step was taken early is proved by the fragment of a dramatic version of *Robin Hood and Guy of Gisborne* which has come down to us in manuscript on a half leaf among the Paston papers. From certain memoranda on the other side of this half leaf, one of which is dated 1475, and from the mention of " Robyn Hod and the Shryff off Notyngham " as a play in the letter quoted above, the approximate date of this fragment may be reached. The late Professor Francis James Child informs us that "the grammatical forms of themselves warrant our putting the composition further back." This earliest fragment of an independent dramatic scene founded on folk-lore and free from the pervading religious and ethical purpose of the age is so interesting that I quote it entire. The text is that of Professor Child.[1] The italicized stage directions, which are given for the sake of clearness, are not in the original but have been added by Professor Manly.[2]

Enter a Knyght to the Sheryff.

Knyght.   Syr sheryffe, for thy sąke,
             Robyn Hode wull Y take.

Sheryff.   I wyll the gyffe golde and fee,
             This beheste thou holde me !

The Knyght goes to Robyn Hode.

Knyght.   Robyn Hode, ffayre and fre,
             Vndre this lynde shote we.

Robyn.   With the shote Y wyll,
             Alle thy lustes to full fyll.

They shoot.

Knyght.   Have at the pryke !

Robyn.   And Y cleue the styke.

[1] *Ibid.*, III. 90.
[2] *Specimens of the Pre-Shaksperean Drama*, 1897, I. 297.

Knyght.   Late vs caste the stone.

Robyn.   I graunte well, be Seynt John.

They cast the stone; Robyn is again successful.

Knyght.   Late vs caste the exaltre.

Robyn.   Have a foote be-fore the !

Then they wrestle.

Syr knyght, ye haue a falle.

Knyght.   And I the, Robyn, qwyte shall :
Owte on the ! I blowe myn horne.

Robyn.   Hit ware better be vnborne.
Lat vs fyght at outtraunce.

Knyght.   He that fleth, God gyfe hym myschaunce !

Robyn slays the Knyght.

Robyn.   Now I haue the maystry here.
Off I smyte this sory swyre
This knyghtys clothis wolle I were,
And in my hode his hede woll bere.

He disguises himself.   Meantime the Sheryff has attacked Robyn Hode's men and a fierce battle is in progress.   Robyn meets a man coming from the scene of the battle.

Robyn.   Welle mete, felowe myn :
What herst thou of gode Robyn ?

Man.   Robyn Hode and his menye
With the sheryff takyn be.

Robyn.   Sette on foote with gode wyll,
And the sheryffe wull we kyll.

They come in sight of the battle.

Robyn.   Beholde wele Ffrere Tuke,
Howe he dothe his bowe pluke.

On the battle-field the Sheryff speaks.

Sheryff.   Yeld yow, syrs, to the sheryff[e].
           Or elles shall your bowes clyffe.

One of
Robyn's Men.   Now we be bownden alle in same ;
               Frere [T]uke this is no game.

Sheryff.   Co[m]e thou forth, thou fals outlawe :
           Thou shall b[e] hangyde and ydrawe.

Frere Tuke.   Now, allas ! what shall we doo ?
              We [m]oste to the prysone goo.

Sheryff.   Opy[n] the yatis faste anon,
           An[d] d[oo] theis thevys ynne gon.

Two other specimens of dramatized versions of
ballads of Robin Hood are preserved. Both are
fragments and are printed together under the title *The
newe Playe of Robyn Hoode*, about 1550, though they
must date from a period long prior to that year.
They concern respectively the adventures of Robin
and the curtal friar and his meeting with the potter.
The former contains some lines of great animation
and both furnish abundant action. Following the
title quoted above we have the words : "for to be
played in Maye games." This indicates one of the
most popular uses to which the plays of Robin Hood
were put ; although it by no means follows that these
plays became a constant or typical feature of May Day.
The sports of that day, as is well known, were com-
posed of many and various features in which giants,

the morris dance, St. George and the Dragon, and Robin Hood all figured. That royalty even at times condescended to employ the master theme of popular balladry is indicated by the account which Halle gives of a device for the entertainment of Katharine, the queen of Henry VIII., in which "therles of Essex, Wilshire and other noble menne to the nombre of twelue, came sodainly in a mornyng into the Quenes Chambre, all appareled in shorte cotes of Kentishe Kendal, with hodes on their heddes and hosen of the same, euery one of them, his bowe and arrowes, and a sworde and a bucklar, like out lawes or Robyn Hodes men." On another occasion the king's guard personated Robin and his merry men and entertained the king in Windsor Forest with feats of archery.[1]

Whether these fragments of plays of Robin Hood are to be regarded as sporadic instances of the straying of the epic into the form of the drama or as indicative of a considerable body of like dramatized ballads, now lost but once enjoying popularity, is a question which it would be difficult to decide. It is sufficient for our purpose to note that this step in the direction of the secular drama was actually taken and to recognize therein that when Greene wrote his *Pinner of Wakefield* and Munday his *Robert, Earl of Huntingdon*, each was returning so far as his subject-matter was

[1] Halle's *Chronicle*, ed. 1809, p. 513 and Holinshed's *Chronicle*, ed. 1809, III. 611.

concerned, to a kind of drama which may possibly once have enjoyed a widespread popularity.

Another forerunner of the Chronicle Play now claims our attention. This is the *Hock Tuesday Play*, witnessed by Queen Elizabeth during her visit to Kenilworth in 1575. Of this production we possess two contemporary accounts, the one by the poet, Gascoigne, the other, more complete, by a gossipy clerk of her majesty's council chamber, Robert Laneham, present in attendance. They unite in giving this production a wholly secular character, whilst Laneham's words, " expressed in actionz and rymez after their manner " precludes our acceptance of Collier's idea that it was " merely a dumb show." *The Hock* or *Hox Tuesday Play* was acted at Coventry to commemorate either the Massacre of St. Brice, 1102, or the death of Hardicanute, 1042, opinion differs as to which.[1] We have knowledge of its performance as early as 1416, and there is reason to believe that it had been acted periodically, at times yearly, from that date to the time when Elizabeth saw it. In the absence of any account of this performance except that of the two courtiers, its precise character must remain indeterminable. But I can not agree with Professor Ward in his opinion that *The Hock Tuesday Play* was " in the main a mirthful representation of a fight." [2] The

[1] Sharp, p. 132.
[2] *A History of English Dramatic Literature*, ed. 1899, I. 144.

mirth was in Laneham's attitude throughout his enter-
taining pamphlet, and is precisely that of Theseus and
his Amazonian bride towards Bottom and his scratch
company of handicraftsmen in *A Midsummer Night's
Dream.* To the "good-harted men of Coventree"
their play was unquestionably a very serious and patriotic affair. Its performance evidently impressed its
auditors; for Elizabeth, who was absent during the
greater part of its first presentation, ordered it repeated for her own special behoof.[1] As containing
the representation of an historical event in action by
means of dialogue, of a character altogether secular
and animated by a purpose free from didactic intent,
The Hock Tuesday Play must be regarded as the earliest dramatic production fulfilling, if rudely, the conditions of a national historical drama.

There is nothing to show the existence of a play
prior to the year 1580 which exhibits that freedom
from extraneous and literary influences, that realism
of method, that deep interest in the story for the
story's sake, and consciousness of nationality which
distinguish the Chronicle Plays as a class. The relation of Bishop Bale's vigorous historical morality,
Kynge Johan, to the Chronicle Play is not so close as
some have thought it. The spirit which the old
morality breathes is that of defiance to the Pope and

---

[1] For these particulars see Laneham in Nichols, *Elizabeth*, I. 420–
484, and Gascoigne's account, *ibid.*, 485–523.

the Church of Rome. Its consciousness is theological and polemic, not political and historical ; and its hero is transformed, in open defiance of anything like historical truth, into a champion of " Crysten libertie." Bale seeks, it is true, to represent actual historical characters on the stage in the persons of the King, Pope Innocent, Cardinal Pandulphus and Stephen Langton ; and it is remarkable that he should have done so. But these figures are surrounded by the usual abstractions, Nobelyte, Syvile Order, Sedycyon and Dan Davy Dyssymulacyon. The degree to which these characters partake of abstraction and to which abstractions stand for characters may be learned from a scene in which the Vices, at one as to their plans, severally assume the characters which they typify, and Sedycyon becomes Stephen Langton, Dyssymulacyon, Raymundus of Toulouse, John's brother-in-law, and Usurpyd Power, the Pope.[1]

But one other morality thus combines social satire with a fable rendered concrete by a reference to events supposedly based on the history of an English king. This is the far later *A Knacke to Knowe a Knaue*. This production was printed in 1594, though doubtless much older, and enjoyed great popularity some two years before, as acted by Edward Alleyn and his company " with Kemp's applauded merriments of the men of Gotham." The authorship of *A*

---

[1] *Kynge Johan*, ed. Camden Society, 1838, p. 30.

Knack is unknown.   Ward considers that "the action
and the main characters are historical and the moral
element is secondary only."   On the contrary, it
seems to me that the central design is the exhibition
of a just monarch sustained by a wise churchman.
On the thread of King Edgar's and Dunstan's moral
discourses is strung a series of satirico-moral dialogues
in various typical though disconnected incidents, each
of which illustrates the same theme.   The death of the
wicked Bailiff of Hexham, the adventures of his sons,
who bear the abstract names of Farmer, Courtier, Priest
and Conycatcher or rogue, the unfilial conduct and punishment of Philarchus, the petition of Piers Plowman,
are all of the essence of the morality of social satire.
The episode in which Prince Ethenwald, sent by his
father to court for him the fair Alfrida, falls in love
with her and wooes her for himself represents to us
actual persons, but is also illustrative of the central
theme; while the short scene of the men of Gotham,
the popularity of which must surely have been supplied by Kemp, the famous actor of clown's parts,
with " merriments " which have not descended to us,
and Dunstan's unnecessary lugging in of the devil are
matters extraneous to the story but wholly in the
manner of the morality.   The placing of the scene of
this play in England is purely a matter of accident, a
circumstance the more certain in view of its probable
relation to the not dissimilar productions, *A Knack*

to Know an Honest Man, and *Nobody and Somebody*.
A Knack to Know a Knave marks no step in the development of the Chronicle History. If moralities of
social satire such as *Kynge John* and *A Knack to
Know a Knave*, despite their reference to personages
of English history, are to be excluded from the category of the originals of the Chronicle Play, far less
can we include the fragment, *Albyon Knight*. In this
production Albyon personifies England and is surrounded by the usual abstractions, Justice, Injury and
Divisyon, who is apparently the Vice. The piece is a
morality of political and satirical intent, and shows, as
Professor Brandl has recently observed, a direct influence of Lyndsay's *Ane Satyre of the Thrie Estaitis*.[1]

It is impossible to overestimate the importance of
the position which the tragedy *Gorboduc* holds at
the threshold of the English drama. The composition of gentlemen of the Inns of Court, performed before the queen and following in the wake of the Continental imitations of Seneca, this play is none the less
of moment for the effect which it was to have on the
popular drama to come. The significance of this
tragedy in its choice of English instead of the learned
tongue in which such performances continued often to
be given, in its use of blank verse in place of the usual
riming and tumbling measures, and in its substitution

---

[1] *Quellen des weltlichen Dramas in England vor Shakespeare*, 1898,
p. lix.

of an artistic purpose for the old didactic one, is familiar to every student of English literature. It is the selection of a theme from English historical lore in place of the customary moral, biblical or classical story which gives to *Gorboduc* its special significance in the history of the national drama ; and this importance is not in the least diminished by the likelihood that Sackville and Norton were attracted to their subject because of its superficial resemblance to the story of the *Thebais* of Seneca rather than through any set determination to levy contribution on national sources hitherto untried. Whatever the direct impetus, *Gorboduc* is the earliest of a long list of English dramas which laid under contribution those legendary and pseudo-historical materials of the early chronicles of Britain which emanated from the fertile brain of Geoffrey of Monmouth. The relation of the earliest English tragedy to the English Chronicle Play is sufficiently defined in the recognition of this fact.

In 1570 we meet with the first example of a drama which deals with the biography of an English personage in the Latin play entitled *Byrsa Basilica seu Regale Excambium* by J. Rickets. It was performed probably before Sir Thomas Gresham, who is represented in the piece under the character Rialto. The story is a somewhat intricate one, setting forth contemporary citizen life mixed with farce and full of the technicalities of the business proceedings of the day.

Professor Churchill, of Amherst, who prepared the report of this play for the list of Latin plays lately published in the *Shakespeare Jahrbuch*,[1] notices both morality and Italian influence in it and considers it alone in its kind. This is doubtless true as to plays in Latin, but it might not be difficult to establish a close relation between this play and the later large class of comedies in English dealing intimately with London civic life. Indeed Sir Thomas appears under his own name in a later English play entitled *The Second Part of If You Know Not Me You Know Nobody*, by Thomas Heywood and dating about 1604. In *Byrsa Basilica* we have a transition from that present interest which characterizes any representation of contemporary manners to a case in which the interest is centered in the career of a person of prominence.

Nine years later Thomas Legge's *Richardus Tertius Tragedia* was acted at St. John's College, Cambridge. Legge was a notable man in the Cambridge of his day, and was successively Master of Caius College, Regius Professor of Civil Law, Commissary and Vice Chancellor of the University. This play is the earliest recorded drama dealing with a subject derived from the actual history of England and it remains, except for Lacey's transcription of it in 1586, the only academic play which sought for a subject in the national chronicles. Legge followed his source, More's biog-

[1] XXXIV. 221.

raphy of Richard in Halle's continuation of Hardyng, with great fidelity. But his dramatic models were the Roman tragedies of Seneca. He was drawn to his subject not because of its national character but because the story of the fall of Richard offered a happy English parallel of a favorite Senecan theme. Hence if Legge was "turning the drama of England in an entirely new direction," as has been suggested,[1] his action was doubtless altogether unconscious and affected by no ulterior motives save possibly a wish to compliment the queen by a dramatic picture of the political overthrow of the great rival of the founder of the reigning dynasty. *Richardus Tertius* is said to have been elaborately staged and enjoyed a great academic success, as no less than seven extant manuscripts and many contemporary allusions attest. So great was its reputation that Sir John Harington, writing nearly ten years later, says : " to omit other famous Tragedies : that, that was playd at S. Iohns in Cambridge, of Richard the 3. would moue (I thinke) Phalaris the tyraunt, and terrifie all tyrannous minded men, from following their foolish ambitious humors." [2]   Such a repute must have had no small influence on University men such as Marlowe, Lodge and Peele. But whether *Richardus Tertius* " furnished the direct incitement to that dramatizing from chronicles of the careers of English

[1] See Churchill's *Richard the Third up to Shakespeare*, 1900, p. 270.
[2] *An Apologie of Poetrie*, 1591, ed. Haslewood, 1815, II. 135.

monarchs which established a national historical drama in popular form upon the popular stage " [1] may be questioned in view of the widely different *animus*, method and purpose of the popular chronicle plays. An excellent analysis of the play under discussion will be found in Professor Churchill's monograph already mentioned above, in which the close imitation of Seneca from individual phrases and single passages to the skillful adaptation of whole situations is carefully pointed out. Perhaps the most salient example of the force of Senecan example in this interesting tragedy is to be found in Legge's complete suppression of the motive of conscience which forms so prominent a feature in the chronicler's conception of Richard's character. As Professor Churchill remarks : " Legge's Richard is not only Senecan in conduct but Senecan in essence." [2] That both the biographical and historical form of the Chronicle Play should have been thus first essayed in the learned language and by scholars is in accord with expectation. It is somewhat remarkable, however, that except for Lacey's transcription of Legge's play neither drama should have led, so far as we know, to attempts of the same kind. When the playwrights next turned to English historical themes, they expressed them in English, and left the Latin drama to classical and satirical topics.

[1] Churchill, p. 272.
[2] *Ibid.*, p. 330.

It was in full recognition of the excellence and success of *Gorboduc* that Thomas Hughes and his fellow students of Gray's Inn set about the preparation of *Certaine Devises and Shewes presented to her Majestie . . . at her Highnesse Court in Greenwich*, February 28, 1588, and generally known as *The Misfortunes of Arthur*. This tragedy treats of the story of Mordred's incestuous love for his stepmother, Queen Guenevora, his revolt against his father, King Arthur, his usurpation of his father's throne and the ensuing tragedy. The story, like that of *Gorboduc*, is derived from Geoffrey of Monmouth, and a superficial resemblance to the classic myth of Œdipus must here once more have influenced selection. *The Misfortunes of Arthur* is altogether Senecan, more so even than *Gorboduc*. For while the latter play merely borrows the manner of the Roman poet, the authors of *The Misfortunes* bodily conveyed whole passages from him.[1] In a word none of these tragedies can be considered as in any direct wise contributing to the upgrowth of the English Chronicle Play.

Up to this point our inquiry has resulted only in exclusion; nor is it to be expected that a national drama essentially popular in its appeal should be fostered in the cloistered seclusion of the University or in the polite and artificial atmosphere of the Eliza-

---

[1] See on this Cunliffe, *The Influence of Seneca on Elizabethan Tragedy*, 1893, p. 130.

bethan Inns of Court. In the tragedy of *Locrine*, which may have preceded *The Misfortunes of Arthur* by a year or two, we have a play which essays a union of the Senecan drama with the cruder popular performances which had just begun to present subjects drawn from the prose chronicles of England. The story once more is ultimately traceable to Geoffrey's *Historia Regum Britanniæ*; but *Locrine* owes more than the suggestion of subject to the two plays just discussed, for it agrees with them in the Senecan form and nature of the serious dialogue and in the introduction of dumb shows. The grandiloquent diction, bombast and extraordinary exuberance of classical allusion which characterize *Locrine* point to an acquaintance with *The Spanish Tragedy*, itself a newer and more vital offshoot of the influence of Seneca. On the other hand the mingling of tragedy and comedy, the ruder and less constructive sequence of events, the freer diction and the less chastened rhetoric all disclose a return to the drama of the people. *Locrine* is one of several plays which the uninformed zeal of early scholars attributed to the youth of Shakespeare. The play is with little question the work of George Peele, as its excessive use of "high astounding terms," of classical proper names and of figures of inflated rhetoric attest.[1]

---

[1] This was long ago recognized by Ulrici, *Shakespeare's dramatische Kunst*, 1847, p. 740. Professor Ward is of the same opinion, *Dramatic Literature*, II. 220.

Peele began his dramatic career before he left Oxford, where, between the years 1571 and 1579, he enjoyed much repute for his poetic talent and for his social gaieties. He was associated in the preparation of academic plays with Dr. William Gager, who later achieved a great reputation as a writer of Latin dramas. It has even been said that Peele himself translated one of the Euripedean *Iphigenias*, but whether into Latin or English does not appear. In 1581 his *Arraignment of Paris*, a graceful attempt to rival Lyly in his new court drama, *Endimion*, was performed before the queen, and in 1583 Peele was back again at Oxford assisting his friend Gager in the production of his two Latin plays, *Rivales* and *Dido*. The expenses of Peele at Oxford had been defrayed in part by the governors of Christ's Hospital, which James Peele, the poet's father, had served for many years in the capacity of clerk. Hence the order dated September 19, 1579, that " James Peele . . . discharge his howse of his sonne George Peele and all other his howsold wch have bene chargable to him befor mychellmas day next cominge vppon paine of the gounos [governors'] displeasure," [1] points clearly to the young poet's mode of life immediately upon his leaving the University. A roisterer and a spendthrift, so far as he had to spend, of dramatic talents generally recognized, it was only a matter of time when

[1] Bullen, *Works of George Peele*, 1888, I. xv.

Peele should find his way to the popular theater and seek the career of actor and playwright. The precise date of this we cannot now ascertain, for his dedications to noble patrons and his calls on their charity continue to the errand, in 1596, by "his eldest daughter, Necessity's servant," to Lord Burghley with the manuscript of *The Tale of Troy*. This must have been near the end.

Did Peele conceive the idea of popularizing the courtly Senecan drama of Sackville and Hughes for inn-yards and strolling companies by joining its violent scenes, its inflated lines and orotund classical proper names with the rude humors of the street and the tavern? Or did Peele only combine in *Locrine* the drama of Whitehall and the Inns of Court with what he found already existing in vigorous life at the Bull, the Bell Savage or the Cross Keys? The latter supposition seems the more reasonable, inasmuch as plays dealing with the deeds of kings of England can be shown, with a high degree of probability, to have antedated *Locrine* on the popular stage. Besides, the other historical plays with which Peele's name has been associated and *Edward I.*, his undoubted and unaided work, show a far closer following of popular example and seem to warrant the inference that Peele's contact with the boards on which Tarlton danced led in time to the choice of more familiar subjects and to a style less encumbered by classical lore and inflated rhetoric.

Briefly to summarize : the parent stock of the English Chronicle Play (as of the comedy of manners and some other forms of the realistic drama) is ultimately the comedy element in the old sacred drama.   It was thence that the Chronicle Play drew its sense of comedy and its adhesion to simple realism in the representation of scenes of actual life.   The devices of non-religious pageantry occasionally presented the figures of historical personages, thus marking the first step towards the subject-matter of the Chronicle Play; while in the plays of St. George and Robin Hood we advance to the representation by means of action and dialogue of personages popularly regarded as national heroes.   There was wanting in these representations only the foundation in definite historical fact and what may be termed the historical consciousness. Both were apparently supplied in *The Hock Tuesday Play* which commemorated an actual historical event by means of dialogue and action, and thus for the first time in English literature fulfilled the conditions of a dramatic presentation of history.   In *Kynge Johan* we have a polemical morality in which history is distorted to serve the purpose of theological attack, while in *A Knack to Know a Knave* the story of a Saxon king is employed for a rigidly didactic purpose and the choice of an English historical subject is probably accidental. Before this last morality was performed English tragedy had passed though its earliest Senecan stage and had contributed several dramas to the forerunners of the Chronicle Play. But although the legendary lore of Geoffrey, afterwards to prove so rich a source, was here broached for the first time, and the historical and biographical chronicle presaged in the Latin play *Richardus Tertius*, neither the Latin nor the English imitators of the Roman dramatist produced the earliest chronicle play.

II

GROWTH OF THE CHRONICLE PLAY; ITS DISTRIBUTION AND LITERARY RELATIONS

THE English Chronicle Drama falls naturally into two groups. The one includes those plays which deal with history and the biographies of actual historical persons ; the other those in which the subjects are legendary or at least such as involve a more or less conscious departure from historical fact. Marlowe's *Edward II.* and Shakespeare's *Henry V.* may be taken as illustrations of the tragic and non-tragic types of the first class. Shakespeare's *King Lear* and Greene's *Scottish History of James IV.* as typical examples similarly contrasted of the second. Neither the rigid Senecan manner of *Gorboduc* nor the mixed Senecan and popular manner of *Locrine* were immediately followed in dramas the subjects of which were derived from the mythologic history of the early British times. In *The True Chronicle History of King Leir*, which furnished Shakespeare with the groundwork of his tragedy, *King Lear*, and which has been variously assigned to years between 1588 and 1593, we have apparently the earliest successor of these plays. But *King Leir* is a successor of *Gorboduc* and *Locrine* only in choice of subject. Its style and method are altogether those of the popular dramas which dealt with kings of historical times. Deferring the mythological British chronicle then for the present, we address ourselves first to a consideration of the effects of the awakening spirit of nationality on general literature and then to the plays which concern themselves with the history and the biography of historical personages and form the most persistent type of the Chronicle Play.

It is a commonplace of English history that the vigilant and centralized monarchy of Henry VII. fostered in Englishmen a sense of nationality to which they had become almost complete strangers during the long feuds of the Wars of the Roses. The national consciousness once reawakened, waxed strong in the earlier days of Henry VIII. and, though submitted to a terrible ordeal in the political and religious persecutions that followed, answered with enthusiasm the appeals of Elizabeth and rested firm in its appreciation of her good government at home and her successful rôle in foreign politics. Literature responded at once to this awakened national spirit in a renewed interest in the past evinced in the translation and republication, for example, of such a history as Ralph Higden's *Polychronicon* and in a revival of the popularity of works like Lydgate's *Falls of Princes* and the *Morte Darthur* in which the historical instinct vies with the love of romance. A little later came the heyday of the English Chronicle History which flourished in prose and in verse, *in extenso* and in epitome, in collections and in separate tracts, poems and dramas. Sir Philip Sidney died too early to have felt to the full the literary reflex of this revival of national spirit. But it was this spirit no less than the love of poetry which inspired a familiar passage of *An Apologie for Poetrie* which quotation can never stale : " Certainly I must confesse my own barbarousnes, I neuer heard the olde song of Percy and Duglas, that I found not my heart mooued more then with a Trumpet : and yet is it sung but by some blinde Crouder, with no rougher voyce, then rude stile." [1]

The amount and variety of literature of the sixteenth century which took English historical and legendary themes for its subject-matter are things commonly forgotten. This literature began towards the end of the reign of Henry VIII. with Grafton's printing and continuation of the metrical chronicle of Hardyng and his edition of Halle. In the two succeeding reigns such books were discouraged ; Gardiner even discerned concealed heresy in the political examples of *The Mirour for Magistrates*, and the projected publication of that work in 1555 was stayed. On the accession of Elizabeth the publication of historical literature began anew with a third edition of the *Chronicle* of Fabyan.

[1] Arber's reprint of the edition of 1595, p. 46.

In 1562 Grafton brought out *An Abridgement of the Chronicles of England* which attained a fifth edition in 1572. He was rivalled in this undertaking by John Stow in 1565 with *A Summarie of Englyshe Chronicles* which ran through ten editions up to 1604 and was the accepted short history of England of its day. [1] Before a decade had elapsed John Foxe's *Actes and Monuments*, first published in 1563 and popularly known as *The Book of Martyrs*, had gone into a second edition ; Grafton had abridged his *Abridgement* which still stretched, however, " from the creacion of the worlde to the yere 1565," and extended it into his *Chronicle at large and meere History of the affayres of England and the Kinges of the same*, 1569, while Stow in association with Bishop Parker brought to the press three earlier Latin chroniclers, Matthew of Westminster, Matthew of Paris and Thomas of Walsingham, and was busily at work in gathering materials for his *Annales of England*. In 1577 appeared the most important of Elizabethan prose histories, *The Chronicles of England, Scotlande and Irelande* by Ralph Holinshed. In his labors, Holinshed was assisted by William Harrison, who wrote the racy prefatory *Description of England*, and by the Irish scholar and translator of

---

[1] Mr. Sidney Lee corrects the mistake which confuses *A breviat Chronicle contaynyng all the Kynges*, etc., by J. Mychell, 1561, with a first edition of Stow's *Summarie*. Grafton anticipated Stow in this. See their quarrel carried on in the prefaces of the successive editions of their books and the *Dictionary of National Biography* under Stow.

4

Virgil, Richard Stanyhurst who, working upon material collected as early as 1569 by Edmund Campion, the Jesuit, contributed the greater part of the
history of his own country. The second edition of
Holinshed was at first published under the title,
The First and Second Volumes of Chronicles, etc. in
1587. It was revised and partly rewritten by J.
Hooker alias Vowell and others and in the process was
much altered and modernized. The book suffered
too from excision and in its " corrected " form appeared under the new title, *The Third Volume of Chronicles beginning at Duke William the Norman.* This
edition of 1587 is the chief quarry of Shakespeare and
other contemporary playwrights for the material of
English and Scottish history. To this enumeration of
chronicles may be added the scattered biographies of
historical personages from *The Life of Cardinal Wolsey*
by Cavendish, written in the reign of Mary, to Bacon's
Life of Henry VII., dating from the reign of King James.

Nor was the prevalent interest in English history
less notable among the poets whose flights, if by no
means so sustained as those of the chroniclers, were
far more frequent. *The Mirour for Magistrates* was
one of the earliest fruits of the Elizabethan press.
This work was originally projected in consequence of
the revived popularity of Lydgate's *Falls of Princes,*
which after but one reprinting in 1527, suddenly
attained a fourth issue in 1558. This origin gives to

The Mirour for Magistrates a medievalism of tone which
is enhanced by the sameness of mood, the moralizing,
the somewhat old-fashioned versification of the majority
of the "legends" and their connection by an artificial
thread. *The Mirour* is a growth and accretion. The
nineteen "legends" which constitute the first edition,
that of 1559, are the work of six writers, of whom
William Baldwin is the chief. They concern events
from the days of the two Roger Mortimers and
Thomas of Woodstock (1355–1397) to the tragedy
of George, Duke of Clarence (1478). The second
edition, 1563, reprinted these "legends" and added
eight more by several authors, three of whom had
already contributed to the first. Nearly all these
"legends" concern personages of the time of Richard
III. In 1574 John Higgins added seventeen "legends" of mythical and Roman Britain, and as they
preceded the other stories in point of time called the
new book *The first parte of the Mirour for Magistrates.*
Four years later a rival continuation called *The Sec-
onde part of the Mirrour for Magistrates conteining the
falles of the infortunate Princes of this Lande From the
Conquest of Cæsar unto the commyng of Duke William
the Conquerour* was published, the work of Thomas
Blenerhasset, Baldwin's work thus becoming the
third part. Blenerhasset's collection contains twelve
"legends." In 1587 Higgins added to his "first
part" no less than twenty-three stories, into which

several Roman emperors intrude with a few further tales of modern personages by Churchyard and others. The last edition of *The Mirour*, 1610, picks and chooses from the earlier ones and adds eleven "legends," one by Drayton, the rest by the editor, Richard Niccols. We have thus a *corpus* of nearly a hundred "legends" varying in length from fifty to four hundred lines each, the work of some fifteen authors, extending over a period of fifty years and appearing in eight issues. If excuse be deemed needful for this digression into particulars, the influence which a production so widely read must have exerted on the coming and the contemporary historical drama need only to be stated to be recognized. Upwards of thirty historical plays exist, the subjects of which are treated in *The Mirour for Magistrates*. And although from its meditative and elegiac character it is unlikely that it was often employed as an immediate source, the influence of such a work in choice of subject and, at times, in manner of treatment can not but have been exceedingly great.

The writing of single poems on the model of the separate "legends" of *The Mirour* began about the time of the earliest popularity of the Chronicle Play. The first of these productions apparently is *The Complaint of Rosamond* by Samuel Daniel, which appeared in 1592. In the next year we have no less than five poems of this class treating besides other topics, of

the well-known historical figures of Robert of Normandy, Piers Gaveston and Richard II., and the work
of men like Lodge, Drayton and Giles Fletcher. The
composition of poems of this class continues far into
the reign of King James in the works of obscure as
well as of better known authors and in poems dis-
coursing of Queen Matilda, of "the Love betweene
Owen Tudyr and the Queene," of Edward IV's courtship of Lady Gray, of the Lollard, Oldcastle, of
Humphrey of Gloucester, and above all in the favorite
theme of the age, the rise and fall of Richard III. and
"the Preservation of King Henry VII." The two
famous works, Daniel's *Civile Wars*, enlarged after its
first appearance in 1595 to eight books in the final
edition of 1609, and Drayton's *Mortimeriados*, 1596,
later rewritten as *The Barons Warres*, 1603, are epic
extensions of the single historical "legend" in verse,
showing too the influence of the contemporary versi-
fied chronicle which had been revived a few years
before in Warner's *Albions England*. This episodic
epic poem was published in 1586 and has for its general theme the legendary history of England from
the division of the world after the flood to the coming of the Normans. Warner's book gained an
immediate and deserved popularity from its patriotic
sentiment and its homely and unpretentious style.
He continued his chronicle to the accession of Queen
Elizabeth in the edition of 1592 and a final (sixth) edi-

tion was printed, in 1612, after the author's death, still further enlarged to include some of the events of the reign of James. Although Drayton had already written other "historical" poetry, his *Englands Hero-icall Epistles*, 1597, a series of letters in verse supposedly exchanged between royal and other historical lovers, was doubtless suggested by the serial character of *The Mirour for Magistrates*. Five editions of Drayton's *Epistles* were exhausted in six years. In 1604 an unsuccessful variation on the rimed chronicle was attempted by Sir William Harbert in *A prophesie of Cadwallader . . . containing a comparison of the English kings with many worthy Romanes from William Rufus till Henry the Fift*. Five years later the dramatist, Thomas Heywood, published his *Troia Britanica . . . an Universall Chronicle from the Creation untill these present times*. This work has more merit than has usually been accorded it, but it came too late to have any effect on the drama, as did Thomas Deloney's *The Crowne Garland of Golden Roses*, 1612, a collection of ballads on stories from English history. Of the many scattered broadsides and ballads on topics drawn from the national history it is impossible here to speak. The illustrated doggeral chronicle of Taylor, the Water Poet, although due to the same general impulse, belongs to a later age.

It is of interest to observe that the greatest vogue of epic historical verse precisely coincides with the period of the popularity of the Chronicle Play: the causes which begot the one begot the other. Moreover coincidences in the subject-matter of the two classes and in authorship are by no means wanting. Thus when Chute published his *Shores Wife*, Churchyard reprinted his contribution to *The Mirour for Magistrates* on the same topic and not long after appeared Heywood's dramatic treatment of the story in *Edward IV.* It was at the height of the interest in Richard III., which produced several plays, that Giles Fletcher wrote *The Rising to the Crowne of Richard III.;* and John Weever followed the play on Oldcastle and the trilogy of *Henry IV.* and *V.* with the *Life and Death of Sir John Oldcastle*, a kind of biography in verse. The English Chronicle Play is thus seen to be only one, though incomparably the most vigorous, offshoot of a body of literature of many species and of great variety, the very essence of which was the assertion of the national consciousness in recalling the scenes of the past. It was in the very nature of things that the popularity of the Chronicle Play should find its origin in the burst of patriotism and the sense of national unity which reached its climax in the year 1588 and stirred England to meet and to repulse the Spanish Armada. It was because the Elizabethan stage mirrored the life about it so widely and so minutely that it responded thus readily and deeply to the appeals of patriotism. " How would it haue ioyed braue Talbot (the terror of the French)," exclaims Thomas Nashe, " to thinke that after he had lyen two hundred yeare in his Toomb, he should triumph againe on the Stage and haue his bones new embalmed with the teares of ten thousand spectators at least, (at several times) who, in the Tragedian that represents his person, imagine they behold him fresh bleeding."[1]

To return to the Chronicle Play and to the development of the type in its earliest species, in February 1567, *The Tragedy of the King of Scots*, "to the which belonged the scenery of Scotland and a great castle on the other side," was acted at court, William Hunnis, Master of the Chapel Children, receiving payment therefor.[2] This play has perished. But its title remains the earliest to which we can attach a story drawn from modern British history, although conjecture as to whether it treated of the recently murdered Darnley or " of the death of Duncan and the succession of Macbeth " must be pronounced idle.[3] Turning to plays still extant, three claim our attention on the threshold. These are *The Famous Victories of Henry the fifth, The life and Death of Iack Strawe* and *The troublesome Raigne of Iohn King of England. The Famous Victories* was printed in 1598, but is undoubt-

[1] *Pierce Penilesse His Supplication*, 1592, *Works of Nashe*, ed. Grosart, II. 89.

[2] *Harleian MS.*, 146, fol. 15.

[3] See an article on *William Hunnis, the Dramatist*, in the *Athenæum*, March 31, 1900.

edly the oldest. Collier dated it "not long after 1580," Mr. Fleay a few years later.[1] It was acted by the Queen's players, a company at the height of its prosperity between the years 1586 and 1593, and according to *Tarlton's Jests* at the Bull.[2] It is certain that this play was popular before September 3, 1588, the date of the death of Richard Tarlton, who seems to have achieved a success in the rôle of Dericke, the clown, and to have taken such liberties with the part as to make it entirely his own, if he was not actually the author of the whole play as some authorities believe.[3] *The Famous Victories* deals with much the historical and traditionary material which Shakespeare afterwards utilized in his historical trilogy on Henry IV. and Henry V. The older play includes scenes depicting the wild life of the Prince and his low-lived companions, but differs widely from Shakespeare's in omitting the conspiracy of Northumberland, Mortimer and Hotspur, the character of Falstaff and the interesting group of the soldiers of Henry V., headed by Fluellen. On the other hand *The Famous Victories* devotes a scene to the episode of Prince Henry's commitment to jail for striking Justice Gascoigne in a fit of anger because the Justice had convicted one of Henry's followers of theft. The historical original of

---

[1] *Dramatic Poetry*, III. 70 ; *History of the Stage*, p. 67.
[2] *Shakespeare Society's Publications*, 1844, p. 24.
[3] Cf. Fleay, *Biographical Chronicle of the Drama*, II. 259.

both plays is found in Holinshed, and feeble suggestions of certain passages of Shakespeare in the historical portions of *The Famous Victories* have been frequently pointed out.   Thus although the incident of
the Dauphin's gift of a tun of tennis balls is mentioned
in Holinshed, the familiar lines beginning : " We are
glad the Dauphin is so pleasant with us" certainly
hark back to this passage :

Henry 5.   My lord prince Dolphin is very pleausant with
       me :
       But tel him, that in steed of balles of leather,
       We wil tosse him balles of brasse and yron,
       Yea such balles as neuer were tost in France,
       The proudest Tennis Court shall rue it. [1]

   Other points of contact among several are Shakespeare's passing reference to an embassy sent from
Harfleur to the French King, the bearer of the request being introduced in the old play ; Shakespeare's
expansion of the hint of Dericke's capture by a French
soldier and escape from him into Pistol's episode with
"Signieur Dew" ; King Henry's reproof of his way-
ward son and the famous scene in which Henry V.
wooes the Princess of France.[2]   Scarcely less clear is
Shakespeare's obligation (if obligation we dare call it)
to the suggestions of the comedy scenes of *The*

---

[1] *The Famous Victories*, Facsimile ed., 1887, p. 30.

[2] Cf. *ibid.*, pp. 19, 35, 44 and 46 with *2 Henry IV.*, IV. 5 ; *Henr*
V., III. 3, 45 ; IV. 4 ; and V. 5, 2.

Famous Victories. A companion of the Prince, addressed as Ned, furnishes his name at least to Ned Poins, and shows at times a faint touch of the "humor" of Ancient Pistol. The brief scene in which a captain impresses the thief and John Cobler for soldiers to serve the king in France with the accompanying farewell of Cobler's wife contains the suggestion—and how paltry it is!—of Shakespeare's laughable scenes of the impressing of Falstaff's ragged regiment and the farewell on the road to Staines. More important is the hint which the mock repetition by Dericke and Cobler of the trial before Justice Gascoigne certainly offered Shakespeare for the delightful mockery of Falstaff and Prince Hal, successively enacting the gravity of the king and the levity of his scapegrace son.

Der. Faith Iohn, Ile tel thee what, thou shalt be my Lord chiefe Iustice, and thou shalt sit in the chaire, And ile be the yong prince, and hit thee a boxe on the eare, And then thou shalt say, to teach you prerogatiues Meane, I commit you to the Fleete.

Iohn. Come on, Ile be your Iudge,
But thou shalt not hit me hard.

Der. No, no.

Iohn. What hath he done?

Der. Marry he hath robd Dericke.

Iohn. Why then I cannot let him go.

Der. I must needs haue my man.

Iohn. You shall not haue him.

Der. Shall I not haue my man, say no and you dare :
How say you, shall I not haue my man ?

Iohn. No marry shall you not.

Der. Shall I not Iohn ?

Iohn. No Dericke.

Der. Why then take you that till more come [*the slap*],
Sownes, shall I not have him ?

Iohn. Well I am content to take this at your hand,
But I pray you, who am I ?

Der. Who art thou, Sownds, doost not know thy self?

Iohn. No.

Der. Now away simple fellow,
Why man, thou art Iohn the Cobler.

Iohn. No, I am my Lord chiefe Iustice of England.

Der. Oh Iohn, Masse thou saist true, thou art indeed.

Iohn. Why then to teach you what prerogatiues mean,
I commit you to the Fleete. [1]

This passage is not devoid of humor, and the touch
by which the two simple wags half forget that they are
"making believe" and call each other by their true
names is natural and not altogether unamusing.

In contrast with the unity and dramatic consistency,
the power and the poetry which this species of drama
was soon to acquire in the masterful grasp of Marlowe
and Shakespeare, *The Famous Victories* is unendurably
rude and primitive, devoid as it is of the slightest attempt at dramatic structure and written almost wholly
in a bald and limping prose. But the choice of sub-

---

[1] *The Famous Victories*, p. 15.

ject is noteworthy and the desertion of rimed septen-
aries and four stress tumbling measures for prose is an
evident groping after a fitter medium for the expression of dramatic dialogue than was common earlier.

*The Life and Death of Iack Strawe, a notable Rebell
in England : who was kild in Smithfield by the Lord
Maior of London*, printed in 1593, is so short and slight
a production that it amounts to little more than an
historical interlude. It is divided into four acts of
disproportioned length and shows signs of haste and
immaturity in composition. It was registered in the
Stationers' Company, October 23, 1593, but is evidently of much earlier date. Mr. Fleay assigns it to
the year 1587 because the Armada is not mentioned
in it and because an insurrection of apprentices had
occurred in the previous year.[1] But there is really
nothing to guide us in these allusions and non-allu-
sions. The story is strictly confined to a single event,
the villeins' revolt in Essex and Kent in the year 1381.
The principal rôle amongst the rebels is maintained by
John Tyler, who, according to Holinshed, took upon
him to be their " cheefe capteine, naming himselfe Iacke
Straw."[2] But other rebels of the chroniclers appear,
among them the Wyclifite parson, John Ball. *Jack
Strawe* marks little advance in dramatic grasp or char-

---

[1] *Biographical Chronicle*, II. 153.

[2] *Chronicles of England*, ed. 1809 II. 736. The correction of
Tyler to Jack Straw, which appears in Dodsley's ed. of this play, was
made in ignorance of this fact.

acterization, but the play is vigorous and not ill written. It is the work of a man who could handle English verse, whether blank verse or lines in four stresses, with some fluency. We may share the opinion that "there are passages in *The Life and Death of Jack Strawe* which may lead us to suspect that it might prove to be the early work of some distinguished dramatist." [1] It may be of interest to note that Jack Straw had been a character of early pageantry. In an order of the Inner Temple, 1519, we learn that the king of Cockneys should sit and have due service on Childermas Day and "that Jack Straw and all his adherents should be thenceforth utterly banished, and no more used in this house." [2] Lastly a production called *The Life and Death of Jack Straw* by John Kirke was registered as late as 1638. It is uncertain if this was a play.

The two parts of *The Troublesome Raigne of Iohn King of England, with the discouerie of King Richard Cordelions Base sonne (vulgarly named, the Bastard Fawconbridge): also the death of King Iohn at Swinstead Abbey* were printed together in 1591. With this play we reach a typical specimen of the earlier Chronicle History before it was transformed by the genius of Marlowe and Shakespeare. That it was acted soon after the performance of *Tamburlaine* the prologue

[1] Dodsley, *Old English Plays*, V., p. 376.
[2] Nichols, *Elizabeth*, I. 252.

discloses. Hence unless the play antedate this prologue *The Troublesome Raigne* was first acted in the
year of the Armada. The company which brought it
out was the Queen's, and it has been variously ascribed
to the joint or several authorship of Lodge, Greene and
Marlowe, a matter the decision of which is not perti-
nent to the present enquiry. The sources of this play
have been traced to Holinshed and Halle and a special
interest attaches to it by reason of the fact that it is the
immediate though perhaps not the sole source on
which Shakespeare modelled *The Life and Death of
King John.* Although *The Troublesome Raigne* ad-
heres to epic sequence of event, the material of the
chronicle is treated with some skill and much freedom.
Thus the dramatist suppresses, as did Shakespeare
after him, the fact of the remarriage of Queen Constance and assigns a motive, in his rapacious treatment of the clergy, for the poisoning of John in
Swinstead Abbey, a point omitted by Shakespeare.[1]
The Troublesome Raigne retains the admixture of comic
and serious material which characterized the two older
specimens of its class and which descended to the
regular drama from the earliest times. These comic
scenes are often dependent for their effect on situation,
as is that in which the Bastard, seeking for treasure in
the sack of a monastery, discovers "a smooth facte
[faced] Nunne" locked up in the Prior's treasure-

[1] See Boswell-Stone, *Shakspere's Holinshed*, 1896, p. 45.

chest, whither she had fled, as she says, "to hide her from lay men." But such scenes have become a more natural and essential part of the drama and less a matter of extraneous clown's play. The clown, such as Dericke, is not a character of the *The Troublesome Raigne*, and the step to the comedy of Shakespeare's *Henry IV.* becomes conceivable. Whether from reluctance to offer so great a relief to the dark picture of the unworthy tyrant John or from the example of Marlowe, Shakespeare reduced the comedy element of the older play to the single figure of the Bastard Faulconbridge and ennobled that personage with a deeper and richer character than is his in *The Troublesome Raigne.* To accomplish this last Shakespeare was compelled to omit the finest scene of the older play, that between Philip and Lady Fawconbridge, in which the youth wrings from his reluctant mother a confession of her frailty and the certainty that his real father was King Richard Cordelion. Shakespeare also confined within bounds the staunch and boisterous Protestant spirit with which the earlier play is pervaded, a spirit which in view of the contemporary struggle with Spain assumes a political rather than a polemical bias. It is in the older play that King John exclaims with prophetic vision :

> The Pope of Rome, tis he that is the cause,
> He curseth thee, he sets thy subiects free
> From due obedience to their Soueraigne :

He animates the Nobles in their warres,
He giues away the Crowne to Philips Sonne,
And pardons all that seeke to murther thee :
And thus blinde zeale is still predominant.
Then Iohn there is no way to keepe thy Crowne,
But finely to dissemble with the Pope :
That hand that gaue the wound must giue the salue
To cure the hurt, els quite incurable.
Thy sinnes are farre too great to be the man
T' abolish Pope, and Popery from thy Realme :
But in thy Seate, if I may gesse at all,
A King shall raigne that shall suppresse them all.[1]

This spirit, which does not materially interfere with
the general purpose of the play, suffices together with its
improved style, the greater ease of its verse, its earnest
attempt at consistency and clear outlining of character, to raise this play to a position distinctly above the
two earlier productions of its class. It may not be too
much to affirm that in the personages of *The Troublesome Raigne*, especially in the king and in Fawconbridge (to the vigorous characterization of which
Shakespeare himself owes more than a hint) we have
the earliest vital representation of an historical personage upon the English stage.

From these plays it is clear that the instinctive
end and aim of the English Chronicle Drama from the
first was "the scenic representation of history." It
therefore conformed to the chronological rather than

---

[1] *The Troublesome Raigne*, Part II., facsimile reprint, p. 13.

5

to the logical or dramatic order of events, and often followed its narrative sources with a fidelity absolutely slavish. Moreover the authors of these dramas were unselective in their use of material and uncontrolled by questions of authenticity. For these reasons the legends and digressions of the chroniclers, however improbable or unconnected with the main narrative, were accepted and followed with fidelity or expanded into episodic scenes. Besides all this it is to be remembered that the age of Elizabeth knew no fine distinctions between fact and myth, and was untroubled even in the writing of sober chronicles by the necessity or even the show of a nice adherence to what we now term historical truth. To dramatists as to chroniclers the legends concerning Brute, Cymbeline or King Arthur were not distinguishable in their credibility from the received records of the doings of Harry Monmouth, Richard Crookback of bluff King Henry. They accepted whatever they found and used it as they found it. The consequent diversity of subject-matter in these plays is as great as their want of individual unity. Both of these features are abundantly disclosed in their many quaint titles: "The Famous Chronicle of king Edward the first, sirnamed Edward, Longshankes, with his returne from the holy land. Also the life of Llevellen rebell in Wales. Lastly, the sinking of Queene Elinor, who sunck at Charing-crosse, and rose againe at Potters-hith, now named

Queenehith "; " The First and Second parts of King
Edward the Fourth, containing His merie pastime with
the Tanner of Tamworth, as also his loue to faire
Mistresse Shore, her great promotion, fall and miserie,
and lastly the lamentable death of both her and her
husband. Likewise the besieging of London, by the
Bastard Falconbridge, and the valiant defence of the
same by the Lord Maior and the Citizens." In a word
in plays such as these was developed the most popular and lasting type of the English Chronicle Play, a
type which partook more or less fully of the epic nature of its immediate sources, the chronicles, ballads
and popular "histories" in verse and in prose.

Let us now turn to a general survey of the number of these plays and the distribution of them over
the period to which our attention is confined. Between 1562, the date of the performance of *Gorboduc*,
and the closing of the theaters in 1642 there is record
of more than a hundred and fifty plays dealing with
subjects drawn from the history of England and from
what went for such at that time. Of these about half
are extant; the remainder, of which many never
reached the press, disappeared after having served the
purpose of the moment. If we add to these a few
plays in which a quasi-historical atmosphere is preserved by placing the plot in a definite English reign
of the past, and also the several in which the travels
and adventures of Englishmen abroad (subjects refer-

able to the same general impulse) are the theme, and if we remember that we have reason to believe that here, as in other classes of the drama, the very name and memory of many plays have perished, we may be able to form some conception of what must have been the complete body of the English historical drama.   Every reign, from that of Edward the Confessor to that of Elizabeth herself, is laid under contribution as the scene for these plays.   Some monarchs figure in many plays : John in six, Edward III., Henry V. and Richard III. in seven each, some of them no longer extant; Henry VI. in ten.   Four plays depict events in the reign of Henry VIII. and as many more concern the lives of his children.   The coming of William, English prowess against the French, the Scotch or the Welsh, the struggles of the barons in Stephen's day, in John's or in Henry's ; the renown of Richard Lion Heart, of the Black Prince or of John of Gaunt ; the deeds of lesser heroes such as Talbot, Hereford, Owen Tudor, all come in for their share in this drama of action.   Nor were the heroes of Saxon times forgotten, from Hengist to Earl Godwin, nor yet the early British kings Brute, Lear and Gorboduc to the historical opponents of Rome, Caractacus and Boadicea.

The distribution of these plays over the period of the reigns of Elizabeth and James is significant. About a dozen dramas yet extant fall before the year

1590, one of them, the Latin comedy, *Byrsa Basilica*, two others, the Latin college plays on Richard III., mentioned above. Of the remainder, *Gorboduc* and *The Misfortunes of Arthur* were written, as we have seen, under the immediate influence of Seneca ; *Locrine* partially so. Two more of these plays, *Fair Em* and *James IV. of Scotland*, are pseudo-historical and may date a little later. The three undoubted chronicle plays discussed above make up the count. In the next decade, 1590 to 1600, the Chronicle Play attained its greatest popularity. Nearly eighty plays, less than half of which are extant, fall therein. In this period this species of drama was elevated by Marlowe and Shakespeare from a mere *drame de circonstance*, declaiming against popery as in *The Troublesome Raigne of John*, or abusive of the enemies of England as in the gross misrepresentations of Queen Elinor of Castile in *Edward I.* and of Joan of Arc in *1 Henry VI.*, to an artistic utterance containing a universal appeal.

With the coming of the new century, this class of plays was superseded in popular esteem by the romantic drama and the comedy of manners, and the recorded examples of the Chronicle Play fall to some thirty, most of them acted in the first few years of the century. Of these less than half have survived. After 1610 plays the subjects of which are drawn from English history and myth are rare and the choice of such subjects must be regarded as for the most part accidental, whilst their treatment is not infrequently purely romantic.[1]

Returning to the consideration of the English Chronicle Drama in the heyday of its popularity, it is of interest to note how wholly these plays are of the people. Few were performed at court : none until it had acquired a reputation on the London boards. Scarcely any were presented at the universities or at the Inns of Court, the former turning to dramatic satire, the latter to Senecan tragedy and later to the masque. Apparently the first company of actors to popularize the Chronicle Play was the Queen's which occupied, off and on with other companies between 1584 and 1593, the old Theater in Finsbury Fields, the earliest theatrical structure built in London. This company enjoyed for a short time a monopoly of the stage. Greene, Lodge, Peele and Marlowe all wrote for it, though Greene alone remained with it when fortune had fallen away. Whatever may be their precise and varying relations, it is in the hands of this *coterie* of playwrights that the chronicle play received its earliest development. In the following years by far the largest number of historical dramas of which we have any record were acted by the companies under the control of Philip Henslowe, by the Earl of Pembroke's, the Admiral's, Lord Derby's, Worcester's

[1] See the Table of Extant Plays and the List of Historical Dramas at the end of this book.

and Sussex's men, at the Rose, the Fortune and the theater at Newington Butts. This does not prove that Henslowe's companies monopolized the plays of this kind, for our data are too incomplete for any such generalization. But this certainly does show that the vogue of the Chronicle Play was great with companies which were removed from the influence of the court. Of these plays of Henslowe the greater part is lost. A large number of extant plays remain to attest the rival activity of Shakespeare's company under its various patrons at the Theater, the Globe and Blackfriars. Owing to the fact that we have no record such as *Henslowe's Diary* for this company, what proportion of plays may have perished must remain matter of pure conjecture. Dekker's *Satiromastix*, 1601, is the solitary play remotely of this class which we know to have been acted by a company of children. And the English setting of this play, the purpose of which is wholly satirical, is purely accidental. The absurdity of laying the scene in the England of William Rufus is patent, and unaccountable except on the tradition that Dekker was pressed for time in the composition of his work and under the necessity of utilizing old material. It seems reasonable to infer that the vogue of the Chronicle Play was general and shared in by all the public companies of adult actors.

III

SHAKESPEARE'S PREDECESSORS: MAR-LOWE AND HISTORICAL TRAGEDY

WE have seen the English Chronicle Play originating in the years immediately preceding the coming of the Spanish Armada and have noted that the earliest productions of the type were performed by the Queen's company of which Richard Tarlton died a member and for which Robert Greene was long a playwright. We have also considered in sketch the number of these plays and their distribution over the period of their popularity; so that our enquiry must now fall wholly within the limits of a map already outlined. Let us now enquire more specifically into the part which the immediate predecessors of Shakespeare took in the development of this species of drama. Of the group of dramatists which preceded Shakespeare and rivalled him in the apprenticeship of his career, the names of John Lyly and Thomas Kyd alone have escaped association with the Chronicle Play. No one of the unaided plays of Greene is, strictly speaking, historical; although English kings figure in no less than three of them and a James IV. of Scotland—whose doings belong not to chronicles—gives another its title. The name of Greene as a coadjutor, however, has been associated with three or four of the early chronicle histories. There is nothing to show that he had a hand in *The Troublesome Raigne;* but the general consensus of criticism allots to him a share in the three plays on Henry VI., which in their later revision are commonly included among the works of Shakespeare. But whatever may have been Greene's share in these and in other historical plays,[1] his contemporary reputation must have depended far less on scenes of horror, in which he could but follow where Kyd and Marlowe led, than on episodes of light comedy such as made his repute in fiction.

Thomas Lodge has left no English historical drama wholly of his own composition and his share in *The Troublesome Raigne, 1 Henry VI., The First Contention* (the earlier form of *2 Henry VI.*), the older *Richard III.* and *King Leir* can not but be regarded as largely a matter of conjecture. Lodge's traffic with the stage was of short duration. In his *Scillaes Metamorphosis,* a volume of poetry published in 1589, he declares his determination :

To write no more of that whence shame doth grow :
Or tie my pen to pennie-knaues delight
But liue with fame, and so for fame to wright.[2]

[1] The late Mr. John Addington Symonds considered parts of *Locrine* "much in the manner of Greene." *Shakspere's Predecessors*, p. 308. See the late Dr. Grosart's paper: "Was Robert Greene substantially the Author of Titus Andronicus?" *Englische Studien*, XXII. 389; and also his edition of *Selimus* in the *Temple Dramatists*, 1898.

[2] *Poems of Lodge*, ed. Chiswick, 1819, p. 33.

With Peele and Marlowe we reach firmer ground ;
for each besides the portions which sound or ingenious
criticism has assigned to him in several plays of doubtful authorship, is the unassisted author of one historical drama : Peele of *Edward I.*, Marlowe of *Edward II.*   Of Peele's relation to the earlier dramas of
this class and of the inspiration which *Gorboduc* was to
him in *Locrine* enough has already been said.   There
remain the three plays on Henry VI.   In the long and
intricate discussion as to the authorship of these plays
Peele's claims like those of Lodge and Greene, have
naturally taken a place second to the more important
claims of Shakespeare.   The names of the two lesser
dramatists were first associated with *1 Henry VI.* by
Malone in his famous *Dissertation on the Three Parts
of King Henry VI.*   These claims were soon extended
by others to the two parts of *The Contention betwixt
the two famous Houses of Yorke and Lancaster*, the
two old plays which in fuller form are printed in editions of Shakespeare as *2* and *3 Henry VI.*   This discussion has continued to Mr. Fleay, who assigns to
Peele, as to the other authors whom he thinks concerned, each his part, with a certainty which is alike
the wonder and the despair of other critics.[1]   None the
less the mention of Peele in this connection has been for
the most part faint and uncertain, and in a recent sum-
mary of the whole question by Professor Ward has

[1] See especially his *Life of Shakespeare*, p. 255.

sunk to the statement of a bare possibility.[1] Even
when we add Peele's one undoubted play on an English historical subject, it must be confessed that this is
slender evidence on which to base any theory which
gives to him a prominent place in the early development of the English Chronicle Drama. Peele had
emulated the success of Lyly at Court in his own *Arraignment of Paris*, he had essayed a revival of a time-
honored subject in his dramatized version of biblical
story, *David and Bethsabe*, he imitated *Tamburlaine* in
its extravagance and grandiloquence in *The Battle of
Alcazar*, as to all appearances he had imitated *Gorboduc* or *The Misfortunes of Arthur* in the serious parts
of *Locrine*. Peele's *Chronicle of King Edward I.* is
one more example of the same imitative and adaptable
talent. Here, as elsewhere, he seems to have followed
in the wake of others. This inartificial and hasty production was first printed in 1593, and its original performance probably dates from 1590 or 1591. Frequent mention of a play called "long shankes" in
Henslowe's Diary, which could hardly have been any
other than Peele's, points to a not inconsiderable popularity. The story of *Edward I.* is disfigured by an
outrageous and altogether gratuitous libel on the
memory of Good Queen Elinor of Castile. Peele was
not above utilizing the momentary prejudice of the
populace to the full, and he has in consequence pro-

[1] *Dramatic Literature*, II. 67 and 73.

duced in his "Queen Elinor" a monster of mingled wickedness and absurdity.[1] *Edward I.* marks absolutely no advance on the earliest dramas of its class and, with every allowance for a text hopelessly corrupt, must be pronounced a production far below the grade of *Locrine.* We may then conclude that while Greene, Peele and possibly Lodge were engaged at one time or another in the joint or several composition of chronicle histories they really added little to what had already been accomplished by the unknown author of *The Troublesome Raigne of John.*

Among several plays which have been dated close to 1590, *The Raigne of King Edward the third. As it hath bin sundrie times plaied about the Citie of London,* claims our attention not only from the fact that it is among the most favorable specimens of the English Chronicle Play before its transformation by Shakespeare and Marlowe, but from the additional circumstance that the hand of Shakespeare has been thought by some to be discernible in it. *Edward III.* is exceedingly well written, easily maintaining the literary excellence of the plays on Henry VI. in the qualities of spirited dialogue, picturesque phrase and occasional poetical sentiment. Indeed the incisiveness of King Edward's defiance of the French, with which the first act opens compares not altogether unfavorably with

[1] Cf. the ballad entitled *A Warning-Piece to England against Pride and Wickedness,* reprinted by Mr. Bullen in his ed. of *Peele,* 1888, I. 77.

the similar scene of *Henry V.* But *Edward III.* contains somewhat inorganically within it a romantic episode, albeit of its hero, derived from that storehouse of
romance, Painter's *Palace of Pleasure.*[1] This is the story
King Edward's lawless pursuit of the beautiful and
virtuous Countess of Salisbury, here told with such a
power, with so full a realization of its dramatic capabilities and with so vigorous a portrayal alike of the
amorous king and the true-hearted lady that many
have not hesitated to ascribe these scenes to the pen
of Shakespeare. Edward has rescued from the be-
leaguering Scots the castle of Lady Salisbury, who in
gratitude and loyalty courteously entertains him. Here
are the sure words with which this earlier Imogen
meets the advances of her royal guest, who has taken
an unworthy advantage in gaining her oath before-
hand to "redeeme" a wrong which he declares he is
suffering in her house :

Countess. As easie may my intellectual soule
          Be lent awaie, and yet my bodie liue,
          As lend my bodie, pallace to my soule,
          Awaie from her, and yet retaine my soule.
          My bodie is her bower, her Court, her abey,
          And shee an Angell, pure, deuine, vnspotted :
          If I should lend her house, my Lord, to thee,
          I kill my poore soule, and my poore soule me.
King. Didst thou not swere to giue me what I would ?
Countess. I did, my liege, so, what you would, I could.

[1] *Novell XLVI.*, ed. Jacobs, 1890, I. 334.

King.　I wish no more of thee then thou maist giue :
　　Nor beg I do not, but I rather buie,
　　That is, thy loue ; and for that loue of thine
　　In rich exchaunge I tender to thee myne.
Countess.　But that your lippes were sacred, my Lord,
　　You would prophane the holie name of loue.
　　That loue you offer me, you cannot giue ;
　　For Cæsar owes that tribut to his Queene :
　　That loue you beg of me, I cannot giue ;
　　For Sara owes that duetie to her Lord.
　　He that doth clip or counterfeit your stamp,
　　Shall die, my Lord : And will your sacred
　　　selfe
　　Comit high treason against the King of heauen,
　　To stamp his Image in forbidden mettel,
　　Forgetting your alleageance and your othe ?[1]

From the perpetuation of the old epic type of the
English Chronicle Play nothing artistic could be expected and nothing came. Save for a more finished
diction, more fluent verse and a clearer perception of
the historic scenes delineated, the latest plays of the
type offer little or no advance, dramatically considered,
beyond the first beginnings. The unifying artistic

---

[1] *Edward III.*, Warnke and Proescholdt, ed. II. 1, 235–259.　With
this passage compare *Measure for Measure*, II. 4, 42–46.

　　　It were as good
　To pardon him, that hath from nature stolne
　A man already made, as to remit
　Their sawcie sweetness, that do coyne heauens Image
　In stamps that are forbid.

motive that crystallized this amorphous mass into a form of beauty came in the first instance from Marlowe, and secondly from Shakespeare himself. With Marlowe it took a concentrated and tragic form, which Shakespeare at first followed. But it attained at last in the hands of the master dramatist a comprehensiveness in which comedy and tragedy become reconciled and the whole range of human life is represented in its political and social relations. It is to the consideration of the tragic type of the Chronicle Drama as developed by Marlowe in his *Edward II.*, to Shakespeare's successive practice of the older epic manner in those plays in which he worked over the material of others, his following of Marlowe in *Richard III.* and his growth through *Richard II.* to the realization of the higher ideal just mentioned in the trilogy of *Henry IV.* and *V.* that we must now address ourselves.

The name of Marlowe has been associated with several chronicle plays. We may reject as untenable the notion that Marlowe had a part in *The Troublesome Raigne of John*, together with the theory that much of an original *Richard III.* was actually written by him.[1] But we must accept the prevalent opinion which awards to that poet a part in the joint authorship of the two old plays commonly known as *The First* and *Second Contentions* together with a probable

---

[1] Fleay, *Life of Shakespeare*, p. 276, and Halliwell-Phillipps, *Outlines*, ed. 1898, I. p. 148.

share in *1 Henry VI.* The full titles of the former two plays runs : *The First part of the Contention betwixt the two famous Houses of Yorke and Lancaster, with the death of the good Duke Humphrey : And the banishment and death of the Duke of Suffolke, and the Tragicall end of the proud Cardinall of Winchester, with the notable Rebellion of Iacke Cade : And the Duke of Yorkes first claime unto the Crowne :* and *The true Tragedie of Richard Duke of Yorke, and the death of good King Henrie the Sixt, with the whole contention betweene the two Houses Lancaster and Yorke.* These plays were printed in the years 1594 and 1595, respectively, and have been variously regarded as earlier, ruder drafts or as later and defective copies of *2* and *3 Henry VI.* Neither nice limitations of the extent of Marlowe's authorship in these three plays nor a precise determination of their chronology need concern us here. It has been held that Marlowe's one unaided chronicle play, *Edward II.,* followed the two *Contentions,* and that the many parallel passages between these plays and *Edward II.* are to be referred to Marlowe's borrowings from that earlier work.[1] This view Professor Ward combats with the argument that the *Contentions* " unmistakably represent in some respects, more especially in the treatment of the humorous element, an advance which had not been reached

[1] See Halliwell-Phillipps in the *Shakespeare Society's Papers,* 1844, I. 5 and Miss Lee, Transactions of the New Shakspere Society, 1875–76, pp. 219–311.

in *Edward II.*"[1] Whatever may be the relation of
these borrowed passages, this last opinion we must
absolutely reject, for nothing can be clearer as a result
of the study of the English chronicle plays than the
fact that the humorous element is present in their
earliest type and common to the whole species throughout the period of their popularity, except where occasionally deliberately rejected. *Edward II.* was registered for publication in July, 1593, less than two
months after the poet's tragic death at Deptford. His
play could not have been above two or three years old
at that time. It seems reasonable to regard such a
triumph of dramatic art as Marlowe's crowning work
in this species of the drama, rather than to suppose
that he subsequently returned to collaboration in plays
of a less organic structure and of a literary quality
generally inferior.

The descriptive title of Marlowe's play runs *The
troublesome raigne and lamentable death of Edward the
second, King of England : with the tragicall fall of proud
Mortimer. . . . Written by Chri. Marlow Gent.*, 1594.
The title of the second quarto, of 1598, adds *And also
the life and death of Peirs Gaueston, the greate Earle of
Cornewall, and mighty favorite of king Edward the
second.* The subject of this play is substantially that
of Shakespeare's *Richard II.:* the struggle of a weak
and unprincipled king, a prey to favorites, to maintain

[1] *Dramatic Literature,* I. 349.

6

his will and later his crown against a group of rebellious nobles whom his arrogance and injustice has estranged and incensed. The parallel is historical, and the tragic element lies in the inherently unkingly nature of both the royal protagonists. Each is odious in his prosperity, but each rises to dignity when the flood of misfortune flows full upon him and claims our compassion in his overthrow. The period of the action of *Edward II.* extends over the events of twenty years and has been condensed into dramatic cohesion with no common skill. As Mr. Verity points out, the troubles in Ireland in 1315 and 1316 and the Scottish border raids of 1318 are made to agree in time, and are referred to the evil counsels of Gaveston, who had actually paid the forfeit of his enmity to the rebellious nobles several years before.[1] Similarly " Warwick, who died in 1315, is made to take part in the battle of Boroughbridge, and afterwards atone for the execution of Gaveston, so that poetic justice may be satisfied : the younger Spencer is represented, with great gain to the continuity of the drama, as succeeding Gaveston immediately in the favor of the king; whereas for several years after Gaveston's death in 1312 he sided with Lancaster's party, was the object of Edward's bitter hostility, and did not change till about 1318." [2] Other departures from the historical sources are the degrading of the social rank of the Spencers to

[1] *Edward II.*, *Temple Dramatists*, p. ix.
[2] *Ibid.*, p. viii.

match that of the upstart Gaveston, and the suggestion of a motive for Queen Isabella's faithlessness to
her royal husband in his indifference and neglect of
her. As Mr. Verity says : " these . . . are in the main
only changes of time or place and do not involve misrepresentation of character." [1] We have here, in a
word, the artist's use of material, whereby the essential
is distinguished with unerring tact from the non-essen-
tial and a truer and severer logic imparted to the sequence of events and to the characters and their relations to each other than can ever exist in life. The
constructive excellence of *Edward II.* is unusual :
when we consider its early date and the exuberant
and lyric quality of the genius of Marlowe, the play in
its restraint becomes worthy of the highest possible
praise. No one will deny that in Marlowe the poet
is greater than the dramatist. But to say that his
work " was cast by accident and caprice into the imperfect mould of the drama " [2] is to say too much.
For in a comparison with his peers Marlowe holds his
own as a constructive dramatist, and is not among the
least in power of characterization. If we feel in-
stinctively that he is not at his best in the glowing
extravagance of *Tamburlaine* or even in the at times
too palpable restraint of *Edward*, it is because we remember the ravishing melody and rare poetic flights

[1] *Ibid.*, p. ix.
[2] Saintsbury, *Elizabethan Literature*, p. 79.

of *Hero and Leander* or the deeper-toned lyrical passages of *Faustus*. In view of these heights and bursts of melody the conscious restraint of *Edward II.* becomes the more noteworthy and the more significant in its promise of the harmonious growth of Marlowe into a world-dramatist as well as a world-poet, a growth unhappily blighted in its spring and destined never to reach fulfilment.

Although the main source of *Edward II.* is Holinshed, Marlowe took certain particulars from Fabyan and Stow and condensed and rearranged his materials as we have already seen, omitting the customary clownage. So that in place of a series of events, connected solely because they all happen to one protagonist and alternated with scenes of mere comic diversion, each scene and character is grouped about the central idea, the struggle of Edward with his barons, and unfolded in such a manner as to lend to the total effect. Up to the turning point of the play (Edward's triumph over his rebellious peers in the third scene of act third) the king is consistently presented to us in a light disadvantageous to our conception of his character as a man and as a sovereign. His vacillation, tergiversation and cowardice are vividly displayed, and his lavish and wanton generosity to Gaveston, the unworthy favorite, whom he permits to insult the noblest men of the realm and even his queen in the royal presence. His childish threats, his injustice and outrage to the church, his want of royal dignity in permitting his barons to quarrel in his presence and bandy abuse, his unchivalrous neglect of his queen and brutal innuendoes as to her relations with Mortimer—all are artfully employed to throw the weight of the spectator's sympathy against this unregal sovereign. On the other hand no sooner has fortune turned against Edward and he is surprised in the Abbey of Neath, " heavy with drowsiness of woe," than the weight is shifted and our attention is drawn away from the king's misdeeds and arrogance to the selfishness and disloyalty of his enemies : to Mortimer, who is no passionate lover chivalrously in arms to right the wrongs of his queen and beloved, but a vulgar intriguer for the crown, playing on the starved affections of a weak woman, seeking to pervert the young prince ; to Isabella herself, long faithless, now become vindictive and conniving at the murder of her lord ; to the hard jailer, Berkley, and Matrevis, Gurney and their hired assassins. The king's brother, Kent, a just man and siding with the barons against the royal abuses, returns to allegiance when Edward's sorrows increase upon him and falls a sacrifice to the royal cause. As to Edward, his faults are forgotten and our attention is riveted on the fading dignity of misused kingship, now slipping away from his reluctant grasp. Face to face with the inevitable, Edward moralizes on the vanity of kingship :

> But what are Kings, when regiment is gone,
> But perfect shadowes in a sun-shine day?

And cries out in anguish :

> Ah Leister, weigh how hardly I can brooke
> To lose my Crowne and Kingdome without cause,
> To giue ambitious Mortimer my right,
>
> .   .   .   .
>
> Here take my Crowne, the life of Edward too.

Then taking off his crown and holding it in his hand, he pleads :

> Let me be King till night,
> That I may gaze vpon this glittering Crowne,
> So shall my eyes receiue their last content,
> My head the latest honour due to it,
> And ioyntly both yeeld vp their wished right.
> Continue euer thou celestiall Sunne,
> Let neuer silent night possesse this clime,
> Stand still you watches of the Element,
> All times and seasons rest you at a stay,
> That Edward may be still faire Englands King!

At length discrowned forever by his own involuntary act he turns his back on his court and exclaims :

> Now, sweete God of Heauen,
> Make me despise this transitory pompe,
> And sit for aye inthronized in Heauen,
> Come death, and with thy fingers close my eyes,
> Or if I liue let me forget my selfe.[1]

Deeper and deeper are the drafts of this royal ill-doer upon our sympathy up to that supreme scene in which

[1] *Edward II.*, V. 1, 26–111.

a violent and horrible death overtakes him discrowned, dishonored and overwatched.

Many details might be cited to show the dramatic aptitude of Marlowe. Such is the brief episode of the opening scene in which three poor men seek the service of Gaveston. Such is the dramatic foreshadowing of the character of Spencer before he succeeds to the precarious honors of that favorite, and the skilful interweaving of the two "favorite threads." [1] Such too is the postponement of Gaveston's death [2] to heighten its effect, and the employment of the report of it to enflame Edward to the climax of the play, his momentary triumph and abuse of that triumph in the execution of Warwick and the banishment of Kent. [3] The latter's attempted rescue of his brother, the king, too, is opportunely introduced to supply what is technically known as "the force of final suspense." More delicate is the touch by which at the very moment that the reverse action (the queen's and Mortimer's conspiracy hatched in France) is set in motion, the young Prince is made to utter the first note of "the sentimental fallacy of the king's real openness to kind management" which is so effectually employed during "the decline." The success too with which the Prince is kept clear of the intrigue and made to assert his sense of justice and his kingship in the end is as

[1] *Ibid.*, II. 1.
[2] From II. 5 to III. 2.
[3] *Ibid.*, III. 3.

worthy of praise as the artful manner in which the
dramatist has contrived to maintain our interest in
the unworthy king when the catastrophe shortly to
overwhelm him has become inevitable.

Well conceived and strongly outlined as are the
characters of Edward, the boyish Prince, the haughty
insurgent Mortimer and the judicious Kent, it must be
acknowledged that in this particular Marlowe does
not stand so clearly the superior of his contemporaries
as in dramatic constructiveness and poetic richness and
vigor of thought. There are breaks and inconsequences
in characterization in all Marlowe's plays, and in *Edward* the figure of Queen Isabella seems especially defective in portrayal and is certainly not to be named with
the fresh and breathing women of Greene, Margaret of
Friar Bacon and Ida of *James IV.*, or even with Marlowe's own Zenocrete or Abigail. Isabella is at first
weak and affectionate, content to endure her loveless
life in quiet and uncomplaining suffering. In the end
she has become a woman hardened in sin and abetting
her paramour in his murder of her husband. This
transition is not delineated in the play, and the transformation if admitted as psychologically possible is in-
defensible dramatically, especially when unexpressed.
In a series of notes (which contain the best dramatic
analysis of this play with which I am acquainted) the
late Professor McLaughlin has suggested : "In Marlowe's plan of building up sympathy against the king

until the tragedy was prepared for, he wished to enlist
the audience on the queen's side at first, as a loving
and injured wife, then after the reverse action was
under way, he aimed to intensify pity for the victim
by every device ; and what would create a stronger
reaction in his favor than the shamelessness of such a
woman as this later Isabel? So with this ultimate
treatment in mind, and as if to give a clue to what is
coming, he tainted her early innocence by slanderous
blemishes, which her transformed nature afterward
proceeded to verify." [1] This is probably the true so-
lution and may likewise account for the fact that
Marlowe has been content to assert rather than to
delineate the guilty passion of Mortimer and the
queen. Inconsequence and sketchiness remain none
the less essential defects of Marlowe's portrayal of historical personages, and it is not in the delineation of
character that his service to the English Chronicle
Drama is to be recorded. When all has been said,
it is the fine restraint, the artist's feeling of fitness,
which has given us in its best scenes no word too
much or word irrelevant, the sense of a general design
and the severity with which it is carried out, above all
the distinction of style and the impelling force of its
sheer poetry that distinguishes this remarkable tragedy
not only from what had gone before it in its own
kind but from its few peers in the English drama.

[1] *Edward II.*, ed. McLaughlin, 1894, p. 163.

Edward II. may be considered the final evolution of the tragic type of the English Chronicle Play. The qualities which differentiate it from the class of plays out of which it was evolved are, briefly to summarize, its superior selectiveness of material, its suppression of scenes of comic diversion and of all matter extraneous to the central idea, its conscious constructiveness and self-restraint, all tending towards a fuller artistic and dramatic unity; lastly its attempt at a higher and more serious conception of character and the infusion of an elevated poetical spirit throughout the whole.

IV

THE MARLOWE–SHAKESPEARE PLAYS

WE turn now to a consideration of the plays on
Henry VI. and Richard III., the dramas in which
Shakespeare, whether in revision or in independent
authorship, was working either with Marlowe or
directly under his influence. We shall defer Shakespeare's independent development of the possibilities
of the Chronicle Play to a later treatment since such
was the order of time. Unedifying and wearisome as
the intricate crimes and sufferings of the houses of
York and Lancaster must seem to the reader of history to-day, this subject had a present interest to the
Elizabethan from the fact that these internecine civil
feuds were to him the latest events in which English
prowess and heroism had displayed themselves in full
glory, and from the additional circumstance that out
of these political upheavals had been evolved the
stable Tudor dynasty under which Englishmen were
then enjoying a national prosperity hitherto unknown.
The popularity of the Wars of the Roses and the ac-
companing events as subjects for historical, epic and
dramatic treatment is attested by numerous contemporary books. Aside from the parts of general chronicles like those of Grafton, Stow and Holinshed which

are employed with this period, Halle's *The Union of the two noble and illustrate famelies of Lancastre and Yorke*, 1548, is devoted wholly to this theme, and Sir Thomas More's fragment of a *History of Richard III.*, authentically published in 1557, to a later portion of it. In narrative verse the events of the reigns of Henry VI. and his two successors may be affirmed to have been for years the most popular of all subjects. In the first edition of *The Mirour for Magistrates* there are eleven stories of historical personages who figured in the Wars of the Roses, nearly half of the whole collection. The second edition added six such stories, and that of 1587 two more, giving us a total of all but twenty "legends" devoted to this one period. Besides this Daniel's *Civile Wars*, three of Drayton's *Heroicall Epistles* and several chapters of *Albions England* concern characters of that age, and some half dozen single poems by lesser men treat of Jane Shore, Edward IV. and his brother Richard. In the drama besides the three parts of *Henry VI.* and the two *Contentions*, the scene of *The Blind Beggar of Bednall Green* by Day and Chettle, 1600, is laid in Henry's reign though it deals little with any real historical event, and a play entitled *The Battle of Hexham* by Barnaby Barnes of uncertain date was extant in manuscript in 1807. An eighth play, the plot of which must have fallen within the reign of Henry was *Duke Humphrey*, one of the many old dramas destroyed by

that menial Omar of English dramatic literature, Warburton's cook, and dating 1625, beyond the period
with which we are here concerned. Turning to *Edward IV.*, Heywood's two plays on that monarch and
a non-extant *Shores Wife* by Day and Chettle are the
only dramas wholly concerned with Edward's reign.
The rise and fall of the portentous figure of Richard
III. was by far the most popular of English dramatic
historical subjects, a fact proved by no less than seven
plays between Dr. Legge's Latin tragedy in 1579 and
the lost *Richard Crookback* of Jonson, 1602. An
eighth play on this subject was *A Tragedy of Richard
the Third or the English Prophet with the Reformation*
by Samuel Rowley, licensed in 1623 and long since
perished. Most of these plays must have made the
ill-favored figure of Richard their chief study. Such
is certainly true of the several which have come down
to us. But one of those now lost but mentioned by
Henslowe appears to have centered attention on one
of the most prominent of Richard's victims, the Duke
of Buckingham, another on Richard's victor and successor, Henry, Earl of Richmond.[1] In short we have
in existence or on record a *corpus* of at least twenty
dramas busy with the various events and persons
which the tetralogy of the three plays on Henry VI.
and Richard III. sought to cover. A passage from *The*

[1] Cf. *Henslowe's Diary*, Sh. Soc. Pub., 1845, pp. 31 and 159. The
dates of these plays are 1593 and 1599. Mr. Fleay assigns the latter
to Robert Wilson the Younger; *Biographical Chronicle s. v.* Wilson.

Epistle to the Reader prefixed to *The Ghost of Richard III.*, by Christopher Brooke, published in 1614, recognizes how thoroughly the topic had become " staled on the common stage." " And when I undertook this I thought with myselfe, that to draw arguments of invention from a subject, new and probable, would be farre more plaucible to the time, then by insisting upon narrations, made so common in playes and so notorious among all men, have my labour slighted, and my pen tax't for triviall." [1]

The essential epic unity of the plays on Henry VI. and their sequel *Richard III.* has long been recognized. The first of these plays is taken up with the successive steps by which the English lost the conquests of Henry V. in France. The main figures here are the brave and honorable Talbot, Earl of Shrewsbury, about whom cluster most of the finer scenes, and Joan la Pucelle, whose career is in the end distorted into that of a witch whose converse with evil spirits and whose loose life and denial of her own father go far to explain if not to justify the terrible fate that overtook her.[2] In this matter the dramatist was merely following the chroniclers, his sources; who

---

[1] *The Ghost*, Shakespeare Society, 1844, p. 6.

[2] See a recrudescence of the extraordinary idea once advocated by Malone, that Joan was thus misrepresented because of the insular prejudice that believed " that nothing not tending to British glory was worthy to be recorded at all," in the introduction to the nineteenth volume of *The Bankside Shakespeare*.

had in turn derived this misrepresentation of the glorious Maid of Orleans from Englishmen, Joan's enemies in the field, to whom she had been a veritable scourge. The superstition of an age that witnessed a French king on his knees in prayer before the pewter images of saints pinned on his hat, and the *amour propre* of warriors defeated by the nation which they had habitually scorned from Creçy to Agincourt are alone responsible for these distortions of truth. But these subjects are not all. The larger theme of the tetralogy, the discord of Lancaster and York, takes its rise in the disunion of the young king's kindred, Humphrey Duke of Gloucester, the Lord Protector, and Henry Beaufort, afterwards Cardinal, and the popular feuds which their disunion fostered. In the fine scene in the Temple Garden this *motif* assumes a definite and picturesque form.[1] It receives a deeper significance in the succeeding scene between the politic Richard Plantagenet and the "Nestor-like aged" Edmund Mortimer, here represented contrary to the historical fact as ending a long life of imprisonment and persecution at the hands of the reigning house. The latter assumes at once a position of contrast, in his practical sagacity, his calculating diplomacy and his bold decision of character, to the saintlike and impotent Henry, the royal puppet of the house of Lancaster, whose illadvised choice of "the badge of Somerset" in his fu-

[1] *1 Henry VI.*, II. 4, 11–76.

tile attempt to reconcile the quarrel of two followers of Richard and Somerset, widens the breach beyond repair. The discord rises until Talbot, the noblest and most chivalrous of Englishmen, is sacrificed to it and the English are all but completely driven out of France. The play ends with the personal quarrel of Duke Humphrey and Cardinal Winchester unabated and the political dissensions of York and Somerset gathering force. We have thus two threads with which to connect the first and the second parts of *Henry VI.* The last act of the former play supplies us with a third in Suffolk's capture of Margaret, the daughter of the impoverished Reignier, Duke of Anjou and Maine, and the king's acceptance of Suffolk's plan by which Margaret becomes queen of England. The whole story of Margaret of Anjou's guilty love for Suffolk is characterized by Mr. Boswell-Stone as " sheer fiction." None the less there are passages in Holinshed and Halle out of which such " fiction " may not unnaturally have taken its rise.[1]

In *2 Henry VI.* the quarrel of Duke Humphrey and Cardinal Winchester is rapidly developed to a climax by the aid of two new elements, Queen Margaret's eagerness to supplant the Protector with her favorite and paramour, the Earl of Suffolk, and her jealousy of Eleanor Cobham, the imprudent and ambitious wife of Duke Humphrey. In the upshot Dame

---

[1] *Shakspere's Holinshed*, p. xiv; Holinshed, II. 220; Halle, p. 218.

Eleanor is disgraced and compelled to do penance in a sheet, for her traffic in the black art. Her husband, popularly revered as the Good Duke Humphrey, is deposed from the Protectorship and murdered by Suffolk's and the Cardinal's procurement. The latter dies of remorse for his crime, and Suffolk, banished the realm, is captured and slain by pirates. In the midst of all stands the saturnine figure of the Duke of York, content to "be still awhile, till time doth serve," but ever plotting, strengthening his party and abetting discontent. Entrusted at length with a military expedition into Ireland because of his seeming loyalty, the tool of treason is thrust into his hand and the play ends with the Battle of St. Albans in which York slays his old enemy Somerset. Nearly the whole fourth act of this play is given over to a fresh and admirable dramatic portrayal of the rising of Jack Cade, an episode, like several minor ones in the same play, illustrative of the main theme, but not directly conducive to the unfolding of it. Here, as in the case of Joan of Arc, the alleged misrepresentations of the actual Cade are referable to the sources of the dramatist, who has somewhat confused this uprising of Kentish men in 1450 with the villeins' revolt of 1381.[1]

The third part of *Henry VI.* begins with the agreement forced from that unhappy monarch by which he accepted the Duke of York as heir to the throne of England and disinherited the young Prince Edward,

[1] See *Shakspere's Holinshed*, p. 271.

7

his and Margaret's son. The civil war is at its height
and the first act concludes with the capture, mockery
and wanton murder of the Duke of York by "bloody
Clifford" and Margaret, "the she-wolf of France."
In rapid succession now follow the rallying of the
York side, the crowning of Edward IV., his subsequent deposition by Warwick, the king-maker, for the
insult offered to the latter's embassy to France, Edward's precipitate marriage with Lady Gray, his overthrow of Warwick and the second coronation, the
murder of Henry by Richard and the postponed but
terrible retribution that overtook Queen Margaret in
the violent death of her only son, the young Prince
Edward. On the death of the Duke of York, Richard,
his youngest son, succeeds to his father's earlier attitude of temporizing duplicity, uniting this play with
the play bearing his own name, as York links the
second and third parts of *Henry VI.* The Richard
of *3 Henry VI.* and of *Richard III.* are the same person, and his final overthrow by Henry of Richmond,
who, free from the crimes of both parties, is able to
unite in his marriage with Elizabeth of York the claims
of each, is a satisfactory close to this long and terrible
epic of fratricidal war.

Omitting for the nonce all reference to Shakespeare's *Richard*, such unity as these shifting scenes
and interspersed episodes possess is wholly epic. It
subsists in the general conception, and is main-

tained by the linking of characters sketched in successive plays. Thus Queen Margaret figures in all four plays. Henry, York and Warwick in three; Duke Humphrey, the Cardinal and Suffolk in the first two; Somerset and Clifford in *2* and *3 Henry VI.;* Edward and his brothers in *3 Henry VI.* and *Richard III.* Of specific or dramatic unity there is none. The sequence of events is hopelessly jumbled. The episodes are, for the most part, conveyed bodily from the chronicles, although several of them, such as the trial by combat [1] and the miracle wrought by the Protector upon the impostor at St. Albans [2] disclose the hand of a dramatist of unusual promise. It is noteworthy that, save for a paltry scene in the first part, [3] the employment of comedy is substantially confined to the second play of the series. In the earlier parts of that play the comedy scenes are all episodic. Even those dealing with Jack Cade, excellent as they are, might be cut out of the play and in no wise impair its epic completeness.

Similarities between passages of Marlowe's *Edward II.* and passages of the two *Contentions* have already been mentioned. It has also been suggested above that these two plays must have preceded *Edward II.,* although the composition of what cannot but be regarded as their later revisions, namely *2* and *3 Henry*

[1] *2 Henry VI.,* II. 3
[2] *Ibid.,* II. 1.
[3] *1 Henry VI.,* II. 1.

VI. and their continuation or sequel, Shakespeare's *Richard III.*, must have followed Marlowe's tragedy. That these similarities are due to the hand of Marlowe either in the original plays (as held by the late Richard Grant White) or in their revision (the theory of Miss Jane Lee) may be accepted, in accord with the best criticism, as all but certain. [1]   The relation of the characters Suffolk, Margaret and King Henry is superficially that of Mortimer, Isabella and Edward, here delineated with fullness and power, but relegated to the background as the plan of *Edward II.* demanded.

That Shakespeare's hand is evident in every play of the finished tetralogy is patent and beyond cavil.   The printing of the two *Contentions* side by side with *2* and *3 Henry VI.* discloses a revision line by line, the repression of a passage here, a judicious expansion there. Yet he is a bold critic who dares venture an opinion as to the precise limits of authorship.   Let us take a typical passage.   Suffolk pursued almost into the presence of the king by Warwick and the commons who are crying out against him for the murder of Duke Humphrey, is banished the realm by Henry, who with Warwick sweeps out of the presence chamber followed by his train, leaving Suffolk and Queen Margaret alone.   In the older version of the play, Margaret thus wreaks imprecation on her foes:

[1] See White's *Essay on the Authorship of King Henry the Sixth*, Vol. VII. of his edition of Shakespeare, 1859, and Miss Lee's *On the Authorship of the Second and Third Parts of Henry VI. and their Originals*, Transactions of the New Shakspere Society, 1875-76.

Queene. Hell fire and vengeance go along with you,
Theres two of you, the diuell make the third,
[*Turning to Suffolk.*]
Fie womanish man, canst thou not curse thy
enemies?
Suffolke. A plague vpon them, wherefore should I curse
them?
Could curses kill as do the Mandrakes groanes,
I would inuent as many bitter termes
Deliuered strongly through my fixed teeth,
With twise so many signes of deadly hate,
As leaue fast enuy in her loathsome caue.[1]

As expanded in revision this passage reads:

Queene. Mischance and Sorrow goe along with you,
Hearts Discontent, and sowre Affliction,
Be play-fellowes to keepe you companie:
There's two of you, the Deuill make a third,
And three-fold Vengeance tend vpon your steps.
Suffolke. Cease, gentle Queene, these Execrations,
And let thy Suffolke take his heauie leaue.
Queene. Fye Coward woman, and soft harted wretch,
Hast thou not spirit to curse thine enemy.
Suffolke. A plague vpon them: wherefore should I cursse
them?
Would curses kill, as doth the Mandrakes grone,
I would inuent as bitter searching termes,
As curst, as harsh, and horrible to heare,
Deliuer'd strongly through my fixed teeth,
With full as many signes of deadly hate,
As leane-fac'd enuy in her loathsome caue.[2]

[1] *1 Contention*, facsimile of the quarto of 1594, p. 39.
[2] *2 Henry VI.*, III. 2, 299-315.

The improvement in the revision is greater than may at first appear. The first gain is in dignity ; a fish-wife might have screamed the original execration. A second gain is in dramatic sensibility whereby Suffolk's "Cease, gentle Queen," with its ring of unconscious irony marks him as, for the instant, oblivious to his enemies, to the question addressed him, to all, in the overwhelming sense of the doom that is to part him from the woman he so fiercely loves. It is the queen's coarser nature that recalls him to the thought of vengeance. Once more, the revised passage has gained in quality of diction. Compare especially the concluding lines of the two passages. Lastly the passage has gained in figurative force : "fast (*i. e.*, fastened, tethered, if indeed the word be not a misprint) enuy" is replaced by the picturesque epithet "leane-fac'd;" "many bitter termes" becomes "bitter-searching termes" and the poetical thought which likens "hearts Discontent and sowre Affliction" in their daily companionship to the intimacy of playfellows has been added.

Farther on in the same scene we meet the following passage in the older play :

Queene.　No more, Sweete Suffolke, hie thee hence to France,

Or liue where thou wilt within this worldes globe,

Ile haue an Irish that shall finde thee out,

And long thou shalt not staie, but ile haue thee repelde,

> Or venture to be banished my selfe.
> Oh let this kisse be printed in thy hand,
> That when thou seest it, thou maist thinke on
>   me.
> Away, I say, that I may feele my griefe,
> For it is nothing whilst thou standest here.

Suffolke. Thus is poore Suffolke ten times banished,
>   Once by the King, but three times thrise by
>   thee.[1]

In the revision, in which " an Irish " ceases to suggest a faithful servitor of a ubiquitous race and is transmuted into the familiar Homeric messenger goddess Iris, this passage is transferred to the very end of the scene and made in its undertone of fatalism to forebode Suffolk's approaching death. The character of the revision of this passage, which is too familiar and readily accessible to require quotation here, should alone be sufficient to refute once and for all the notion that Shakespeare is the author of both versions, or that the shorter copy is a pirated edition of the text afterwards printed in the folio.[2] The clumsiest of reporters could scarcely have contrived to omit with unfailing regularity the words and phrases which transform many passages of the older play from dead material into poetry instinct with dramatic life and vigor.

But an interesting question arises at this point as to

---

[1] *1 Contention*, p. 40.

[2] See Fleay, *Biographical Chronicle*, II. 63 ; and his *Life of Shakespeare*, p. 255.

the relation of *3 Henry VI.* and its forerunner, *2 Contention* to Shakespeare's *Tragedy of King Richard III.* and to *The True Tragedy of Richard III.*, an earlier play distinguishable alike from Shakespeare's and from *The True Tragedy of Richard Duke of York*, the fuller title of *2 Contention*. The full title of this earlier play runs : *The True Tragedie of Richard the Third : Wherein is showne the death of Edward the fourth, with the smothering of the two yoong Princes in the Tower : with the lamentable ende of Shores wife, an example for all wicked women, And lastly the coniunction and ioyning of the two noble Houses, Lancaster and Yorke. . .* 1594. Collier's assignment of this play to a date prior to the year 1588 certainly places it too early.[1] Mr. Fleay and Professor Churchill agree in dating it three or four years later and after the earlier plays on Henry VI.[2] The title page of *The True Tragedy of Richard III.* states that it " was playd by the Queenes Majesties Players." There is reason to believe that *1 Henry VI.* and *1 Contention* (*i. e.*, *2 Henry VI.*) were both earlier plays of the same company.[3] The *2 Contention* was acted by the Earl of Pembroke's company and has therefore been regarded as a continuation by that rival company of the Queen's company's play, *1 Contention*. Pembroke's men thus borrowed the title

---

[1] Collier's ed. of *Shakespeare*, 1842, V. 344.

[2] *Biographical Chronicle*, II. 315 ; and *Richard III. bis Shakespeare*, p. 38.

[3] *Ibid.* and Fleay, *Stage*, p. 406.

of the Queen's company's play in the word " Contention." The Queen's men now retorted with a further
continuation of the story of *The True Tragedy of the
Duke of York* and also played on the title by calling
their new play *The True Tragedy of Richard III.*

That the Richard of *3 Henry VI.* is developed from
the preparatory sketch of the *2 Contention* even a cur-
sory examination of the two texts in parallel will disclose. The alterations in this revision are less than
those which were made in the revision of *1 Contention ;* and the changes, so far as they concern Richard,
all make for distinctness and vividness, and generally
consist in additions. Thus Richard left alone after
witnessing his brother Edward's courtship of Lady
Gray soliloquises in the older play :

> I, Edward, will vse women honourablie,
> Would he were wasted marrow, bones and all,
> That from his loines no issue might succeed,
> To hinder me from the golden time I looke for,
> For I am not yet lookt on in the world.
> First is there Edward, Clarence, and Henry
> And his sonne, and all they lookt for issue
> Of their loines ere I can plant my selfe,
> A cold premeditation for my purpose.[1]

In the revision these few lines are transformed :

> I, Edward will vse women honourably :
> Would he were wasted, Marrow, Bones, and all,
> That from his Loynes no hopefull Branch may spring,

[1] *2 Contention*, facsimile ed. of the quarto of 1595, p. 47.

To crosse me from the Golden time I looke for :
And yet, betweene my Soules desire, and me,
The lustfull Edwards Title buryed,
Is Clarence, Henry, and his Sonne young Edward,
And all the vnlook'd-for Issue of their Bodies,
To take their Roomes, ere I can place my selfe :
A cold premeditation for my purpose.
Why then I doe but dreame on Soueraigntie,
Like one that stands vpon a Promontorie,
And spyes a farre-off shore, where hee would tread,
Wishing his foot were equall with his eye,
And chides the Sea, that sunders him from thence,
Saying hee'le lade it dry, to haue his way :
So doe I wish the Crowne, being so farre off,
And so I chide the meanes that keepes me from it. [1]

In a word the impression conveyed in this comparison gives to the Richard of the *2 Contention* and of *3 Henry VI.* the same general features, but to the latter a quality of deeper subtlety and a higher intellectuality.   Now if we turn to the Richard of *The True Tragedy of Richard III.* we find an uncouth if powerful figure, swayed between an absorbing ambition for kingly power and the torments of a guilty conscience, striding through scenes which are presented with the looseness and want of unity which marks the earlier type of the Chronicle Play, but tinged with a color of the Senecan influence whereby the play becomes alike a history and a tragedy of revenge.   If this play was written in continuation or rivalry of the *2 Contention,*

[1] *3 Henry VI.*, III. 2, 124–141.

the author certainly missed the earlier conception of the character of Richard; while Shakespeare (or Marlowe and Shakespeare as the case may be) caught it with a spirit that made certain the development of its possibilities to the full in the later *Richard III.*

In a recent monograph on *Richard III. up to Shakespeare*, Professor Churchill shows that the author of *The True Tragedy of Richard III.* and Shakespeare used the same materials, More, Halle and Holinshed, excepting that Shakespeare did not have recourse to *The Mirour for Magistrates*, which the minor playwright may have used for the scenes concerning Jane Shore. Professor Churchill further affirms that Shakespeare did not know the Latin play of Legge, but that the author of *The True Tragedy* may have used it as a source.[1] Be all this as it may, *The True Tragedy of Richard III.* is a production of little intrinsic worth. I cannot agree with Professor Churchill, who finds in this play the history of a character, not a reign.[2] Such unity as exists is due to the commanding personality of the protagonist and the play marks no step in dramatic development beyond the primitive type, far less a step beyond Marlowe's *Edward II.* Professor Churchill seems on firmer ground when he assigns a peculiar interest to *The True Tragedy* from the fact that it is the earliest to

[1] *Palæstra*, X. 1900.
[2] *Ibid.*, p. 299.

unite the English historical drama with the tragedy of revenge. Here again the subject-matter is partly responsible, though the influence of Senecan traditions and models is clear.

As we pass from *3 Henry VI.* to Shakespeare's *Richard III.* the bandying of taunts and defiances and the clash of steel is succeeded by the stealthy tread of murder, the pathos of innocent suffering and the shrill lyric wailings of the widowed and child-bereft queens, Elizabeth and Margaret, the latter more terrible in her impotence than in her power. Crowning all and dominating all, is the deformed and monstrous Richard Crookback, insinuating, fascinating in his intellectual poise and subtlety, reptilian alike in his cunning and in his charm, sinuously working his way about obstacles till the moment is ripe, then striking with murderous and triumphant fangs, remorseless and terrible. We have emerged from the epic chronicle into the domain of tragic history, from the kaleidoscope of shifting colors huddled together by chance to the carefully painted portrait of a unified personality.

The essential difference between Shakespeare's *Richard III.* and his other historical plays has long been recognized. There is a tragic unity which centers in the Titanic person of the deformed king and whirls all the other characters of the play into the vortex of his crimes. Richard, it has been observed, is not so criminal as he is diabolical. The overpowering force

of his nature, his amazing audacity and remorseless
energy, his bold hypocrisy, and brutal cynicism and
impiety are all of superhuman dimensions and dilate
into the heroic.   We lose ourselves in wonder before
this stupendous instrument of Fate making for evil,
and wonder rises almost to admiration, the admiration
with which we contemplate some overwhelming mani-
festation of the power of nature, an avalanche or an irresistible stream of molten lava.   It is precisely this
concentration of interest in the heroic dimensions of a
unified personality whose master passion carries the
auditor's sympathies with it, at times despite his judgment, which characterizes the drama of Marlowe from
imperious Tamburlaine to piteous Edward.   Nor does
the likeness of *Richard III.* to Marlowe's work in plan
and conception end here.   Not to mention the employment of blank verse and the total absence of the
slightest gleam of comedy, this likeness extends to a
certain fixity of character, a coarseness of stroke, violence of speech and deed and to a lyricism which con-
verts whole scenes into the expression of a single
emotion.   Such are the recurrent soliloquies of Richard and such is the all but purely lyrical scene in
which the queens Margaret and Elizabeth and the
Duchess of York, three wretched women bereft of
husband and child, oblivious of former rivalry and
recrimination, sit on the ground in complete abandon-
ment to sorrow and give themselves up to an almost

choric expression of hopeless woe.[1]   It would be difficult to find in the range of the English drama a
scene reproducing so completely the nature and the
function of the Greek choric ode.

All this has been a frequent theme for comment
and has been variously explained : some assigning to
Marlowe a hand in *Richard III.* and regarding it as a
joint production of Shakespeare and Marlowe ; others
denying Marlowe's hand, but confessing his influence.
The latter is assuredly the wiser view.   While the
precise degree of Marlowe's influence upon Shakespeare and the actual share which each may have had
in the writing of the plays which constitute the tetralogy of Henry VI. and Richard III. must remain indeterminable, in these earlier chronicles better than
elsewhere can we discern what must have been the
successive stages of the greatest of all literary appren-
ticeships.   To *1 Henry VI.* Shakespeare contributed
isolated scenes, those concerning Talbot and the
quarrel in the Temple Garden.   Such would be the
work assigned to a young and yet untried hand on
the revival of an old play, the text of which commanded respect because of its authorship or (what
was far likelier) on account of its former success on
the boards.   Those who accept the claims of a Shakespearean authorship which have been advanced for the
romantic scenes in which Lady Salisbury is courted

[1] *Richard III.*, IV. 4.

by King Edward III., may offer this as another example of this earliest state of Shakespeare's dramatic authorship. When the preparation of *2* and *3 Henry VI.* followed, emboldened by the popular approval of his interpolations (sufficiently attested in the case of 1 Henry VI. by the passage concerning Talbot from the pen of Nashe quoted above), the young aspirant would demand a freer hand and submit these plays to a line for line revision, though still leaving the essential fabric of his original untouched and retaining a large part of the text. Chronologists of Shakespeare are in doubt as to the order of *King John* and the two *Richards.* All we know is that they all must have followed the three plays on Henry VI. and certainly preceded the trilogy on Henry IV. and V. Be this order what it may, these plays must have come close together and they mark, however ordered, Shakespeare's gradual progress from mere apprenticeship to complete freedom in the practice of his art. In *King John*, Shakespeare took two old plays and welded them into one, for the first time treating his material with freedom. We have no longer mere expansion, selection and revision of matter suggested in the older play, but an all but complete rewriting of the text, a suppression of what is trite and unfitting, an elevation of the characters to lifelikeness and dignity and the infusion throughout the whole of a spirit of poetry for which we may look in vain in the

original play.   The similarity of the dramatic method
of much of *2* and *3 Henry VI.* to that employed by
Marlowe has just been noticed, together with the debt
which such a personage as Richard owes to Marlowe's
gigantic conceptions of the unbridled lust of power.
This play shows the influence of Marlowe to a greater
degree than any play of Shakespeare's shows any
single influence, and displays to us the young dramatist advanced a further step and seeking to rival his
most successful competitor with his own weapons in
his own field.   In *Richard II.* Shakespeare passes beyond the period of interpolation, revision and imitation, but he still has his great rival in view.   The subject of *Richard II.* as already mentioned, is that of
Edward II. : the struggle of a weak and unprincipled
sovereign to maintain his will and finally his crown
against a group of rebellious nobles.   But Shakespeare has treated this subject in a manner wholly his
own.   He has rivalled his competitor in his own field
but with weapons, this time, of Shakespeare's own
choosing.   He has added to Marlowe's power, com-
pression and unity of dramatic structure, poetic delicacy and a more searching insight into character.
But Shakespeare has not surpassed the tragedy of
Marlowe in *Richard II.*   This was yet to come in the
greater plays of maturity, in the powerfully contrasted
effects of temptation, crime and remorse, in the conception of the delicately adjusted temper of Lady

Macbeth and of her coarser-fibered if more imaginative husband, and in the deeper doubts and psychologic questionings of Hamlet.

V

SHAKESPEARE AND THE TRIUMPH OF THE EPIC TYPE

BEFORE taking up Shakespeare's tragedy of *Richard II.*, his earliest independent venture in English historical drama and a realization of the highest capabilities of the tragic type of the Chronicle Play, let us turn to an earlier tragedy, the events of which also concern Richard of Bordeaux. The consideration of this play has been deferred to this place because of its subject, although it probably belongs, in point of time, before *Richard III.* and synchronizes with *Edward II.* and *2 Henry VI.* It seems almost incredible that a play dealing with the earlier events of the reign of an English king whom Shakespeare has immortalized in drama, and a play too of merit, should have been allowed to remain in manuscript and practically unknown until the year 1899. In 1870 Halliwell-Phillipps printed eleven copies of this play, which he entitled *A Tragedy of King Richard the Second concluding with the Murder of the Duke of Gloucester a Calais. A Composition anterior to Shakespeare's Tragedy on the same Reign.* His original was a manuscript since acquired by the British Museum.[1] The

---

[1] *Egerton MS. 1894.* Mr. Bullen printed several of the plays of this MS. in his *Old English Plays,* 1882.

editor furnished no account of it or comment on his
"find" save a few words in the *Athenæum* for April
1, 1871, offered in reply to one who had declared the
production " a very close imitation of an old drama,
but not the old drama itself." Thus the play has remained a mere title even to scholars until its republication with a serviceable commentary by Dr. Wolf-
gang Keller, one of the editors of the *Jahrbuch der
deutschen Shakespeare-Gesellschaft* in a recent volume
of that valuable journal.[1] The manuscript is without
title and the authorship of the play is beyond ascertain-
ment. The query of Mr. Fleay as to the possible performance of this play by the Queen's company appears as likely as any other guess.[2] While King Richard
seems the protagonist in the earlier acts, the play is
really the tragedy of Thomas of Woodstock, Duke of
Gloucester, youngest uncle to the king. The story is
concerned with the youth of King Richard, who is
represented surrounded by favorites and sycophants
and as turning a deaf ear to the counsels of his uncles,
the three brothers of the Black Prince, his father.
These personages are well drawn and clearly individu-
alized, and the youngest, conceived as an outspoken,
shrewd, but single-hearted patriot, falls in the end a
victim to the malice of his enemies who surround the
king. The play is well written and not badly con-

[1] XXXV., pp. 3–121.
[2] *Biographical Chronicle*, II. 320.

structed and displays a regularity of form which suggests acquaintance with classical examples.   The unknown author handles his material with skill and is
happy in the lighter dialogue of comedy as he is successful in the more exacting demands of tragic representation.

Woodstock delights in the name " plain Thomas "
and clothes himself habitually " in frieze coat."   He
is mistaken by a foppish messenger from court for a
groom, and bidden walk his horse.   The Duke falls in
with the humor of the situation and thus communes as
he walks the beast to and fro :

Is't possible that this fellow that's all made of fashions
should be an Englishman ? no maruell if he knewe not me,
being soe brave and soe beggarlye.   Well I shall earne
money to inritch me now, and tis the first I earnt, bith
rood, this (40) yeare.   Com on, sir [*to the horse*], you
haue sweat hard about this hast, yett I thinke you knowe
little of the busines.   Why so I say ; youre a very indif-
ferent beast, you'le followe any man that will lead you.
Now trulye sir you looke but ene leanely an't ; you feed
not in Westminster Hall adays, wher so many sheepe and
oxen are devoured. . . .   You knowe not the duke neither,
no more then your master, and yett you haue as much
witt as he.   Ifaith, say a man should steale ye and feed ye
fatter : could ye rune away with hime?   Ah your silence
argues a consent, I see.

Soon after, the courtier, having discovered his mistake, returns and this dialogue ensues.

Woodstock.   Now sir, your busines !

Courtier.   His majestie commends hime to your grace—

Wood.   [*Noting the Courtier's pointed shoes, the 'pick' or toe supported by a chain attached to the knee.*] This same's a rare fashione you haue gott at courte. Of whose deuiseing was't? I pray.

Cour.   I assure your grace king Richards counssell satt (3) dayes about it.

Wood.   By my faith ther wisdomes tooke great paines I assure ye.

      The state was well imployd the wilse, bith rood. Then this at courte is all the fashione now?

Cour.   The king hime self doth weare it : whose most gratious maiestie sent me in hast—

Wood.   This picke doth strangly well becom the foote.

Cour.   This picke the king doth likewise weare, being a Polonian picke : and me did his highnes picke from foorth the rest—

Wood.   He could not have pickt out such another, I assure ye.

Cour.   I thanke your grace, that picks me out so well : But as I sayd, his highnes would request—

Wood.   But this most fashionable chayne, that linckes, as it were, the tooe and knee to gether—

Cour.   In a most kynd choherence, so it like your grace. For these (2) parts being in opperatione and quallity different, as for example : the toe a disdayner, or spurner, the knee a duetyfull and most humble oratour, this chayne doth, as it were, soe tooefy the knee, and so kneefye the tooe, that betweene boeth it makes a most methodicall coherence or coherent method.

Wood.   Tis most excellent, Sir, and full of art.[1]

---

[1] *Egerton MS. 1894,* edited as to punctuation. Cf. *Jahrbuch,* p. 80.

Such an attempt to give historical color by allusion to a passing fashion in the dress of a former age is rare if not unparalleled in the popular historical drama, and might be regarded of greater importance did we not find a passage in Stow's *Abridgement of English Chronicles* which must have suggested it.[1]

Dr. Keller has investigated the sources and dramatic influences upon this play. Into the intricacies of this investigation it is impossible here to follow him. He finds the general sources in Holinshed and Stow and the author's special dramatic inspiration in *2 Henry VI.* and *Edward II.;* and he shows that not only are certain passages apparently suggested by the older plays, but that situations and conceptions of character are borrowed. For example, the general situation of Edward and Richard is the same with respect to the contrasted groups of the king's flatterers and the rebellious nobles. The attitude of Queen "Ann a Beame" in the earlier part of the play (which was not her historical attitude) is much that of Queen Isabella; and young Richard's assumption of his crown seems suggested by young Prince Edward's throwing off of the yoke of Mortimer. The whole conception of Thomas, Duke of Gloucester, as a bluff, independent and honest patriot, the idol of the common people and Lord Protector of the realm is without basis in

[1] See ed. 1611, p. 143: In her [Queen Ann of Bohemia's] daies began the vse of piked shooes, tied to their knees with chains of siluer and gilt.

history and is evidently derived from the character of
Good Duke Humphrey, also a Duke of Gloucester, in
2 Henry VI. or the older play on that theme.[1] But
perhaps the most striking instance of a parallel between this play and Marlowe's—and one not mentioned by Dr. Keller—is found in the two catastrophes,
the murders respectively of Woodstock and of King
Edward.   In Marlowe's tragedy we have the murder
of a discrowned king.   The pathos of the situation
lies in the contrast between his regal and his fallen
state.   Our sympathies are aroused for the wretched
if unworthy victim of cruel and extraordinary indignities ; and our feelings rise to the pitch of indignation
when we find these indignities instigated by the self-
seeking schemer, Mortimer, who has alienated the
queen's affections from her unhappy husband and
usurped his throne.   In the catastrophe of Woodstock, on the other hand, we have the murder of an
innocent man, procured by flattering sycophants at
the hands of an unjust king.   In the deed he dishon-
ors age and kindred as he has violated hospitality ;
for he has seized the Duke in his own house, having
gained admittance for the royal party by the device of
a masque offered for the Duke's entertainment.   The
pathos lies in the wrong that innocence should suffer,
for Woodstock's deeds, according to the play, have
been those of a true and patriotic man and are in no

[1] *Jahrbuch*, pp. 27–32.

wise contributory to his fall. In the tragedy of Edward the interest centers in the victim with that singleness and intensity that is one of the striking traits of the genius of Marlowe as a dramatist. The murder of Woodstock, on the other hand, is worked up into greater intricacy. In Lapoole, the custodian of the castle of Calais in which Woodstock is immured, is presented as a loyal man constrained though reluctant to do the bidding of his sovereign and stricken with remorse in the very act. He is watching for a favorable moment, his assassins in waiting, but the old Duke, presaging his doom, is wakeful and Lapoole quails before his princely eye. At last wearied with watching Woodstock falls asleep and as Lapoole withdraws to call the murderers the spirits of Edward I., his father and of his brother, the Black Prince, appear to the sleeping man and warn him of his impending fate.

He starts from his sleep and cries :

> Oh, good angells, guide me, stay thou blessed
>   speritt,
> Thou royal shadow of my kingly ffather,
> Returne agayne ; I knowe thy reverent lookes.
> With thy deere sight once more recomfort me,
> Putt by the feares my trembling harte foretells,
> And heere is mayd apparant to my sight
> By dreams and visions of this dreadfull night :
> Vpon my knees I beg it : ha : protect me
>   heauen !

> I heere remayne
> A poore old man, thrust from my natiue country,
> Kept and imprisond in a fforrayne kingdome.
> If I must dye, bear reccord, righteous heaven,
> How I haue nightly waked for Englands good,
>
> *Enter Lapoole and murderers.*
>
> And yet to right hir wrongs would spend my
> blood.
> Send thy sadd doome, king Richard, take my
> life :
> I wish my death might ease my countryes griefe.
> *Lapoole.* We are preuented, backe retire agayne,
> Hees ryssen from his bed, what fate preserues
> hime ?
> My lord, how faire you ?
> *W.* Thou canst not kill me villayne !
> Gods holly angle guards a just mans life,
> And with his radient beames as bright as fire
> Will guard and keepe his righteous innocence.
> I am a prince ; thou darst not murder me.
> *L.* Your grace mistakes my lord.

Urged by Lapoole to plead his own case, Woodstock consents to sit down to a table to write to the
king and Lapoole withdraws. While Woodstock is
writing, both murderers enter.

> *1M.* Creepe close to his backe, ye rogue ; be readye with
> the towell, when I have knockt hime downe to
> strangle hime.
> *2M.* Doe it quickly while his backe is towards ye ; ye
> dambd villayne, if thou lettst hime speake but a
> word, we shall not kill hime.

1 M.   Ile watch hime for that ; downe on youre knees and
creepe ye rascall.

W.   Haue mercye god ! my sight oth sudden fayles me,
I cannot see my paper, my trembling fingers will
not hold my pen, a thicke coniealed mist ore-
spreds the chamber.   Ile ryse and view the roome.

2 M.   Not to fast for fallinge.   *Strickes hime.*

W.   What villayne hand hath done a deed soe badd,
To drench his blacke soule in a princes blood ?

1 M.   Doe ye prate sir, take that, and that ; zounes, putt the
towell abouts throat and strangle hime, quickly
ye slaue : or by the harte of hell, Ile fell thee too.

2 M.   Tis done, ye dambd slaue, pull ye dog : and pull
thy soule to hell in doeing it, for thou hast kild
the truest subiect that euer breathed in England.

1 M.   Pull, rogue, pull ; thinke of the gould we shall haue
for doeing [it], and then lett hime and thee goe
toth devell to gether.   Bring in the fether bead,
and rowle him vp in that till he be smothered
and stiffled and life and sowle prest out to
gether : quickly, ye hellhound.

2 M.   Heere, heere, ye caniball.   Zounes, he kickes and
spralls ; ly ons breast, ye villayne.

1 M.   Lett hime sprall and hang.   Hees sure enough for
speakeing.   Pull of the bed now, smooth downe
his hayre and beard, close his eyes and sett his
necke right : why so : all fine and cleanely.   Who
can say that this man was murdered now ?

Enter Lapoole.

L.   What, is he dead ?

2 M.   As a doore nayle, my lord.   What will ye doe with
his bodye ? [1]

---

[1] *Ibid.*, and cf., *Jahrbuch*, p.   8, 110–111 ; pp. 105–111.

In the sequel the actual perpetrators of the deed are slain as Lightfoot, the murderer of King Edward, is slain in Marlowe's play.   Indeed the analogy between the two plays might be easily extended to further details.   But enough has been said to show that we have before us a striking example of a thing common to the dramatic literature of many ages, the practice of writing scenes—sometimes whole plays—in direct emulation of a successful drama already well known to the boards.   The overpowering pathos of the scenes depicting the murder of King Edward must have created a lasting impression on the play-goers and dramatists of the time and affected subsequent treatment of like situations.   The murder of Clarence in *Richard III.* presents a situation not dissimilar.[1] Here, as in the tragedy of Woodstock, the murderers are distinguished, one showing qualms of conscience. Clarence, too, discovers murder in his executioner's face as do both Edward and Woodstock.[2]   In *Richard II.*, because written in direct emulation of Marlowe's tragedy, Shakespeare has varied the catastrophe and made Richard precipitate his death by a characteristic display of hasty temper.[3]

---

[1] Cf. *Richard III.*, I. 4, 84ff. and *Woodstock*, as quoted above.

[2] *Richard III.*, I. 4, 169; *Edward II.*, V. 5, 44; *Woodstock*, V. 1, 130–134.

[3] See the scene in which the king belabors and kills his keeper for refusing to taste his meat, and thus precipitates his own death. *Richard II.*, V. 5, 98–115.

As to the relations of the tragedy of *Thomas of Woodstock* to Shakespeare's *Richard II.*, it is all but certain that Shakespeare's is the later play. We may agree with Dr. Keller that neither did Shakespeare write *Richard II.* as a continuation of the tragedy of *Woodstock* nor did the unknown author of the latter play follow Shakespeare in an endeavor to write a first part to a play already staged. In substantiation of this want of relation between the two plays Dr. Keller notes especially that in the anonymous play Lapoole is made the plotter of Woodstock's death, whilst Shakespeare, following the chronicles, charges Thomas Mowbray, Duke of Norfolk, with that crime.[1] If Shakespeare knew this tragedy, he was content to disregard it and return to the usual sources in the chronicles.

Besides Shakespeare's *Richard II.*, the play just described, and *Jack Strawe*, which, as we have seen, concerns the early popular rising in Richard's time, there are other mentions of plays in which Richard II. figures. Shakespeare's play was first printed in quarto in 1597 and is usually dated about 1594. On the afternoon of February 7, 1601, one Sir Gilley Merrick, a conspirator with the Earl of Essex, procured the performance of a play described as *The Deposing of King Richard II.*, by the payment of a fee of forty shillings to Augustine Phillips, a fellow sharer with Shakespeare in the Globe Theater. The addi-

---

[1] See *Jahrbuch*, p. 39, and *Richard II.*, I. 1, 99.

tional fee was paid because the play was described as old,[1] and the actors were seemingly unwilling to undertake the risk of performance unless thus assured against loss. This performance was attended by Merrick and his fellow conspirators, and was intended by the representation of the deposition and killing of a king to enflame the auditors to courage in a similar undertaking. Although the actual scene of the deposition of Richard does not appear until the third quarto edition of Shakespeare's play, printed five years after the death of Queen Elizabeth, as this scene contains the climax of the whole matter and the scene is seriously impaired dramatically by its omission, there is every reason to believe that the omitted scene was written when the rest of the play was written, and suppressed in publication, though probably not in the original performance, either by command or from motives of prudence. It is difficult to escape the conviction that the *Richard II.* which thus figured in the conspiracy of Essex was Shakespeare's when we recall " the lower but loving likelihood," in which he compares the royal entry of Henry V. into London after the victory of Agincourt with the expected return of Essex,

> The Generall of our gracious Empresse
> .   .   .   . from Ireland comming,
> Bringing Rebellion broached on his Sword ;[2]

[1] Camden calls it "exoletam tragœdiam de tragica abdicatione Regis Richardi Secundi." *Annales Rerum*, ed. 1625, p. 810.

[2] *Henry V.*, Chorus to Act V.

and further remember that Southampton, Shake-speare's patron, was involved with Essex and suffered imprisonment in his cause.

Among the anecdotes that cluster about the end of the old queen's reign, when the courtiers and even statesmen that she had made were covertly plotting treason or at least unloyally coquetting with the shadow of the coming rule of James which cast itself before, there is one which touches the subject of this play. Some months after the execution of Essex the queen was looking through the digest of her Rolls in the Tower, which had been compiled and presented to her by William Lambarde, Keeper of the Rolls. On reaching the reign of Richard II., she remarked : " I am Richard II., knew ye not that ?" To which Lambarde replied : " Such a wicked imagination was determined and attempted by a most unkind gentleman, the most adorned creature that ever your Majesty made." And the queen rejoined : " He that will forget God will also forget his benefactors, this tragedy was played forty times in open streets and houses." [1]

From *The Book of Plays* of Dr. Simon Forman, under date of April 30, 1611, it appears that the company of Shakespeare acted another play on the events of the reign of Richard II. A synopsis of its contents which the diarist made shows, however, that it was neither

[1] Nichols, *Elizabeth*, as above, III. 552.

Shakespeare's tragedy, *Jack Strawe*, nor the anonymous
tragedy of *Woodstock*, but a play including apparently
a wider range of events than any of these and present-
ing more particularly Richard's relations to his uncles,
especially Lancaster, the father of Bolingbroke.[1]

As already intimated above in *Richard II.* Shakespeare passes for the first time in the Chronicle Play
beyond the shadow of Marlowe's influence and essays
to rival him not by recourse to Marlowe's methods, as
in *Richard III.*, but by means wholly his own. That
there might be no mistake as to his intent, Shakespeare boldly chose as his theme the history of the only
English king whose fall paralleled that of Edward II.
and confined himself rigidly to tragedy as Marlowe
had done before him. Constructively *Richard II.* is
less closely knit than *Edward II.* in which Marlowe's
method demanded the intensest concentration of interest on the royal central figure. In Shakespeare's
tragedy the effect is produced by means more varied,
and the contrasted kingly personages grow by delicate
recurrent touches rather than by means of bold outline and heightened light and shade. Mortimer is a
mere instrument whereby the fall of Edward is brought
about. Richard's fall on the other hand involves the
rise of Bolingbroke, and Bolingbroke by his abilities
and the specious justice of his cause, dilates into the
image of the just and moderate sovereign in whose

---

[1] *Transactions of the New Shakspere Society*, 1875–76, Part I., p. 415.

success we can not but feel the deepest interest, despite our knowledge that his claim to kingship is not founded on hereditary right.   Richard is shallow, heartless and callous, a man of many words and brimming over with fantasy and eloquent imagery.   It is a necessity of his nature that he fill at all times the central rôle.   Whether in the lists of Coventry, wantonly throwing his warder down and turning into wandering exiles two champions armed to decide their differences by the arbitrament of the sword, or whether shaking the dust of humiliation from his comely, discrowned head as he rides with silent Bolingbroke through London streets, Richard is always the center of a canvas picturesquely conceived and artistically appreciated by himself.   In the very moment of his deposition he calls for a mirror in which to behold the fading lineaments of royalty, and when inevitable death is near, he hurries its oncoming with an impatient daring which would be admirable were it not for its suspicion of melodrama.   Over against this figure stands the politic and unimaginative Bolingbroke,[1] a man taciturn and reserved, and yet solicitous to conciliate even the humblest.   Single in his aim and not to be swerved, he shows an exhaustless patience among the intricacies that lead to attainment.   A dauntless warrior and capable of rigor where rigor is imperative, yet temperate in the moment of triumph ; a politician, yet jealous of his country's honor and respecting her

[1] See *Richard II.*, I. 3, 294–303.

institutions, he commands the respect of all though he gains the love of no one, and stands the embodiment of worldly sagacity and circumspection, a usurper in his conscience, a capable and dreaded sovereign before the world. This contrast reaches its climax in Richard's enforced and reluctant resignation of his crown. In this great scene Richard plays with his sorrow as if it were a bauble, wrapping it in innuendo and word-play and expanding it in similitude and hyperbole. His enemies are Pilates, and he dares impiously to liken himself to Christ betrayed by the kiss of Judas.

Nothing could present a wider contrast to Richard's torrent of excited eloquence than the calm and half-contemptuous restraint of Bolingbroke throughout this scene. To Richard's conceit, in which the crown is likened to a well and its two claimants to the full and empty buckets, Bolingbroke's only reply is:

I thought you had been willing to resigne:

When Richard, calling for a mirror, descants upon the flattery of its reflected image of his face and says:

A brittle Glory shineth in this Face,
As brittle as the Glory, is the Face,

and, dashing the glass to pieces on the ground, exclaims:

For there it is, crackt in an hundred shiuers.
Marke silent King, the Morall of this sport,
How soone my Sorrow hath destroy'd my Face,

9

Bolingbroke's answer comes, the cold analysis of the practical man of the world :

> The shadow of your Sorrow hath destroy'd
> The shadow of your Face.

And even Richard is startled at this searching glance into his shallow soul.   Recovering from the shock he has but one desire : to go,

> Whither you will, so I were from your sights.[1]

The connection between *Richard II.* and the trilogy of plays consisting of the two parts of *Henry IV.* and *Henry V.* is patent.   The obvious link is the character of Bolingbroke, who forms, as King Henry IV., the center of the main historical action.   But the key-note of Henry's relation to his son, the latter's popular repute as a roisterer and unclean liver with its suggestion of comedy is foreshadowed in *Richard II.*

> *King H.*   Can no man tell me of my vnthriftie sonne?
> Tis full three moneths since I did see him last,
> If any plague hang ouer us tis he :
> I would to God my Lordes he might be found :
> Inquire at London, mongst the Tauernes there,
> For there (they say) he daylie doth frequent,
> With vnrestrained loose companions,
> Euen such (they say) as stand in narrow lanes,
> And beate our watch, and rob our passengers.[2]

It is significant that the answer to Henry's enquiry should be put into the mouth of the Prince's

[1] *Ibid.*, IV. 1.
[2] *Ibid.*, V. 3.

later rival, Harry Hotspur. Although he has shown
his very enemies his fitness to rule, King Henry remains throughout the victim of Nemesis, which seeks
him out in the many guises of ingratitude and rebellion,
in the lawless conduct of the Prince and in the cease-
less gnawings of the king's own conscience. It was
the irony of fate that he whose insinuating address
and unerring tact had gained him a crown, should remain a stranger to his own son and mistrustful of him ;
and that the intervention of death should deprive him
of the expiation which he had so frequently desired
and long had planned to seek in an attempt to recover
the Holy Sepulchre to Christendom.

In *1 Henry IV.* Shakespeare continues to practise
the method of dramatic contrast of character which he
had employed so effectively in *Richard II.* Hotspur,
the impelling force of the conspiracy against Henry,
is of a nature so engaging, so hearty and honest that
his very faults endear him to all who know him. He
is arrogant and domineering, headstrong and impetuous, capricious of temper and possessed of a restless-
ness of thought almost amounting to an infirmity. In
speech he is boisterous, sharp-tongued and given to
exaggeration, and so voluble that at times he speaks
thick from the excessive flow of words. But Hotspur
is also eloquent, finely imaginative, despite his undis-
guised contempt for poetry, honorable, generous,
brave in a battle to intrepidity, and " doubly charged,"

as it has been well put, "with the electricity of chivalry." The momentary glimpses which we get into
the daily life of Percy and his Lady are delightful in the
picture which they present of the absent-minded, impatient, self-willed warrior and his devoted wife, who,
secure in the love which she knows to be hers, meets
her husband's bluntness of speech with equal directness and with a charming playfulness even when her
heart is anxious for his safety and mistrustful of the
issue of his hidden plans. It is characteristic of Hotspur that he should chide his Lady for her mincing
oath, "in good sooth."

Not yours in good sooth, Hart, you sweare like a
comfit-makers wife, not you in good sooth, and as true as
I liue, and as

> God shall mend me, and as sure as day :
> And giuest such sarcenet surety for thy oathes,
> As if thou neuer walkst further then Finsbury.
> Sweare me Kate like a ladie as thou art,
> A good mouthfilling oath, and leaue in sooth,
> And such protest of peper ginger bread
> To veluet gards and Sunday Citizens [1]

Shakespeare has given us these brief suggestions of
the home life of the Percys further to heighten the
contrast between Harry Hotspur and the Prince. The
court of Henry IV. is represented as totally without
the grace of woman's presence. Bereft of a mother's
love and solicitude, with a father absorbed in cares of

[1] *1 Henry IV.*, I. 252–261.

state and a brother, Prince John (the only other son
of King Henry represented in the first part of the play),
precociously betraying that hardness and abstractedness
of character which had estranged the Prince from his
father, it was inevitable that one of so warm and ex-
pansive a nature should seek for light and sustenance
beyond the somber precincts of the court. It was the
love of freedom, the zest for adventure, an intellectual
appreciation for the fascinations of Falstaff, not moral
depravity, which drew such a nature temporarily into
the vortex of a wild and reckless life. Shakespeare,
as is notorious, departed from the Prince Henry of
tradition, which makes his reformation of character
miraculous or at least unaccountable, by representing his delight in low associations to consist in the
diversion which such life afforded and then inventing
the captivating personality of Falstaff to account for
the attraction. Henry, like his creator, was possessed
of " an experiencing nature," as Bagehot puts it in another connection. His delight was in reality, in life
and the fulness thereof. With the unreality of the
court he had neither sympathy nor patience ; and he
was perhaps too young to see under its irksome forms
their causes and justification. The course of the two
plays from the plot of Poins and the Prince to rob the
robbers on Gadshill to Falstaff's scenes with Doll
Tearsheet (in which the Prince is little more than an
onlooker) discloses the latter gradually withdrawing

himself from Falstaff and his associates, as his princely
nature matured and developed and in consequence of
the approaching responsibilities of kingship.

But it is in his relations to his father that the true
metal of Henry of Monmouth is most completely re-
vealed.   His frank acknowledgment of fault and his
dutiful behavior under rebuke, even when likened to
Richard, "the skipping king," who "mingled his roy-
altie with capring fooles"; the modest fervor of his
reply to his father's parallel between himself, landed
at Ravenspurgh, and Richard on the one hand and
Hotspur and Prince Henry on the other; his filial
piety to the father who on his very death bed continued to misunderstand his son and wrong him in
his judgment—all mark a character as unaffected as
honest, as gentle as magnanimous.   Whether we behold the Prince rescuing the king, brought to his knee
by the thundering blows of Douglas; whether we
listen to him exchanging chivalrous taunts with Hotspur, meeting and overwhelming his impetuous on-
slaught with a loftier self-contained valor; or witness
him magnanimously delivering Douglas in generous
admiration for his enemy's prowess, "ransomless and
free"—we have ever before us the very ideal of young
chivalry, sound in body and trained to efficiency in
arms, keen, provident, with a mind tempered to the
elasticity of a rapier, tender of heart and unaffected,
graced in every act with that simplicity which is

born of true nobility and greatness. It was from such a man, once entered gravely upon his office of sovereign, that we should look for a magnanimous recognition of the integrity and propriety of the conduct of the Lord Chief Justice who sent him as Prince to prison for his affront to the law in striking its recognized representative, his Lordship. We feel too that the same high sense of right which confirmed the Lord Chief Justice in his office, demanded the absolute repudiation of Falstaff and his godless rout of folly.

In *Henry V.*, which is knit to the two plays of the previous reign by the royal central figure, the paragon of chivalry expands into the hero king. Here as before he is possessed of the fulness of life and brushes aside peremptorily all unrealities as trifling and of no value. There are few finer passages even in Shakespeare than that in which Henry metes out justice to the traitors, Scroop, Gray and Cambridge, for their plot to kill him at Hampton before his departure for France. All three have advised severity in the punishment of a common fellow who when heated with wine had railed against the king. Whereupon the king hands each a paper declaring his treason and judges them unfalteringly as they grovel at his feet. Their treason against his person is of little moment to him in comparison with the depths of human faithlessness and ingratitude which that treason discloses.

Oh, how hast thou with iealousie infected
The sweetnesse of affiance? Shew men dutifull,
Why so didst thou: seeme they grave and learned?
Why so didst thou. Come they of Noble Family?
Why so didst thou. Seeme they religious?
Why so didst thou. Or are they spare in diet,
Free from grosse passion, or of mirth, or anger,
Constant in spirit, not sweruing with the blood,
Garnish'd and deck'd in modest complement,
Not working with the eye, without the eare,
And but in purged iudgement trusting neither?
Such and so finely boulted didst thou seeme:
And thus thy fall hath left a kinde of blot,
To mark thee full fraught man, and best indued
With some suspition, I will weepe for thee.
For this reuolt of thine, me thinkes is like
Another fall of Man.

But the king takes no step of false lenity. Although
his words kindle the spark of loyalty in the hearts of
traitors, their lives must pay the penalty of the offended
majesty of the law :

Touching our person, seeke we no reuenge,
But we our Kingdomes safety must so tender,
Whose ruine you sought, that to her Lawes
We do deliuer you. Get you therefore hence,
(Poore miserable wretches) to your death :
The taste whereof, God of his mercy giue
You patience to indure, and true Repentance
Of all your deare offences.[1]

[1] *Henry V.*, II. 2, 126–181. This passage occurs first in the folio.
Cf. with this the paltry treatment of the same historical fact in *Oldcastle*,
V. 1.

In war, as in counsel Henry's straightforwardness and homely honesty shatters all illusions and makes direct for the point at issue. It was this which gained for him his triumphs in war and the devotion of his subjects. It was this "fidelity to fact," as it has been called, turned into an irresistible force by the king's enthusiasm for military exploit and his patriotic love of country, which translated a vulgar lust of mere conquest into a great national war and transformed a feudal war-lord into the crowned genius of impassioned victory. To such a man it is the weight of the duties and responsibilities of sovereignty rather than its rights and dignities that are ever present. The latter are to be guarded only as the outward and visible signs of that majesty which he represents; and a sincere humility comes over him which seeks expression in a simple faith and trust in God. Henry's piety, like his other virtues, is honest and unaffected, even if it does seem somewhat too outspoken in these modern days in which we are wont to cherish our virtues in private, not without some anxiety lest we be caught practising them.[1]

The trilogy of *1* and *2 Henry IV.* and *Henry V.* may

[1] I am not unaware that this orthodox view of Henry of Monmouth has fallen of late into disrepute. In a recent book (*The Later Renaissance*, 1898, p. 256) Henry is summed up in the words : "a perfect portrait of the unconscious hypocrite." It is a consolation to remember that the same writer has given to Euphuism the illuminating definition, "this square-toed finical vacuity," in which it must be agreed that even Sir Percie Shafton is outdone.

be regarded as representing the height to which the
English historical drama attained. These plays are
less condensed and unified by singleness of purpose
and force of tragic passion than either *Richard II.* or
Richard III., which in these very particulars rise
out of the specific class of chronicle history into
the wider sphere of tragedy. The plays of *Henry
IV.*—especially the second one—are wanting in incident, and the substitution of an interest in character, however absorbing in the main historical thread
and in the interwoven strand of comedy, by no
means suffices to remedy this defect. In *Henry V.*
there is more stirring action, and a sort of unity re-
sults from the inspiring personality of the king. But
this unity is epic, not dramatic. No one felt more
deeply than did Shakespeare himself the complete in-
adequacy of scenic and theatrical devices for the visual
representation of a theme of such magnitude and splen-
dor. Well might he exclaim:

> O for a Muse of Fire, that would ascend
> The brightest Heauen of Inuention :
> A Kingdome for a Stage, Princes to Act,
> And Monarchs to behold the swelling Scene.
> Then should the Warlike Harry, like himselfe,
> Assume the Port of Mars, and at his heeles
> (Leasht in, like Hounds) should Famine, Sword, and
>   Fire Crouch for employment.

Well might the imaginative dramatist conjure his auditors to

Suppose within the Girdle of these Walls
Are now confin'd two mightie Monarchies,
Whose high, vp-reared, and abutting Fronts,
The perillous narrow Ocean parts asunder.
Peece out our imperfections with your thoughts :
Into a thousand parts diuide one Man,
And make imaginarie Puissance.
Thinke when we talke of Horses, that you see them,
Printing their prowd Hoofes i' th' receiuing Earth :
For 'tis your thoughts that now must deck our Kings,
Carry them here and there : Iumping o're Times ;
Turning th' accomplishment of many yeeres
Into an Howre-glasse.[1]

In this great trilogy we find Shakespeare returning to the type of the earlier chronicle history, in its epic quality, in a marshaling of material arranged in a natural order rather than dramatically, and in the admission among serious historical events of a comedy of fiction, conceived to relieve and lighten the somberness of the council chamber and the taunts and alarms of battle.   It is in the last of these things that Shakespeare has contrived once more to show that supreme originality which is ever his.   Working upon the slender suggestions of the trivial old play, *The Famous Victories of Henry the fifth*, he expanded the customary interludes of farce and horse-play into a connected series of scenes of comedy, and transformed the clowns, Dericke and his mates, into a group of humorous and yet realistic figures, the equal of which

[1] *Prologue*, 1–8 and 19–39.

English literature knows nowhere else save in Chau-
cer. In this play Shakespeare has done more than
return to the type of the old Chronicle Play ; he has
absolutely wedded two types of the drama ; the Chronicle History and the realistic comedy of everyday life.
There are no scenes in Dekker, Middleton or Jonson
which so consummately depict the humors and droll-
eries of the low life of contemporary London. In
them Shakespeare was the Dickens of his age ; but
where Dickens permitted his unparalleled power of
caricature to run away with his imagination, and to
weaken by an exuberance of amusing detail the verisimilitude of his picture to life, Shakespeare has always remained true to the verities and escaped not
only this but also the chief snare of what is commonly
and erroneously called "realism," a *penchant* for the
abnormal, the brutal or the lewd. Falstaff, Bardolph,
Mistress Quickly, Nym, the preternaturally puny and
witty page, of none of them save perhaps of Ancient
Pistol can we say : this is caricature ; and even Pistol
with all his bravado, his jargon of play-house bombast
and his woeful want of the spark of valor, remains
poised dizzily on the brink of actual caricature.

The popularity of *1 Henry IV.*, which was evidently
originally written without thought of a second part,
was immediate and extraordinary. Six quarto editions
of it were printed before the folio of 1623 ; the first of
them registered in 1598. In the very next year Jon-

son mentions Falstaff in *Every Man Out of His Humour*
and there is no character in all Shakespeare that was
so frequently alluded to in his age.   A continuation
was at once demanded and enjoyed almost an equal
success.   Whatever the interest in the Prince, this
popularity was largely due to the superlative wit and
enchanting personality of Falstaff, who held the stage
year after year and inspired many imitations.   Nor is
it difficult to believe the tradition first related by Den-
nis that Queen Elizabeth " was so well pleased with
that admirable character of Falstaff, in the two parts of
Henry IV., that she commanded the author to continue it for one play more, and to show him in love,"
whence came *The Merry Wives of Windsor*.[1]

The association of the character Falstaff with the
name of Sir John Oldcastle, the famous Lollard leader,
condemned for heresy and burnt at the stake in 1417,
calls for a word.   In the old play *The Famous Victories
of Henry fifth*, one of the companions of Prince Henry
is Sir John Oldcastle, in this following the chronicles.
In it Oldcastle plays no important part and is distinguished neither for his wit nor for his corporal dimensions.[2]   The single instance in which this character

[1] *Epistle Dedicatory to the Comical Gallant*, an adaptation of *The
Merry Wives*, acted in 1702.   A condensation of the two parts of
Henry IV. into one play, transcribed before 1644, was printed from
MS. for the Shakespeare Society in 1845.

[2] Collier's notion that the Oldcastle of the earlier play was " a fat old
knight " is not borne out by an examination of the play.   See his
Dramatic Literature, III. 69.

exhibits "the least glimmer of humor" is that in which the Prince says : "If the old king my father were dead, we would be all kings." To which Oldcastle replies : " Hee is a good olde man, God take him to his mercy the sooner." In *1 Henry IV.* Prince Henry calls Falstaff "my old lad of the castle."[1] In Field's *Amends for Ladies*, printed in 1619, there is an allusion to " the play where the fat knight, hight Oldcastle, did tell you truly what his honor was" ; a plain reference to Falstaff's soliloquy in the fifth act.[2] In one place the quarto of *2 Henry IV.*, the abbreviation *Old.*, for *Oldcastle*, has been allowed to stand by mistake prefixed to one of Falstaff's speeches ; and elsewhere Falstaff is described as having been, when a boy, page to Sir Thomas Mowbray of Norfolk, which the real Oldcastle actually was.[3] All this establishes that Shakespeare derived the character, Falstaff, from the Oldcastle of the earlier play, and in his earlier draft retained the name Sir John Oldcastle. That the change to Falstaff was subsequent to the earlier performance of both parts of *Henry IV.* seems highly probable from the allusion of the epilogue of part second, where, mentioning the possible continuance of the adventures of Falstaff in France, the speaker adds : " For Oldcastle died a Martyre, and this is not the man.[4]" We

[1] I. 1, 149.

[2] *Amends for Ladies*, IV. 3 ; and ct. *1 Henry IV.*, V. 1.

[3] *2 Henry IV.*, facsimile ed. of the quarto of 1600, p. 11 ; and *ibid.*, III. 2, 27 ff.

[4] V. 4, 33.

may agree with those who believe that it was never
the intention of Shakespeare to cast ridicule upon the
historical Oldcastle, Lord Cobham, and that the change
in the name of his character was made to avoid such
an inference or perhaps in reply to it.   It may be remembered that a Sir John Fastolfe, an historical personage, figures—doubtless unjustly to his memory—
as a coward in *1 Henry VI*. and is disgraced and degraded by Talbot before the king after Joan's relief of
Rouen.[1]   It is likely that the similarity of the names,
Fastolfe and Falstaff is accidental.   That Oldcastle
and Falstaff continued to be confused in the public
mind is proved by Field's words quoted above.   The
Jesuit, Father Parsons, too, who as a Roman Catholic
must have relished seeing the old hero of Lollardry
gibbetted as a gross sinner and perverter of youth,
alludes to Oldcastle as "a Ruffian-Knight, as all
England knoweth, commonly brought in by comme-
dients on their stages."[2]

The trilogy of plays on Henry IV. and V. led to
many imitations, and Falstaff with the group sur-
rounding him gave new life and a more definite form
to the comic underplots of the serious drama.   As
remarked above, the element of comic relief is a prominent feature of the Chronicle Play from the first.   It is
only in plays of the tragic intensity of *Edward II*. or

[1] *1 Henry VI.*, III. 2, 103 ff. and IV. 1.
[2] See Father Parsons, *Three Conversations*, 1603, quoted in *Fresh Allusions to Shakspere*, New Shakspere Society, 1886, p. 30.

Richard II. or *III.*, with a few others that we find this element wholly suppressed. In the earlier plays of the chronicle type this feature varies from the introduction of a mere clown like Miller in *Jack Strawe* or a single scene of drollery such as that in *Edward III.*, in which Douglas and David are represented dividing the spoils of a castle which they have not yet succeeded in taking, to a string of rude scenes in which a whole group of humorous characters appear. Into *Locrine,* with all its Senecan terrors, an elaborate string of farcical scenes is interwoven depicting the humors of Strumbo, a cobbler, and his man, Trumpart, and involving the song, the mock flight, the use of dialect and horse-play, all of them stock devices of later comedy. Even in so serious a play as *Thomas of Woodstock* the element of comic relief is variously supplied by Nimble, a direct descendant of the old Vice, by the courtier-gull, a not unworthy predecessor of Shakespeare's Osric, and by the several scenes which concern the market-folk and the arrest of a country bumpkin on the charge of whistling treason.[1] Peele's *Edward I.* contains all the devices noted above, and besides, the device of disguise, borrowed in this particular case perhaps from the ballads of Robin Hood.

The comedy scenes of *Henry IV.* and *Henry V.* as well, in which Shakespeare gives us a fresh and enter-

[1] *Jahrbuch*, XXXV., p. 87.

taining group centered in the fiery and loquacious Welsh
captain, Fluellen, wholly admirable as they are, are
only the crown and perfection of what had gone
before. Without going into particulars, Pistol and
Falstaff himself are merely idealized forms developing
in different directions of the braggart soldier whose
English literary original may be sought in plays like
Thersites or *Ralph Roister Doister* if not in the Herod
of the mysteries, although the type is as constant to
one age and nation as to all others. Again, the puny,
clever-tongued page before whom Falstaff walks, as he
expresses it, " like a sow that hath ouerwhelmed al
her litter but one," is the pert youngster which Lyly,
amongst others, helped to popularize in the three witty
pages of *Endimion* or in Cryticus of *Sapho and Phao*,
and which Shakespeare had already used in the character of Moth in *Love's Labour's Lost*. Falstaff and Doll
are paralleled in the earlier " Dolls " of Strumbo and
of the Friar in *Edward I.*, and in the later " Doll " of
Sir John of Wrotham in *Oldcastle*. The situation of a
prince amusing himself, in familiar discourse, with the
humors of a man of lower station was a favorite one
on the Elizabethan stage, as it had been in the earlier
ballad literature. It recurs again and again : in Edward IV. and the Tanner of Tamworth, in George
a Greene and Edward III., in Strumbo and King
Albanact, and in Prince Edward and Margaret of

[1] See *Der Miles Gloriosus bei Shakespeare*, *ibid.*, Vol. XIII.

10

Fressingfield. To these may be added Vortigern and Simon, the Mayor of Queenborough, in the play of the latter title, and Simon Eyre, Mayor of London and the king of *The Shoemakers' Holiday*. Both these plays must have been almost contemporary with Shakespeare's plays on *Henry IV.* and *V.* As to the "foreign wit" supported by Fluellen, and Jamey Macmorris, the Welshmen, the Scotchman and Irishman of *Henry V.*, and Dr. Caius, the French doctor of *The Merry Wives*, such obvious butts of sport have been the commonplaces of the drama since the days of Aristophanes.

The success of *Henry IV.* inspired the production of two plays entitled respectively *The first part of the true and honorable historie of the life of Sir John Oldcastle, the good Lord Cobham,* and *The Second Part of Sir John Oldcastle, with his Martyrdom.* According to Henslowe these plays were the joint work of Monday, Drayton, Wilson and Hathway. They were acted in the autumn of 1599 by the Admiral's company, and the earlier was printed in the next year with the name of Shakespeare on the title, a circumstance due to the confusion between Falstaff and Oldcastle already described, and one of which an enterprising publisher would be loath to disabuse the public mind. [1] Only this first part has come down to us, although it is certain that the second part was acted, as we hear

[1] *Oldcastle* was reprinted in the third folio of Shakespeare, 1663–64.

that Henslowe possessed properties for it in March, 1599.[1] It has been suggested that *Oldcastle* was written immediately after the first performance of *1 Henry IV.* and before the second part of that play was written, perhaps even before the name of Oldcastle was changed to that of Falstaff. This seems borne out by the circumstance that there are several allusions to *1 Henry IV.; e. g.*, to the Prince as "a perfect night walker" and a taker of purses, to "Falstaffe that villain so fat he can not get on's horse"—a plain reference to the old knight's fretting "like gumd Velvet" when his horse was "remouede" by the Prince on Gadshill ; while none of these allusions refer to any of the personages or events which belong distinctively to *2 Henry IV.*[2] In the prologue to *Oldcastle* the note of relation to the popular play of a rival company is struck :

> The doubtfull Title (gentlemen) prefixt
> Upon the Argument we have in hand,
> May breed suspence, and wrongfully disturb
> The peacefull quiet of your setled thoughts :
> To stop which scruple, let this brief suffice.
> It is no pamper'd Glutton we present,
> Nor aged Counsellor to youthfull sin ;
> But one, whose vertue shone above the rest,
> A valiant Martyr, and a vertuous Peer.
>
>   .   .   .   .   .   .
>
>   Let fair truth be grac'd
> Since forg'd invention former time defac'd.[3]

[1] *Henslowe's Diary*, p. 166.
[2] See *Oldcastle*, IV. 1 ; II. 1 ; III. 4 ; and *1 Henry IV.*, II. 2.
[3] *Oldcastle*, I. 1, text of the Shakespeare folio, 1663-64.

But Falstaff had made too good a hit to be represented in a rival play only by contrast with "a valiant
Martyr and a vertuous Peer." Sir John of Wrotham,
the knavish, lecherous priest and highwayman, a
personage of much vigor and some originality, is
modelled directly on the more famous and infinitely
more witty Sir John of Shakespeare. Among the parson's escapades is his robbery of the king, who in disguise had wandered by night beyond the precincts
of his camp. Attracted by the rattle of dice on a drum's
head, Sir John enters the camp and, joining in a game
of chance, loses the king's money to the king. His
identity as the robber who had just bade King Henry
stand is disclosed when he offers a broken angel as a
stake, the half of one which he had given Henry to
insure that his victim should not be "held up" a
second time by one of Sir John's pals. The most
diverting scene of this play is one which is borrowed
outright from Greene's *Pinner of Wakefield*. In it
Harpool, a faithful but eccentric servant of Oldcastle,
plays a trick of the Pinner's in forcing a summoner of
the Bishop of Rochester, his master's enemy, to eat
the seals of his summons.[1] The last act of *Oldcastle*
is made up of a series of mystifications and disguisings,
a departure from the usual practice of the Chronicle
Play, but one not entirely unknown to previous dramas
of the class. As a whole the play of *Sir John Old-*

[1] *Ibid.*, II. 1.

castle seems hasty and far from well written.   It is not impossible that the wit of three kingdoms exemplified in Henry's captains, Fluellen, Macmorris and Jamy, may have been Shakespeare's way of outdoing Davy, the humorous Welsh servant of Oldcastle and the cut-throat, Mack Chane, who begged that he might be " hang'd in a wyth after my country the Irish fashion."[1] The similarity, too, between the night meeting of King Henry with John a Wrotham and his acceptance of a broken angel from that thief as a token, and the meeting of Henry on the eve of the battle of Agincourt with the soldier, Williams, and the latter's acceptance of the royal glove, unknowing the king's identity, as a like token is assuredly a similarity not founded on mere accident.

[1] *Ibid.*, I. 1, V. 11.

VI

POPULAR PLAYWRIGHTS; MODIFICA-
TIONS OF THE TYPE

As we have seen above, it was during the last decade of the century that the Chronicle Play flourished
in its greatest luxuriance. We have already investigated the part which Shakespeare's earlier contemporaries, Marlowe, Greene and Peele, played in the development of this species of drama. Let us now consider
the authors of chronicle plays in the later years of this
decade and then proceed to the treatment of those species of this drama which fell away in one particular or
another from the earlier epic type and from the historical tragedy and later comedy form which we have
seen developing in the hands of Marlowe and Shakespeare.

Robert Greene died in September, 1592, leaving behind him in his *Groats-worth of Wit* the notorious address " To those Gentlemen his Quondam Acquaintance, that spend their wits in making Plaies," which
contains the earliest allusion to the great sovereign of
the Elizabethan drama. In this much-quoted passage
it will be remembered that Shakespeare is called " an
vpstart Crow, beautified with our feathers " and it is a
line from *3 Henry VI.:* " O Tygres Heart wrapt in a

134

Womans Hide," which in its parody: " His Tygers heart wrapt in a Players hide, " declares Greene's enmity to Shakespeare to have been caused largely by the success with which the new dramatist was working over the old historical dramas to fit them for reproduction on the stage. But now Greene was in his grave. Marlowe was killed in the following June, and Peele wrote no chronicle history after *Edward I.*, which was printed in 1593 and must have been first acted three or four years earlier. The chief playwrights, other than Shakespeare to take up the Chronicle Play when Greene, Peele and Marlowe left it, were Anthony Munday and Thomas Heywood. Munday was more than ten years older than Shakespeare and appears to have begun life as a Protestant spy on the English Jesuit college at Rome. He was known as an actor as early as 1575 and continued a busy pamphleteer, small poet and dramatic writer throughout a long life which extended into the reign of King Charles. Munday enjoyed some contemporary repute and was commended by Meres in his *Palladis Tamia* as " our best plotter," praise which his extant dramatic work by no means warrants.[1] On the other hand Munday was lampooned as Antonio Balladino by Jonson in *The Case is Altered.*[2] Munday's career as a playwright began with a translation entitled *Fidele and Fortunio* in

[1] See Haslewood, *Art of English Poetry*, II., 154.
[2] On this topic see Penniman, *The War of the Theatres*, p. 37.

1584.   His first work in the general class of chronicle plays was *John a Kent and John a Cumber*, a departure, as we shall presently see, from the contemporary type of the historical drama.   Six other plays, supposedly chronicle histories, have been attributed to Munday in joint authorship with Henry Chettle and others.   Of this number *1 Oldcastle*, and the two parts of *Robert Earl of Huntington*, are still extant; the non-extant plays were *2 Oldcastle, Owen Tudor* and *The Rising of Cardinal Wolsey*.   Our knowledge of all of these plays is derived from Henslowe.

Thomas Heywood is in many respects the most typical of Elizabethan playwrights.   He was an actor also and a defender of the " qualitie " he professed as appears from his *Apology for Actors*, a pamphlet of great interest.   Heywood's career as a dramatic writer and general pamphleteer is traceable back certainly to 1596 and his earliest chronicle history is that of *Edward IV.*, in two parts, printed in 1600 though doubtless several years older.   Between this play and *If You Know Not Me*, Heywood's dramatic chronicle of the chief events in the earlier life of Queen Elizabeth, acted in 1604, we have record of two non-extant plays of this class, *The Bold Beauchamps*, 1599, and *1 Lady Jane Grey*, 1602, the work of Heywood and others.   Passing *The Valiant Welshman* which may possibly be capable of identification with *The Welshman*, performed by the Admiral's and Chamberlain's companies at Newington in 1595, we reach several new names in Henslowe. Henry Chettle has been associated with eighteen plays, nearly all of this class ; Thomas Dekker and Michael Drayton were part authors of fifteen and thirteen dramas of the chronicle type respectively ; Robert Wilson the Younger and John Day were employed on nine and seven chronicles each. The habit of collaboration was general with the playwrights of this group and no one of them save Dekker has left a chronicle play of undivided authorship. Hence the number of these productions seems greater than it really is. Among the slender remains of these plays which are still extant are the two parts of Munday's *Robert Earl of Huntington*, mentioned above, in both of which Chettle had a share ; *The Blind Beggar of Bednall Green*, in which Day was Chettle's collaborator ; the two plays on Sir Thomas Wyatt in which Webster served an apprenticeship with the older dramatist Dekker ; and *Oldcastle* which, as we have seen above, was the joint effort of no less than four writers. Dekker's one independent play of this general class is *The Whore of Babylon*, and it is a departure from the type. His *Satiromastix*, the plot of which is laid in the court of William Rufus, and his *Old Fortunatus*, the later scenes of which are laid in the England of Athelstan, may be accounted on the border of this class.

Henry Chettle first appears in the history of the

drama as the publisher of Greene's *Groats-worth of Wit*, for the violence of the language in which with regard to Shakespeare he apologized in his *Kind-Harts Dreame*, printed almost immediately after. Within the decade of his thraldom to Henslowe, 1597–1607, Chettle contributed nearly fifty plays of various kinds to the drama of his time.[1] Of Robert Wilson, usually distinguished from the author of *The Three Ladies of London* and designated "the Younger," we know little beyond what Henslowe tells us.[2] This Wilson was active in the writing of chronicle plays but appears to have essayed no unaided effort. Michael Drayton's traffic with the stage rests likewise almost solely on the evidence of Henslowe's old book of accounts in which Drayton's name recurs again and again as the associate of Dekker, Chettle, Wilson and others during a period from December, 1597, to May, 1602.[3] Drayton's "well written tragedies" are also alluded to in an anonymous book entitled *Poems of Diverse Humours*, 1598,[4] although this may have been no more than a reference to his epical histories such as that of Meres who called Drayton, "Tragœdiographus, for his passionate penning of the downfals of valiant Robert of Normandy, chast Matilda, and great Gaueston."[5] Henslowe mentions

[1] See Henslowe, pp. 93 *et passim*, and the list of his plays in Ackermann's ed. of *Hoffman*, 1894.

[2] Henslowe, p. 153, etc.

[3] *Ibid.*, pp. 95, 96.

[4] Reprinted in *Shakspere Allusion Books*, p. 186.

[5] *Palladis Tamia*, ed. Haslewood, as above, II. 151.

twenty-four plays in connection with Drayton's name, of which number about half concern English historical subjects and but one, *William Longsword*, was written by Drayton alone. Drayton had been intimate with Lodge and Daniel, with both of whom he vied, at first in carrying on the pastoral mode which Sidney and Spenser had rendered popular and, after the publication of the former's *Astrophel and Stella* and Daniel's *Delia*, in his own sonnet-sequence *Idea*. In the writing of narrative history, too, Drayton imitated Daniel, whose *Complaint of Rosamund* appeared in 1592 and was succeeded in the next year by Drayton's *Legend of Piers Gaveston*, the subject of which may have been suggested by the contemporary popularity of Marlowe's *Edward II.* This coincidence taken with some others, such as the appearance of Daniel's *Civile Wars* in the same year, 1594, with a revived popularity of the plays dealing with the contention of the houses of York and Lancaster, has been thought by some to point to a rivalry between the stage and the epic in this species of literature.[1] Be this as it may, *The Legend of Robert Duke of Normandy*, the *Mortimeriados* (later remodelled as *The Barons Warres*), together with *Englands Heroicall Epistles* and the far later *Battle of Agincourt*, all attest Drayton's fertility and perseverance in the epic presentation of subject-matter drawn from the old

[1] Elton, *An Introduction to Michael Drayton, Spenser Society's Publications*, 1895, p. 24.

chronicles. Nothing could have been more natural
than that Drayton should have transferred his interest
in chronicle history epically told to the planning and
penning of historical dramas when the temporary failure of patrons and the stress of circumstances drove
him to a temporary coöperation with men his inferiors
in birth, station and celebrity..

Dekker and Day call for no word here. Other
names which *Henslowe's Diary* has associated with the
Chronicle Play are William Haughton, who had a
hand in eight such plays, besides some others during
the years 1600 and 1601 ; Henry Porter, the author
of the delightful comedy of situation, *The Two Angry
Women of Abington ;* Richard Hathway whose name
suggests a possible Shakespearean relation ; Wentworth
Smith whose initials have created some confusion with
William Shakespeare and William Smith, the author
of the sonnet-sequence, *Chloris ;* and lastly William
Rankins, the satirist. The works of these writers of
chronicle plays have perished save for the now indistinguishable part which Hathway had in *1 Oldcastle.*

John Webster and Thomas Middleton are both
mentioned in *Henslowe.*[1] William Rowley is not so
mentioned but claims a place here. The part of these
three dramatists in the Chronicle Play was slight.
Middleton in *The Mayor of Queenborough* and Rowley in *The Birth of Merlin* meet on common ground

[1] Henslowe, pp. 110 and 227.

in offering legendary chronicles reconstructed from earlier dramatic material. Neither author has written any other play of the chronicle type, if we except Middleton on the basis of Henslowe's association of his name with a play no longer extant called variously *Chester Tragedy* and *Randall Earl of Chester*. Webster's share in the Chronicle Play is confined to the assistance rendered Dekker in the extant play on Sir Thomas Wyatt and the two non-extant plays on Lady Jane Grey, if indeed these two titles are not referable to the same production.[1] Samuel Rowley covenanted in 1599 to act for a year for Henslowe,[2] but his one unaided play of the chronicle type *When You See Me You Know Me or the Famous Chronicle History of Henry VIII.*, printed in 1605 and performed not long before, was not written while he was in Henslowe's employ. Finally Jonson's name has been attached to three plays of the chronicle class. Henslowe mentions *Robert II. of Scotland*, written by Jonson in conjunction with Chettle and Dekker in 1599, and *Richard Crookback*, 1602, the work of Jonson alone.[3] Neither of these is extant. The fragment of *Mortimer his Fall* which appears in Jonson's works was possibly once complete and may be identified with the play of *Mortymore* for which Henslowe provided "ij sewtes a licke" (*i. e.*, two suits alike), in

[1] Fleay, *Biographical Chronicle*, I. 130 and II. 269.
[2] Henslowe, p. 260.
[3] *Ibid.*, pp. 156 and 223.

September, 1602.[1] By the fragment, which is preceded by an argument of the five acts, it is manifest
that this play must have exhibited a complete departure from the customary traditions of the popular
Chronicle History. If we are to judge by the indicated
choruses " of Ladyes celebrating the worthinesse of
the Queene," of " Countrey Justices and their Wives
telling how they were deluded and made beleeve the
old king lived, etc.," Jonson's *Mortimer his Fall* must
have been an attempt to carry the English Chronicle
History back to a stricter accord with the classical
traditions and usages which obtain in Jonson's Roman
tragedies, especially *Cataline*. Such an attempt is
precisely what we might expect of Jonson's theories
as to literature and the drama, theories which combine an intelligent and independent appreciation of the
excellence of ancient literature with an equally intelligent and independent desire to adapt whatever was
adaptable to English conditions. It is much to be
regretted that we have not Jonson's experiment of an
English chronicle play conformed to classical usage
in its fulness.

In the treatment of Shakespeare's and of Marlowe's
part in the evolution of historical tragedy of passion
out of the epical Chronicle Play, special mention was
made of the popularity of the Wars of the Roses, particularly the events involving the rise to power of Richard

[1] *Ibid.*, p. 226.

III., as a theme for both epic and dramatic poetry.
We have seen too how the reviser of *The True Tragedy
of Richard Duke of York* (otherwise called *2 Contention*) heightened the portrait of Gloucester, how *The
True Tragedy of King Richard* sketched in rivalry a
gross if vigorous picture of the same deformed usurper,
and how Shakespeare's *Richard III.* surpassed as it
succeeded these three earlier plays, not only in the
presentation of the protagonist but in the conduct of
the whole story as well.   This working over of material
of approved popularity is one of the most usual as it
is one of the most interesting characteristics of the
Elizabethan drama, although there are few instances
in which it can be traced with the certainty which the
case before us exhibits.   To the succession of plays
just enumerated must be added Heywood's two chronicle histories on the reign of Edward IV.   Here the
author gathered up whatever was left by his predecessors
and presented what he was compelled to repeat in a
guise at once familiar and yet novel.   Moreover this
play, while representing in a sense a return to the epic
type of the Chronicle Play of mingled history and
comedy, marks likewise a falling away from that type,
because of the prominence which it gives to the element of pathos and to the picturing of contemporary
London life.   The elaborate title of the two plays of
Heywood on the reign of Edward IV. has been given
above and need not be repeated here.[1]   The two parts

[1] See p. 51.

contain no less than five different stories more or less loosely connected by personages which take part in two or more.   On the more strictly historical side we have the attack on London by rebels under the adventurer Falconbridge, the last feeble attempt of the defeated Lancastrians to restore saintly and incapable Henry to his crown;[1] secondly, Edward's abortive expedition into France with what the title calls "the trecherous falshood of the Duke of Burgundie and the Constable of France"; and thirdly, the events which immediately preceded and followed the death of Edward, including the murder of the Duke of Clarence and of the young princes and Richard's succession to the crown.   To all this is added the episodic scenes of King Edward's diversions with the loyal, outspoken Hob, the Tanner of Tamworth,[2] and the pathetic story of Jane Shore, the king's mistress, her temptation and fall and her pitiful death. Of these stories the last alone finds place in both parts. Except for the scenes with the Tanner which the author had from a contemporary ballad, and barring a few modifications (among them the harrowing details of the deaths of the Shores), the material is derived directly from the *Chronicle* of Holinshed which includes, as is well known, Sir Thomas More's *Life of Richard III.*, although the intervention of an earlier play, such as *The Siege of London*, mentioned as revived by Hens-

[1] Holinshed, III. 321.
[2] See Child, *Popular Ballads*, V. 67.

lowe in 1594, is not impossible.[1] That the author of this facile production is Thomas Heywood cannot admit of a moment's doubt. The manner is uniformly his in its ease, its unaffectedness and its freedom from the gawds of contemporary poetic diction. In the scenes which concern Shore and his wife, we meet again and again Heywood's generous conception of character and that wholesome and unrestrained pathos which is peculiarly his. Indeed the whole treatment of that delicate subject, the relation of a true and honorable man to the wife who has wronged him, but whom he continues to love in a spirit chastened by his wrongs, is handled with the same innate delicacy, the same wide tolerance and sympathy and yet with the ethical soundness, which Heywood displays with such effect in his characters, the Franklins, in *A Woman Killed with Kindness*—qualities in which Heywood is practically alone amongst his contemporaries. The changes which Heywood made in the story of Jane Shore are significant. Shore, the husband, is dignified with an important part in the defense of London against Falconbridge by a transfer to him of the rôle actually played in the chronicles by Alderman Basset.[2] This links the story of the siege with that of Jane and leads naturally to her meeting with the king at a civic feast.[3] Once more Shore is identified with a party of ships-

[1] Henslowe, p. 46, and Fleay, *Biographical Chronicle*, I. 288.
[2] Cf. *1 Edward IV.*, I. 3 and I. 6, with Holinshed, III. 323.
[3] *1 Edward IV.*, IV. 2.

11

men who have become constructively pirates, though really innocent, and Jane, unknowing, becomes instrumental in saving her husband's life.[1]   Lastly the story of the murder of the young princes is linked with that of Jane by the device by which Shore, as the assistant of Sir Robert Brackenbury, Keeper of the Tower, falls into an altercation with Tyrrel and his cutthroats and receives a dagger thrust in the arm.[2]   In the upshot Heywood departs from all the chronicles, narratives and ballads, in making Shore defy Richard's tyrannical command that no one offer relief or harborage to Jane after her public penance with sheet and candle, and in the final tragedy by which the reunited husband and wife perish of want and hunger together.[3]

These are examples of that instinctive insight into the possibilities of a subject which mark the born dramatist.   Not less successful is Heywood's adaptability evidenced in the evasion of repetitions where repetition seems all but unavoidable, and in throwing a new light on incidents already treated by others in a previous play.   The events of the two parts of *Edward IV.* range from a scene in which King Edward's mother, the Duchess of York, is represented chiding Lady Grey for her marriage with Edward to the moment when King Richard, secure as he thinks in the possession of his ill-gotten throne, disregards the

[1] *2 Edward IV.*, II. 1 and II. 4.
[2] *Ibid.*, III. 4.
[3] *Ibid.*, IV. 3, V. 1 and 2.

ominous mention of Harry Richmond's name to proceed to "the princely ceremonies" of the founding of
the Order of the Bath. Between these extremes there
are several points at which Heywood's play comes
into contact with Shakespeare's *Richard III.* and *The
True Tragedy of Richard III.*, the latter of which treats
not only the steps of Richard's rise to power but the
consequences of Edward's death on the fortunes of
Jane Shore. In each of these cases it is Heywood's
cue to avoid the actual repetition of scenes already
part of the earlier plays and to illuminate well-known
events with the side light of novelty. In the induction
of *The True Tragedy* the ghost of the Duke of Clarence
appears, after the Senecan manner, to call for vengeance
on his murderer. In *Richard III.* Clarence is shown
face to face with his murderers in agonized pleading
for his life, while in *Edward IV.* the news of his death
by drowning in a butt of malmsey is thrown into a
conversation between Lovell and Dr. Shaw, two creatures of the usurper, and thus presented in contrast
with the natural sympathies of the beholder.[1] *The
True Tragedy of Richard III.* devotes many scenes to
the intrigues and subterfuges by which the young
princes are separated from their friends, their mother
and from each other, to fall into Richard's hands.
Shakespeare subordinates all this to the higher unity
in which Richard becomes the center of the stage,

[1] *Richard III.*, I. 4; 2 *Edward IV.*, III. 1.

while *Edward IV.* goes at once to the imprisonment
of the princes in the Tower.   There is a simple pathos
in this short scene between the motherless little princes
which exhibits Heywood at his best.   The scene is a
bedroom in the Tower.   The young princes Edward
and Richard enter "in their gowns and caps, vnbut-
toned and vntrust."

Ric.   How does your lordship?
Ed.   Well, good brother Richard.
          How does yourself? you told me your head aked.
Ric.   Indeed it does, my Lord feele with your hands
          How hot it is.
          He laies his hand on his brothers head.
Ed.   Indeed you haue caught cold,
          With sitting yesternight to heare me read.
          I pray thee go to bed, sweet Dick, poore little
            heart.
Ric.   Youle giue me leaue to wait vpon your lord-
            ship.
Ed.   I had more need, brother, to wait on you.
          For you are sick; and so am not I.
Ric.   Oh, lord, methinks this going to our bed,
          How like it is to going to our graue.
Ed.   I pray thee, do not speake of graues sweetheart,
          Indeed thou frightest me.
Ric.   Why, my lord brother, did not our tutor teach
            vs,
          That when at night we went vnto our bed,
          We still should think we went vnto our graue?
Ed.   Yes, thats true,
          If we should do as eu'ry Christian ought,

> To be prepard to die at euery hour,
> But I am heauy.
>
> *Ric.* Indeed, and so am I.
>
> *Ed.* Then let vs say our prayers and go to bed.
>
> *They kneel, and solemn musicke the while within. The musicke ceaseth, and they rise.*
>
> *Ric.* What, bleeds your grace?
>
> *Ed.* I two drops and no more.
>
> *Ric.* God blesse vs both ; and I desire no more.
>
> *Ed.* Brother [*Opening his prayer-book*], see here
>   what Dauid says, and so say I :
>   Lord ! in thee will I trust, although I die.[1]

In *The True Tragedy* the innocent doubts and apprehensions of the young princes with their murderers' contrasted brutality and flickering qualms of conscience had entered as elements in a rude but effective scene.[2] Shakespeare reduced all this to a score of pathetic and poetic lines which he put somewhat unfittingly into the mouth of Tyrrel, the instrument of the children's death.

> The tyrannous and bloodie Act is done,
> The most arch deed of pittious massacre
> That euer yet this Land was guilty of:
> Dighton and Forrest, who I did suborne
> To do this peece of ruthfull Butchery,
> Albeit they were flesht Villaines, bloody Dogges,
> Melted with tendernesse, and milde compassion,
> Wept like to Children, in their deaths sad Story.
> O thus (quoth Dighton) lay the gentle Babes :

[1] *Ibid.*, III. 5.

[2] *The True Tragedy*, ed. Shakespeare Society, 1844, p. 42.

Thus, thus (quoth Forrest) girdling one another
Within their Alablaster innocent Armes :
Their lips were foure red Roses on a stalke,
And in their Summer Beauty kist each other.
A Booke of Prayers on their pillow lay,
Which one (quoth Forrest) almost chang'd my minde :
But oh the Diuell, there the Villaine stopt :
When Dighton thus told on, we smothered
The most replenished sweet worke of Nature,
That from the prime Creation ere she framed.
Hence both are gone with Conscience and Remorse,
They could not speake, and so I left them both,
To beare this tydings to the bloody King.[1]

In like strait, while the very deed is doing, Heywood's Tyrell thus communes with his own blackened
soul :

I haue put my hand into the foulest murder
That euer was committed since the world.
The very senselesse stones here in the walles
Breake out in teares but to behold the fact.
Methinkes the bodies lying dead in graues,
Should rise and cry against vs—O hark, [*a noise within*]
    harke,
The mandrakes shrieks are music to their cries,
The very night is frighted, and the starres
Do drop like torches, to behold this deed :
The very centre of the earth doth shake,
Methinks the Towre should rent down from the toppe,
To let the heauen look on this monstrous deede. [2]

[1] *Richard III.*, IV. 3, 1–23.   In the folio, the text of which is here
followed, this passage forms part of the second scene.
    [2] *2 Edward IV.*, III. 5.

" Heywood," says Charles Lamb, in a much-quoted passage, " is a sort of *prose* Shakespeare.   His scenes are to the full as natural and affecting.   But we miss *the Poet*, that which in Shakespeare always appears out and above the surface of *the nature*." [1]   Is it too bold to query whether the poet in Shakespeare's Tyrrel, taken with the beauty of " the gentle Babes " more than is a murderer's wont—" their Alabaster innocent Armes " and lips, " foure red Roses on a stalke "—" appears out and above the surface of *the nature* " somewhat to that nature's detriment ?

It is in such touches of nature as these that Heywood excels and it is with expectation rather than with surprise, therefore, that we record the play of *Edward IV.* as a notable example of the falling away from the epic type of Chronicle Play by the substitution of interests of diverse kind from that which centered in the delineation of events which appealed to patriotic spirit and national feeling.   The central story of *Edward IV.* is, after all, that of Jane Shore.   The scenes of the rise of Richard are repetitions in sketchy outline; the siege of London and the king's journey into France possesses next to no power of dramatic appeal.   In short the romantic tale of a kingly and conquering lover with the involved emotion of a woman's remorse for sin and a man's constancy and magnanimity have outweighed political intrigues and

[1] *Specimens of English Dramatic Poets*, ed. 1893, I. 213.

the bluster of arms. To posit strict chronological order in developments and changes of literary taste and form such as this is to lose sight of the facts and obscure their true relations in the attempt to work out a theory. That later chronicle plays were more exposed to the intrusion of extraneous influences than the earlier ones is, however, undeniable; although this species of drama was open from the first to admixture and to modifications from without, most of them referable to two influences : the emphasis of the element of comedy, and the centralization of the whole play in biographical particulars which concerned a single individual.

Of the several classes of quasi-chronicles in which the comedy element has gained an ascendancy, an interesting though limited group has its basis in stories of the heroes of popular balladry. Though the direct evidences are slight, we have already seen that there is much reason to believe that mummings, dialogues and interludes celebrating the deeds of Robin Hood and his associates enjoyed at one time considerable prevalence and popularity. It is then a return to an old and tried subject and the adaptation of it to altered conditions that we recognize in the appropriately named *A pleasant conceyted Comedie of George a Greene, the Pinner of Wakefield*, the work of Robert Greene. This play is mentioned three times by Henslowe, [1] under

[1] See pp. 31–33.

date of December, 1592, and the January following.
The external evidence attributing this play to Greene
is slight; but its style and manner are all but indubi-
tably his.   In this play the dramatist has drawn the
ideal of the sturdy English yeoman of his day.
George a Greene is faithful and loyal to his king
though independent in his bearing before him, daring
in open fight yet sagacious in stratagem against his
sovereign's enemies and magnanimous to them in their
overthrow.   The Earl of Kendall has revolted from
his allegiance to King Edward and sends Sir Nicholas
Mannering to Wakefield to demand supplies for the
rebel army.   On being refused, Mannering threatens
the citizens and George a Greene interposes :

George.   Proud dapper Iacke, vayle bonnet to the
            bench
         That represents the person of the King ;
         Or sirra, Ile lay thy head before thy feete.
Man.   Why, who art thou?
George.   Why, I am George a Greene,
         True liegeman to my king,
         Who scornes that men of such esteeme as these,
         Should brooke the braues of any trayterous
            squire :
         You of the bench, and you my fellowe friends,
         Neighbours, we subiects all vnto the King
         We are English borne, and therefore Edwards
            friends,
         Voude vnto him euen in our mothers wombe;
         Our mindes to God, our hearts vnto our King,

> Our wealth, our homage, and our carcases,
> Be all King Edwards : then, sirra, we haue
> Nothing left for traytours, but our swordes,
> Whetted to bathe them in your bloods, and
>   dye
> Gainst you, before we send you any victuals.[1]

In the upshot Mannering is compelled by George to swallow the seals of his rebels' commission and is thrust out of Wakefield.   Mention has already been made of the borrowing of this incident by the authors of *Oldcastle*.   The trick of his namesake is related by Nashe as having been actually performed by the dramatist Greene on an apparator come to serve a citation on him.   As pinner, penner or impounder of Wakefield, it is George's duty to impound all strays and to prevent trespass on the crops and the commons of the town.   He finds the horses of the Earl of Kendall in the town's corn and orders them to the pound, but is immediately surrounded by the Earl's followers. Craftily pretending to yield to the rebels' invitation to join them, George induces the Earl to visit a holy hermit of the neighborhood to consult him on the prospect of the success of his revolt.   The Earl comes with but two attendants.   The hermit, who is none other than George in disguise, kills one and puts the other to flight, and makes the Earl his prisoner. King Edward now happens into the neighborhood and comes to "merrie Bradford" in disguise.   There he

[1] *George a Greene, Works of Greene*, ed. Grosart, XIV. 126.

and his courtiers are compelled to trail their staves by
the stalwart shoemakers of that town, who will permit
no man to carry his staff on his shoulder in traversing
the town unless he fight for that right. George enters
at this juncture with Robin Hood, Much and Scarlet,
who have just tasted to their sorrow of the pinner's
valor at quarter-staff, and the disguised king and his
nobles are put to the dilemma of fighting the shoemakers for carrying their staves on their shoulders or
George and Robin for trailing them. After a merry
fight which comes to an end on the shoemakers' dis-
covery of the identity of George, a keg of ale is
broached in the street and all join in merriment. To
the king's praises for his capture of the rebel Earl,
George modestly replies :

> I humbly thanke your royall Maiestie.
> That which I did against the Earle of Kendal,
> It was but a subiects duetie to his Soueraigne,
> And therefore little merit[s] such good words.[1]

The king of Scots is among the royal prisoners and
King Edward asks George to fix his ransom. This
after some reluctance George consents to do. But instead of seeking a large sum of money for himself,
after the custom of his time, the honest pinner only
demands :

> Then let king Iames make good
> Those townes which he hath burnt vpon the borders ;
> Giue a small pension to the fatherlesse,

[1] *Ibid.*, p. 176.

Whose fathers he caus'd murthered in those warres ;
Put in pledge for these things to your grace,
And so returne.[1]

Just before this, when urged to ask something for
himself, George begs for the king's intercession in pro-
curing the consent of the father of Bettris, his sweetheart, to their marriage.   But the king is not content
thus to leave the young hero, and after bestowing upon
him some of the estates of the rebels, bids him kneel.

George.   What will your maiestie do ?
Edward.   Dub thee a knight, George.
George.   I beseech your grace, grant me one thing.
Edward.   What is that ?
George.   Then let me liue and die a yeoman still :
          So was my father, so must liue his sonne.
          For tis more credite to men of base degree,
          To do great deeds, than men of dignitie.[2]

We can imagine how such an apotheosis of the
yeomanry of England must have stirred the audience
of the Earl of Sussex's servants at the Rose.   Indeed
it would be difficult to find in the plays of the period
a happier realization of that honest loyalty, that spirit
of fair play and generosity of heart, which are among
the best as they are among the most enduring qualities of the English people.

If we turn to the sources of this comedy we meet
with some difficulty.   In English balladry only one

[1] *Ibid.*, p. 181.
[2] *Ibid.*

fragment remains to associate George a Green with the Robin Hood ballads. That fragment exists in several copies but in only two versions, little differing. "It is thoroughly lyrical, and therein 'like the old age,' and was pretty well sung to pieces before it ever was printed," says the late Professor Child.[1] *The Jolly Pinder of Wakefield*, as the ballad is entitled, relates how the report had gone abroad that such was the prowess of George a Green that none

> Dare make a trespasse to the town of Wakefield,
> But his pledge goes to the pinfold.

Robin Hood and his men, Scarlet and John, determine to test this report. They "make a path over the corn" and are challenged by George, who fights each of them in turn until Robin calls for a truce. After bread, beef and ale at the pinner's house, Robin makes his usual offer that George go the greenwood with him, which George accepts upon condition that he first fulfil the obligation of his engagement to his master to serve him till Michaelmas Day. The subject-matter of this ballad forms the tenth and twelfth scenes of the play but is given a turn, not in the ballad though in the romance presently to be noticed, by making the enmity which the reported beauty of Bettris Grimes, the "leman" of George, has inspired in Maid Marian the cause of Robin's trespass. The immediate source usually ascribed to Greene's play is a prose romance

[1] *Popular Ballads*, III. 129.

entitled *The History of George a Greene, Pinder of the Town of Wakefield, his Birth, Calling, Valor, etc.*, a late version of which is printed by Thoms.[1] This editor's preface contains mention of an earlier extant version of 1632, and it is altogether likely that still earlier versions once existed. Although the play and the story exhibit such striking likenesses that it may be regarded as certain that they are either dependent, the one on the other, or referable to a common source, there are points of difference. The chief divergence consists in the introduction into the play of the episode of Lady Barley's spirited resistance to the suit of King James and the subsequent capture of that monarch. Neither of these matters immediately concerns the story of the pinner and both are subversive of unity. These things with the change of the king from Richard I. to Edward, presumably Edward III., and some minor differences seem to point to the fact that here, as is the more usual course, the play followed the tale. On the other hand, the Robin of the play is "poor Robin," and Marian seems reasonably jealous of her equal in station, Bettris, the squire's daughter; while in the story the rank of Robin Hood as Robert Earl of Hunting-ton and Marian as "Matilda daughter to the Lord Fitzwalters" is carefully set forth with a reference to the solicitations of Prince John under which the fair lady was still suffering. These things it is well known

[1] *Early English Prose Romances*, ed. 1858, II. 150.

are late sophistications of the old ballads, though it must be confessed not too late for Greene to have met.   Lastly, it may be noted that in the scene in which George forces Mannering to swallow the seals of his commission, the playwright (supposing that he had the story before him) appears to have thrown away a point which heightens the climax by omitting the mock courtesy of a cup of ale wherewith to wash down the unusual diet.   Altogether it would be difficult to determine whether Greene founded his material on an earlier version of the prose tale or adapted his play from more general sources and was copied by later prose romancers.

That the most popular hero of the old ballads was not unknown to the Elizabethan stage in a treatment more complete than that accorded him in this minor rôle in *George a Greene* is proved by an entry at the Stationers' Register of *A Pastoral Pleasant Comedy of Robin Hood and Little John* in May, 1594.   In December, 1600, Henslowe records a play of Haughton's which he calls *Roben hoodes penerthes*.[1]   None the less it is somewhat remarkable that two plays of Munday and Chettle should be the only ones now extant in which the deeds of Robin Hood are treated *in extenso* as the major theme of a drama.   The complete titles of these plays run : *The Downfall of Robert, Earle of*

[1] See Arber's *Reprint of the Register of the Stationers' Company*, II. 649 ; and *Henslowe*, p. 174.

Huntington, afterwards called Robin Hood of merrie Sherwodde: with his love to chaste Matilda, the Lord Fitzwaters Daughter, afterwarde his faire Maide Marian; and *The Death of Robert, Earle of Huntington, Otherwise called Robin Hood of merrie Sherwodde: with the lamentable Tragedie of chaste Matilda, his faire maid Marian, poysoned at Dunmowe by King John.* Both were published in 1601 and are mentioned by Henslowe under date of February, 1598, as acted by the Admiral's company. These plays are disappointing for several reasons, but chiefly because of their inadequate handling of a topic rich in dramatic possibilities and their total failure to reproduce the fresh atmosphere of Sherwood Forest which breathes through the ballads. The authors of these plays laid under contribution many ballads, reproducing one of them at least in full and quoting snatches of others.[1] But they have employed their materials carelessly, adapting at will and seldom for the better; and they have subordinated the deeds of Robin, who as an earl loses half his interest, to the story of " Matilda Lord Fitzwater's daughter " in whose dignified repulse of the solicitations of the Prince John and tragic death we lose the sprightly maiden companion of Robin. The general sources of the historical parts of these plays have been traced to Holinshed and Grafton. The story of Matilda, explained as a composite picture of

[1] See *Dodsley*, VIII. 138, and cf. Child, *Popular Ballads*, III. 177.

the adventures of no less than three maidens of that name has been referred to the recently published treatment of that theme by Drayton in *Englands Heroicall Epistles* and to a passage in Stow's *Annales* which is quoted from the *Chronicle of Dunmow*.[1] *The Downfall* is set in an Induction in which the poet Skelton is represented as conducting the rehearsal of a performance intended for the ear of his master, King Henry VIII. An inartificial device for merriment is that by which Skelton is made to forget from time to time his part of Friar Tuck and fall into Skeltonic doggerel. Several clumsy attempts are made to utilize the device of disguise, whilst among the personages of the elaborate and abortive dumb shows Ambition and Insurrection, personified abstractions of the old drama, still linger. These remnants are doubtless Munday's, for he had been bred in an earlier school. The occasional rise in dignity and the improvement in diction which some scenes display may be confidently attributed to the abler hand of the author of *Hoffman*. But *The Death* is little better than *The Downfall* and the adventures of Matilda, set in an incoherent mass of the bickerings and taunts of characters with difficulty distinguished one from the other, are verily " rough-hewn out by an uncunning hand," as the epilogue ingenuously

---

[1] See a *Dissertation* on the sources of these plays by A. Ruckdeschel, Erlangen, 1897 ; and Mr. H. L. D. Ward, *Catalogue of Romances*, 1883, I. 506, on the three Matildas.

12

informs us.   With a perversity not infrequently born
of unwitting failure, Munday employed the figure of
Robin Hood once more in his masque *Metropolis
Coronata*, 1615.

It is strange that the best dramatic realization of
Robin Hood and his merry men should have come
from the pen of an avowed classicist and should have
been interwoven into that most artificial of all species
of the drama, a pastoral play : for *The Sad Shepherd,
or a Tale of Robin Hood* is commonly so described.
The date of the writing of this fragment of Jonson's is
doubtful.   It was probably acted, if acted at all, earlier
than 1619, for there seems reason in Mr. Fleay's
identification of this play with *The May Lord* mentioned
by Jonson in his *Conversations with Drummond* in that
year and generally supposed to be lost. [1]   As a matter
of fact the "forest element," as it has been not inaptly
called, much prevails over the pastoral. [2]   The scene
is Sherwood not Arcadia, and the story turns upon an
invitation of Robin to the neighboring shepherds to
come to the greenwood and feast a day with him.   It
is difficult for the non-impressionist critic to find any
such "preposterous" and "irritating" incongruity,
any such "inexcusable" and "inexplicable" artistic offence as Mr. Swinburne contrives to discover in all

[1] *Biographical Chronicle*, I. 379.   Symonds accepted this view ;
Ward thinks it not sufficiently proved.

[2] Dr. Homer Smith, *Pastoral Influences in the English Drama*,
1897, pp. 29–32.

this.[1] The juxtaposition of Aeglamour, Robin Hood and Puck-hairy under the beeches of Nottinghamshire seems hardly more startling than that of Titania, Theseus and Bottom in the copses bordering a certain very unclassical Athens. Indeed their fine names and the poetry of their lines alone ally Jonson's shepherds and shepherdesses with the old pastoral conventions. The freshness and naturalness with which the familiar figures of Robin and Marian, and the witch of Papplewicke with her attendants Maudlin and Lorell, are drawn scarcely admit of too much praise. *The Sad Shepherd* is a refreshing piece of open-air realism and is entitled to a place in the drama of English folk-lore with *A Midsummer Night's Dream*, *Friar Bacon* and *Old Fortunatus*.

Robin Hood fills an interesting but minor rôle in the sprightly comedy of disguises, *Look About You*, first printed in 1600 and variously dated between 1594 and that year. Here Robin is represented in his boyhood as the young Earl of Huntington, ward of Prince Richard and the intimate companion and playfellow of the young and virtuous Lady Fauconbridge, whom the prince courts for her love. On the historical side *Look About You* deals with the dissensions between Henry II. and his three sons. But the gist of the matter is in the disguises and opposed mystifications of an eccentric earl, Robert of Gloster, and one Skink, a sharper and creature of Prince John. In this

[1] *A Study of Ben Jonson*, p. 87.

intricate comedy Skink passes through nine disguises, Gloster through four, while the princes Richard and John, Lady Fauconbridge and Robin each plays at least one part other than his own. The clearness of design is not less remarkable than the intricacy of this diverting comedy, which belongs, however, in purpose and in kind, despite the scenes which depict Henry's troubles with his sons, with the comedy of disguise. In the long list of non-extant plays the titles of which betray historical subject-matter there is no other apparently that can be connected with a subject drawn from ballad lore. In November, 1602, Henslowe paid Middleton for a play called *Randall Earl of Chester*. This worthy, known in history as Randulph de Blundevill, is one of the characters in Munday's extant play, *John a Kent*, and is mentioned with Robin Hood in *Piers Plowman*.[1]

One other play fulfils the conditions of a comedy of disguises superimposed upon an historical background. This is *The Blind Beggar of Bednall Green*, the joint production of John Day and Henry Chettle, first recorded by Henslowe in 1600, and printed for the first time in 1659. The popularity of this play, which was great, seems to have depended chiefly on the character of Old Stroud, a hearty Norfolk yeoman. Two other "parts" are named by Henslowe, in both of which Haughton assisted Day. In the first and only extant part, Lord Momford, a deserving but broken soldier

[1] Ed. Skeat, *Early English Text Society*, 1873, p. 121.

in the French wars, assumes the habit of a beggar and a serving-man, as a counterplot to a conspiracy against his fame and the fortunes of his daughter, and much of the comedy is also supported by similar disguisings of other characters. The play is bustling and full of action, and a spirited trial by combat, over which King Henry VI. presides, brings out the climax. Except for the scenes in which Humphrey, Duke of Gloucester, and Cardinal Beaufort play a very undignified and unhistorical part, the drama displays not the slightest basis in even supposed history. Munday's inferior play, *John a Kent and John a Cumber*, is likewise a comedy of disguises in which personages supplied with historical names figure. But here not even the shadow of an actual event enters into the plot, and the mystifications are effected by the supernatural powers of two rival magicians as in *Friar Bacon and Friar Bungay*. It is with this latter play and with *The Marry Devil of Edmonton* that *John a Kent* belongs. The one manuscript of this play is in Munday's own hand, and is dated 1595. Mr. Fleay's identification of it with *The Wise Man of West Chester*, mentioned by Henslowe as acted at the Rose, in December, 1594, by the Admiral's men seems not improbable.[1] The *Ballad of British Sidanen*, on which this play is in part founded, was entered in the Stationers' Register as early as 1579.

[1] *Biographical Chronicle*, II. 114.

In that species of the vernacular drama which seeks
subject-matter in popular folk-lore we have already
found history playing a subordinate part.   That the adventures of the heroes of romance and drama were fictitious mattered little to the novelty-loving Elizabethan.
Other steps in the growth of myth were taken : that
of attributing imaginary events to actual personages of
history and that of adding to the interest of foreign
stories by giving them an English coloring or setting.
Thus we find Greene, in his search after novelty, not only
attempting a revival of the Robin Hood play but also
endeavoring to enhance popular interest in his dramas
by both of these devices.   In the best of his comedies,
Friar Bacon and Friar Bungay, he heightens the effect
by introducing into a tale of magic a story of romantic
love and generosity told of an English prince.   King
Henry III. and Edward his son both appear in this
play : but the events in which they figure might with
equal irrelevancy attach to any English or other prince.
In *The Scottish Historie of Iames the fourth, slaine at
Flodden.   Entermixed with a pleasant Comedie presented by Oboram King of Fayeries* we have a play
the title of which clothes, besides much else, a romantic tale of love and jealousy until then unconnected with the historical King James.   The composition of this play has been assigned to various
dates from 1589 to 1592.   It was most likely earlier
than *George a Greene* and subsequent to *Alphonsus*
and *Orlando*.   There seems no reason to question the

view of Storojenko, "that Greene, dissatisfied with
his former plays in which he had imitated the style
of Lyly [a point decidedly questionable] and the
manner of Marlowe, decided on striking out a new
and independent course." [1]   There is no mention of
The Scottish History in Henslowe, and though the play
was registered in 1594, the earliest extant edition is
that of 1598.   A wider departure from history, even
from the liberal type of the chronicles, than that of this
play it would be difficult to find.   The events of two
different reigns are confounded and crimes imputed to
King James of which he never could have been guilty.
But neither intentional misrepresentation nor sheer ignorance need be attributed to the playwright for all
that.   It was his task to write a play which should
strike the fancy of the moment.   " James IV., slain at
Flodden " was a pure catchpenny, for James is not
slain and Flodden does not form a part of the play.
Under this misleading title the author set forth a romantic drama which he borrowed entire from a
romance of Cinthio's *Hecatomithi*, although the Irish
and Scottish kings of his original may have suggested
his fathering the story on James and making Henry
VII., of England, a character in it. [2]   Further into the

---

[1] See Grosart's ed. of Greene, I. 184.

[2] The source of this play was discovered by Mr. P. A. Daniel and
communicated to the *Athenæum*, Oct. 8, 1881.   There is a play on
the subject by Cinthio, entitled *Arenopia*.   Greene follows the story,
not the play.   Creizenach's paper in *Anglia VIII.*, p. 419, is later
188(5) and adds nothing.

characteristics of this curious and by no means inferior production it is not necessary to go here as in the mingled elements of romance, melodrama, fairy-lore and comedy which form its components the historical is the least conspicuous.

An example of the assignment of fictitious adventures to a well-known name which is even more striking is to be found in a play which may possibly antedate *The Scottish History*. This is *A Pleasant Comedie of Faire Em, The Millers Daughter of Manchester. With the Love of William the Conqueror,* the main plot of which is a wholly absurd quest into Denmark undertaken by King William in search of a fair lady whose face he has beheld painted on the shield of one of his knights. The source of this story, which suggests the extravagance of degenerate heroic romance, has not been traced although Simpson thought that he discerned "some distant resemblance" to Greene's *Arbasto*.[1] The two plots, which are remarkable for their complete independence, may well have been invented by the author of the play whoever he was. *Fair Em* is one of several plays which the credulity of Tieck assigned to the authorship of Shakespeare on the strength of a book-binder's blunder. This notion Simpson supported with painstaking and futile ingenuity.[2] Mr. Fleay attributes this comedy to Robert Wilson the Elder, the known or putative author of several early

[1] *The School of Shakspere*, II. 341.
[2] *Das altenglische Theater, Kritische Schriften*, 1848, I. 279, and Simpson, as above, II. 337.

plays, the diction and general nature of which are not altogether unlike those of *Fair Em.*[1] This is not the place in which to discuss the question of personal satire and controversy supposed by some critics to be involved in this play. The thing which allies it to the group of chronicle histories—as with *The Scottish History of James IV.*—is the use in the title of a well-known historical name to cloak adventures altogether fictitious, a relationship surely very slight. A later instance of the assignment of apocryphal adventures to an actual historical personage may be found in Anthony Brewer's mediocre tragedy *The Lovesick King*, in which King Canute is represented as reaching the tragedy of his life through an unholy infatuation which impels him to force the beautiful nun, Cartesmunda, to become his wife. This play, although not printed before 1655, has been assigned by Mr. Fleay, not without a show of reason, to about the year 1604.[2] An earlier play on Canute is mentioned by Henslowe in 1597. Even less tied to the merest semblance of history must have been the original English comedy from which was translated *Eine schoene lustige triumphirende Comoedia von eines Koeniges Sohn aufs Engellandt vnd des Koeniges Tochter aufs Schottlandt*, one of a collection of *Engelische Comedien vnd Tragedien* printed in Germany in the year 1620. In this production the English prince is named Serule, the Scottish

---

[1] *Biographical Chronicle*, II. 281.
[2] *Ibid.*, I. 34.

princess, Astrea.   The two countries are at war and
the prince, disguised as a fool, visits the princess, his
beloved.   An element of the supernatural is added in
the black art of one Runcifax.[1]   Tieck regarded this
as one of the oldest plays of the collection.[2]

The chronicle histories in which Dekker had a hand
in his earlier career have perished, but the simplicity
of his nature and the realism of his art made Dekker
precisely the dramatist from whom an adherence to
English scenes might be expected so far as the fashion
of the day might permit.   Accordingly, beside his
share in such non-extant chronicle plays as *The Famous Wars of Henry I. and the Prince of Wales*, the
two plays on Godwin and his sons, *Conan of Cornwall* and *Robert II. of Scots*, we find Dekker contriv-
ing to give an English coloring to several dramas the
actual design of which is wide of the Chronicle Play.
In the fanciful and highly poetical *Comedy of Old Fortunatus* the scene of the adventures of the sons of that
universal personage, who was the hapless possessor of
the inexhaustible purse and the cap which rendered the
wearer of it invisible, is laid in an imaginary England
of Athelstan, while *Satiromastix*, Dekker's reply to
Jonson's satirical attack on his fellow playwrights, as
we have seen, is preposterously placed at the court of
William Rufus.   *The Shoemakers' Holiday*, a happily -

[1] See Cohn, *Shakespeare in Germany*, 1865, p. cviii.
[2] *Die Anfaenge des deutschen Theaters*, 1817, *Kritische Schriften*,
I. 353.

conceived and well-executed comedy of London life, introduces an indeterminable English king whose function it is to straighten out the complications of a troubled course of true love.   Another play in which an English king is employed as a *deus ex machina* to unravel the difficulties of a dramatic situation is the domestic drama, *The Fair Maid of Bristow*, in which, as in *2 Robert Earl of Huntington*, Richard I. so figures.   Equally remote from the genuine Chronicle Play are such productions as *Alphonsus, Emperor of Germany*, "a Machiavelian revenge-play," attributed to George Chapman, in which appear a Richard of Cornwall and a young English Prince Edward; and Heywood's *Royal King and Loyal Subject*.   This last play is referable to the story of the Persian king Artaxerxes and his seneschal Ariobarzanes, as told in Painter's *Palace of Pleasure*.[1]   It is an instance of the sporadic reversion from Italian dukedoms and pseudo-Greek courts to an English scene.   Whether modelled on an earlier play of Heywood and Smith, entitled *Marshall Osric*, referred to by Henslowe in 1602,[2] or a new play a few years before its publication in 1637, the spirit of nationality, if it may so be called, has wholly evaporated from this play, and it may be regarded as a specimen of the final absorption of the Chronicle History into romantic drama.

[1] Ed. Jacobs, 1890, II. 198, and see Koeppel, *Quellen-studien zu den Dramen Ben Jonson's*, etc., 1895, *Muenchener Beitraege*, XI. 133–135.

[2] Fleay, *Biographical Chronicle*, I. 300.

VII

THE LEGENDARY CHRONICLE PLAY

DRAMAS of the chronicle type on subjects derived from the romantic myths of fabulous Britain have already been mentioned, and they have been included in our estimates of the number and distribution of the Chronicle Play. The earliest plays on such subjects, *Gorboduc*, *The Misfortunes of Arthur*, and *Locrine*, have received our attention among the forerunners of the historical drama. The Elizabethan conception of history accepted such tales and gave them the credence which we accord to historical fact. Hence to a certain extent the division of plays of mythical plot from those on later and more genuinely historical topics is defensible only as a means to a clearer understanding of both. That an appreciable loss of historic interest resulted in scenes so remote from their own contemporary life can not admit of doubt, and the playwrights sought in various ways to supply this loss by a heightened and inflated style, by the interpolation of scenes of humor and buffoonery or by an emphasis of the elements of the strange or the supernatural. In truth the chronicle plays the subjects of which are English legend and myth have as deep a root in romance as in history.   The persistence of this variety of play after the subsidence of the more strictly historical drama is due in a large degree to the romantic quality of the myths themselves, whether told in the first instance by Goeffrey of Monmouth or by the sober historians or confessed romancers that followed him.   This romantic quality deeply affected the Elizabethan age as it stirred the ages before and has touched our own century, and it produced a more lasting, if a less vivid, impression on the English drama than direct appeals to the sense of historical reality.

It is somewhat remarkable that the suggestion of *Gorboduc* and of *Locrine* should not have been immediately followed and a tragedy developed which was founded on British myth as the tragedy of Seneca was founded on the myths of ancient Greece.   The divergence of the spirit of the tragedy of Sackville from that of the legends of Merlin and King Arthur was assuredly not greater than the divergence of the spirit of imperial Rome from the anthropomorphic myths of early Greece.   And if the scholars alone had had their way the Chronicle Drama might have presented an analogue to the Roman tragedy of Seneca.   As it was, the Universities preferred classical subjects as well as classical treatment, the court had become thoroughly Italianate, while the popular audiences of the Bankside demanded subjects less remote from their daily habits of thought.   Here alone was a real demand for the

Chronicle Play, and this demand was sufficiently supplied in the earlier years by the chronicles of sovereigns who had reigned since the conquest and by the
pseudo-histories and comedies of folk-lore of Greene
and others. The earliest extant play on a mythological British subject which satisfies the conditions and
retains the general artlessness of treatment which distinguish the earlier type of the Historical Drama is
*The True Chronicle History of King Leir, and his three
daughters, Gonorill, Ragan and Cordella.* This play,
which ends as a comedy, deserves attention not only
as the immediate source of Shakespeare's tragedy
but also because of its genuine intrinsic worth. *King
Leir* was acted according to Henslowe by the Sussex
and Queen's men jointly, April 6, 1594.[1] It is not
stated that this was a first performance. The play
does not appear to have been printed until 1605, when
interest in the story was revived by the appearance of
Shakespeare's tragedy on the stage. The older play
contains only the story of Leir and his daughters:
the parallel underplot of Gloucester and his sons was
added from another source by Shakespeare, as was the
daring picture of madness real and feigned, the pathos
of the contrasted folly of Lear and "the sad-eyed
fool," and the wonderful climax of storm in which
the warring elements of nature unite in subtle sympathy with the wild tumult of human suffering and pas-

[1] See p. 34.

sion.   Yet the old comedy retains a merit of its own, especially in the simple candor and beauty of the character of Cordella—the earlier Cordelia—to the "unaffected loveliness" of whose nature, as Dr. Furness expresses it, "justice has never been done."[1]   In the older play, as befits a comedy, "the Gallian king's" wooing of Cordella is made much of, a feature completely subordinated in the sterner tragedy.   This romantic young prince sets out, like Romeo, disguised as a pilgrim, and attended by a single courtier, Mumford, who is the humorous man of the play.   Chided by the king for addressing him as " my lord," Mumford replies :

> For Gods sake name your selfe some proper name.
> *King.*   Call me Tresillus : Ile call thee Denapoll.
> *Mum.*   Might I be made the Monarch of the World
>   I could not hit upon these names, I sweare.
> *King.*   Then call me Will, Ile call thee Iacke.[2]

The two young Gallians arrive at the British court just as Leir has promulgated his unjust decree disinheriting his youngest daughter.   They overheard Cordella's lament in which daughterly obedience and submission to her sad fortune mingle with heart-broken sorrow.   Seeking to comfort her and yet maintain his disguise, the young king loses his heart, and the matter is concluded in the following little idyl, which

[1] *King Lear*, Variorum ed., 1880, p. 398.

[2] *King Leir*, Hazlitt, *Shakespeare's Library*, 1875, Part II., Vol. II., p. 324.

is as naïve as it is poetical.   Indeed this scene is by
no means unworthy of the pen of Thomas Lodge, the
author of *Rosalynde*, to whom a share in *King Leir*
has been by some assigned.[1]

King.   Sweet Lady, say there should come a king
        As good as eyther of your sisters husbands,
        To craue your loue, would you accept of him ?
 Cor.   Oh, doe not mocke with those in misery,
        Nor do not think, though fortune haue the power,
        To spoyle mine honour, and debase my state,
        That she hath any interest in my mind :
        For if the greatest Monarch on the earth,
        Should sue to me in this extremity,
        Except my heart could loue, and heart could like,
        Better than any that I euer saw,
        His great estate no more should moue my mind
        Than mountaynes moue by blast of euery wind.
King.   Think not, sweet Nymph, tis holy Palmers guise,
        To grieued souls fresh torments to deuise :
        Therefore in witness of my true intent,
        Let heauen and earth beare record of my words :
        There is a young and lusty Gallian king,
        So like to me, as I am to my selfe,
        That earnestly doth craue to have thy love,
        And ioyne with thee in Hymens sacred bonds.
        .   .   .   .   .   .
 Cor.   Ah Palmer, my estate doth not befit
        A kingly marriage, as the case now stands.
        Whilome when as I liued in honours height,
        A Prince perhaps might postulate my loue :
        Now misery, dishonour and disgrace,

---

[1] Fleay, *Biographical Chronicle*, II. 51.

Hath light on me and quite reuersed the case.
Thy King will hold thee wise, if thou surcease
The sute, whereas no dowry will insue.
Then be advised, Palmer, what to do :
Cease for thy King, seeke for thy selfe to woo.[1]

Indeed the gentler, though no less natural, pathos of the situation of the older Leir as compared with the tempest of the passion of Shakespeare's hero, the steadfast fidelity of Perillus, from which character Shakespeare received more than a hint for his Kent, and the womanly tenderness which marks Cordella's conduct towards her broken and repentent old father in the later scenes go far to justify the words of Professor Ward that " while Shakespeare's genius nowhere exerted itself with more transcendent force and marvelous versatility, it nowhere found more promising materials ready to its command."[2]

Of much the same date as *Leir* is the inferior production printed in 1606 and entitled *Nobody and Somebody With the true Chronicle Historie of Elydure, who was fortunately three several times crowned King of England*. From the circumstances that one Archigallo is an important character in this play, Mr. Fleay has identified it with " *Alberte galles*" for which Henslowe paid Heywood and Smith in 1602.[3] Be this as it may, it is of interest to note that *Nobody and Some-*

[1] *Shakespeare's Library*, p. 326.
[2] *Dramatic Literature*, I. 126.
[3] See Henslowe, p. 239, and *Biographical Chronicle*, I. 290.

13

body is one of the plays taken to Germany by English actors and there translated and published in 1620.[1] The main plot of this play is a meagre and inartificial chronicle of the relations of the pious Elydure to his three brothers and the rivalry of the queens of Elydure and Archigallo. The underplot satirizes popular abuses in the adventures of the two personages who give title to the play. According to Simpson, " the early edition contains two woodcuts . . . representing the stage dress of the two chief characters. The picture of Nobody at the beginning represents him in a huge pair of slops, all legs, head and arms, but no body. Somebody has an equally exaggerated doublet, with no legs to speak of." [2] The witticisms of these two worthies may be readily imagined, and must have been of an interest, however farcical, sufficient completely to overbalance the dull " historical " plot. In 1594, too, the Earl of Sussex' players acted a play not now extant entitled *King Lud*.[3]

If a drama fulfilling the conditions of the older type of the Chronicle Play and yet dealing in subject-matter with history treated as legend be sought, no better example could be offered than *The Valiant Welshman*. This play was printed in 1615 and again in 1663 with " by R. A. Gent" on the title page, and this has led to the assignment of it to the authorship of Robert Armin,

[1] Cohn, *Shakespeare in Germany*, pp. cviii and cx.
[2] *The School of Shakspere* I. 272.
[3] Henslowe, p. 32.

the actor and the known author of a comedy entitled
The Two Maids of Moreclacke.   Whatever the facts as
to this, the structure and style of this play point to the
period of the height of the Chronicle Drama, and it
seems not impossible that this was a later form of the
old play called *The Welshman,* acted at the Rose, November 29, 1595.[1]   *The Valiant Welshman ; or, the true
chronicle history of the life and valiant deedes of Caradoc
the Great, King of Cambria, now called Wales,* exhibits
the incessant˙action, the epical nature, the looseness of
construction and the comic relief, all of which will be
remembered as common to the general epic type of the
Chronicle Play.   The interest is sustained by a pre-
senter in likeness of an ancient bard, by dumb shows
and by a masque, but none of these things nor the
comedy which is supported by one Morgan and
Morion his fool, is permitted to interfere with the central interest which lies in the prowess and magnanimity
of the Welsh hero.   As this play, which has not been
reprinted, is inaccessible to the general reader, two
short passages may be quoted.   The first is the reply
of an enchanter whose power over the elements has
been ignorantly questioned ; it exhibits the author in a
typical " King Cambyses vaine."

> Know Gloster that our skill
> Commands the Moone drop from her siluer sphere,
> And all the stars to vayle their golden heads,

[1] Henslowe, p. 61.   This surmise is Malone's.

At the black horrour that our Charmes present,
Atlas throwes downe the twinckling Arch of heauen,
And leaues his burthen [;] at our dreadful spels
This pendant element of solid earth
Shakes with amazing Earthquakes, as if the frame
Of this vast continent would leave her poles,
Neptune swels high, and with impetuous rage
Dashes the haughty Argosey with winds
Against the Christall battlements of heauen,
The troubled ayre appeares in flakes of fire,
That, till about the ayres circumference
We make the upper Region
Thick full of fatal comets, and the skie
Is filde with fiery signes of armed men.[1]

The second passage contains the climax of the play and discloses, if crudely, the animating spirit which was the excuse for the existence of this species of the drama. The scene is Rome. British captives are brought before Cæsar. All bow the knee save Caradoc, whom Cæsar thus addresses :

Ces.   What's he that scorns to bow, when Cesar bids?
Car.   Cesar, a man that scorns to bow to Jove
        Were he a man like Cesar ; such a man,
        That neither cares for life, nor feares to die.
        I was not borne to kneele but to the Gods,
        Nor basely bow unto a lumpe of clay,
        In adoration of a clod of earth.
        Were Cesar Lord of all the spacious world,
        Euen from the Articke to the Antarticke poles,
        And but a man ; in spite of death and him,

1 *The Valiant Welshman*, ed. 1615, III. 4.

Ide keepe my legs upright, honour should stand
Fixt as the Center, at no Kings command.
Thou mayst as well inforce the foming surge
Of high-swoln Neptune, with a word retire,
And leave his flowing tide, as make me bow.[1]

And there is much more of it; well may "Cesar"
have exclaimed at the conclusion of this tirade: "So
braue a Brytaine hath not Cesar heard." In the upshot Caradoc proves to be the British soldier who
earlier in the play disarmed Cæsar in battle and sent
him back to the Roman camp ransomless. Cæsar had
on this occasion pressed upon his generous captor the
gift of a golden lion hung on a chain as a pledge of
gratitude. On the recognition of this talisman a reconciliation ensues which knits Rome and England in
bonds of lasting friendship.

Two plays of this immediate class now claim our
attention; these are *The Mayor of Queenborough*, by
Thomas Middleton, and *The Birth of Merlin*, the work
of William Rowley. They may be best considered
together because both plays treat of the same group
of legendary characters, because of the likelihood that
the earliest performances of them nearly coincided, and
from the circumstance that the versions which we now
have are late revisions and were published after the
Restoration. Between November, 1596, and November, 1601, there are several entries in *Henslowe's Diary*

[1] *Ibid.*, V. 5.

concerning a play variously entitled *Valtiger* or *Vortiger*. This is evidently Vortigern, the legendary king of Kent at the time of the landing of Hengist at Ebbsfleet.[1] In June, 1597, there is entry of a play which Henslowe calls "*Henges*," *i. e.*, Hengist.[2] As it was no unusual thing for Henslowe to call his plays by any catch-word sufficient to identify them, it is more than likely that these two titles refer to the same play and that they constitute an earlier version of the extant romantic historical drama, *The Mayor of Queenborough*, which shows clear evidence of revision and in which both Vortigern and Hengist appear as important characters. Indeed this last identification rises to all but certainty, as Collier found a play entitled *Hengist King of Kent* in a manuscript of several dramas "in the library of an ancient family in the East of England," the prologue of which he quotes, unaware that it is identical with the prologue of *The Mayor of Queenborough*, save for a word or two.[3] In this powerful but unpleasing drama the main story is that of the rise of Vortigern to kingly power by the murder of his saintly sovereign Constantius, his alliance with the newly arrived Saxons under Hengist against the efforts

[1] See pp. 76, 83, etc., to 274.

[2] *Ibid.*, p. 89.

[3] *Early Illustrations of Shakespeare and the English Drama, Shakespeare Society's Publications*, 1846, p. 85 ; and see a note on this subject by the author of this book, entitled *Valtiger, Henges and The Mayor of Queenborough*, in *Modern Language Notes*, May, 1900.

of Aurelius and Uther Pendragon to regain their
brother's kingdom, and the final overthrow of Vortigern with his false and insidious allies by these princes.
The humors of one Simon the Tanner, who is raised
by the Saxons to the dignity of Mayor of Queenborough, relieve the otherwise somber story and give
a new title to the late version which we possess.

*The Birth of Merlin: Or, the Childe hath found his
Father* was first printed by Francis Kirkman, the first
English publisher to evince an interest in the old
drama, in 1662. Kirkman printed on the title page:
" Written by William Shakespear, and William Rowley "; and it is generally admitted on internal evidence
that Rowley, whoever may have been his coadjutor,
had a hand in this play as we now have it. If so, it
must date in its present state from a period subsequent
to 1607, which is the earliest known date of Rowley's
connection with the stage. Considering the universal
custom of revision and alteration and the circumstance
that this prince plays the leading part in Rowley's
play, it is not improbable that in *Uther Pendragon*, a
play several times mentioned by Henslowe during the
year 1597, we have the original of *The Birth of Merlin*.[1] As to Kirkman's assignment of a share in this
revision to Shakespeare, this has seriously imposed
upon the credulity of no one except the German poet
Tieck, whose enthusiasm laid him open to incessant

[1] Henslowe, p. 87.

visitations of the ghost of alleged Shakespearean authorship.[1]   *The Birth of Merlin* is a strange mixture
of legendary chronicle history, romantic comedy, broad
humor and *diablerie*.   The story is occupied with the
deeds of Aurelius, King of Britain, and of Uther Pendragon, his brother, the plot by which the beautiful Artesia, sister to the Saxon general, seeks their ruin and
actually effects that of Aurelius, and the warfare of
Uther against Vortigern and the Saxons.[2]   An underplot depicts the romantic but somewhat unreasonable
preference which two young British maidens display
for the cloister to their faithful lovers.   The rest of
the play is taken up with the birth and prophecies of
Merlin in which are involved many things mundane and
the supernatural interferences of Merlin's father, the
devil.   Notwithstanding this extraordinary diversity
which is enhanced by processions, the raising of spirits,
the appearance of the worthies, Hector and Achilles,
the goddess Lucina with the Fates and even the abstraction, Death, *The Birth of Merlin* is a remarkably clear
and well-written play.   In the grossly represented but
pathetic plight of Joan, Merlin's mother, and in the
coarse humor of her foul-mouthed but faithful brother
we have a favorable specimen of the vigorous comedy of
William Rowley.   Not less excellent in its kind is the
well-drawn character of the artful and merciless Saxon

[1] *Shakespeare's Vorschule, Kritische Schriften*, I. 288.
[2] See Holinshed, I. 564.

princess, Artesia, who lavishes the allurements of her beauty and her genius for intrigue with equal sublety on the weak and infatuated king and on the romantic and virtuous prince, his brother.   Artesia is undoubtedly borrowed from the Rowen or Rowena of the old chroniclers, and the hint of her wickedness is contained in Rowen's poisoning of her step-son Vertumerus.[1] But Rowley transferred the episode which Middleton had used to bring about the death of Vortigern to Aurelius and made his Artesia a Judith who inveigled and slew her people's enemy for her people's sake. Moreover, Middleton, after the taste of a later time, degraded his Roxena to a mere adventuress, brazen, lustful and full of guile, untrue alike to friend and foe, a creature of the type of Tamora, Queen of the Goths, in *Titus Andronicus*, without the dignity of passion that imparts a lurid majesty to that terrible figure.   *Merlin* succeeds *The Mayor* in point of sequence of time, taking up the march of events from the death of Hengist. The plays, however, have no relation one to the other and must have been written independently.   The story of Vortigern forms likewise the subject of an anonymous contemporary Latin tragedy, whether of earlier or later date it seems impossible to ascertain.   This tragedy, which remains in manuscript in the British Museum,[2] is entitled *Fatum Vortigerni Seu miserabilis*

---

[1] *Historia Regum Britanniae*, VI. 14.

[2] *MS. Lansdowne 723.* This play has recently been described in *Die lateinischen Universitaets-Dramen Englands*, Shakespeare Jahrbuch, XXXIV. 38.

vita et exitus Vortigerni regis Britanniae vna complectens aduentum Saxonum siue Anglorum in Britanniam. It follows, like most of its class, the Senecan traditions. The comedy of the underplot which gives *The Mayor* its title is of course wanting and there is no such departure from " history " as that which makes Roxena here known as Ronixa, the paramour of Horsa. An enquiry into the relations of the three plays might be worth the trouble.

The treasures of ancient British mythical lore thus again disclosed to the drama in *King Leir* and the adventures of *Merlin,* several plays from the same general sources followed. Between July, 1598, and March of the following year, five plays, the titles of which suggest such an origin, are recorded by Henslowe. These are *The Conquest of Brute, with the first finding of the Bath,* by John Day, rewritten in two parts shortly after; *The Life and Death of King Arthur,* by Richard Hathway, to which it is not impossible that Justice Shallow refers in reminiscence of his madcap days at Clement's Inn in the words : " I was then Sir Dagonet in Arthurs Show." [1] The others are : *Mulmutius Donwallow,* by William Rankins ; *Conan Prince of Cornwall,* by Dekker and Drayton ; and *Brute Greenshield,* the author not named. It may be worthy of note in passing that Dunwallow was a famous law-giver, restorer of London and father of

[1] See Henslowe, *s. v.* and *2 Henry IV.,* III. 2, 300.

Brennus, the English conqueror of Rome, according to the old story.   Brute Greenshield was the " sixt ruler " of Britain and famous for his attempt to conquer France.[1]   A little later than this Haughton contrived to get Henslowe to accept a play on Ferrex and Porrex, the relation of which to Sackville and Norton's play *Gorboduc* (or *Ferrex and Porrex*, as it was called in the second and authorized edition), must remain to us unknown.[2]

As to the immediate sources of these chronicle plays founded on British myth, it is unlikely that popular playwrights would seek far afield for material. Such sources as the *Historia Britonum* of Nennius and Geoffrey of Monmouth's *Historia Regum Britanniæ* must have been as unknown to them as they are to the casual reader to-day.   Of the popular chronicles of the time Grafton's *Chronicle at Large*, Holinshed, and Stow in his *Annales*, treat of the early mythical period of British history.   Holinshed enters into the fullest detail.   He was, as is well known, the favorite quarry of Shakespeare and other dramatists for later English history.   *Locrine*, *Leir* and the story of Elydure, in *Nobody and Somebody*, are certainly founded on Holinshed.   *Gorboduc* was written too early to have laid under contribution this popular source and with *The Misfortunes of Arthur*, as shown recently,[3] and the

[1] See Holinshed, I. 451 and 445.
[2] Henslowe, p. 166.
[3] See the ed. of *The Misfortunes*, by H. C. Grumbine, *Litterarhistorische Forschungen*, XIV. 17.

Latin *Fatum Vortigerni*, not improbably, is referable
directly to Geoffrey's *Historia*. In *The Mayor of
Queenborough*, although the material is handled with
freedom and the intervention of an older play may be
assumed, the circumstance that " Raynulph Higden,
Monk of Chester," performs the function of chorus
and a recollection that John de Trevisa's translation
of Higden's *Polychronicon* in 1482 is still described as
the least rare of Caxton's publications identifies this
history as the likely original on which the older play
revised by Middleton was founded. The story of Vortigern is told at some length in the *Polychronicon*, but
when the careful old chronicler reaches "the Merlin-
stuff," he balks : " Furthermore, what is i-seide of the
ponde of the tweie dragouns, white and rede, of
Vortigernus his buldynge, of Merlyn his fantastik
getynge, and of his prophecie that is so derk, is con-
teyned in the Brittishe book, and I wolde putte it to
this storie gif I trowed that it be i-holpe by sothenesse."[1]
In *Merlin*, despite the general fidelity with which the
"historical" part of the story is told, we must look
beyond the chronicles, but to which of the innumerable
"lives and prophecies" of the redoubtable wizard would
be a matter difficult, if not impossible, to decide. A
popular book of the kind was *A Lytel Tretys of the
Byrth and Prophecyes of Merlin* first issued by Wynkyn

[1] *Polychronicon, Chronicles and Memorials of Great Britain and
Ireland*, V. 279.

de Worde in 1510 and two or three times thereafter during the century.[1] That the playwright treated the old legend with inventive freedom is patent in the degradation of Merlin's mother from the daughter of the king of Demetia to Joan Go-too-t, whose brother is a country clown, and in the dramatic scene in which the magician defends his wretched, cowering mother from the proffered violence of his father, the devil, and defies his supernatural power. Lastly in *The Valient Welshman* we leave the earlier mythical history for legend which has grown up about an actual historical personage. Although the author refers in his prefatory words to Tacitus, the Caractacus of that historian and of Dio Cassius, who especially related the campaigns of Ostorius against "this patriot chief, the first of our national heroes,"[2] is not Caradoc the Great King of Cambria of Armin's play. And yet the essential lines in the two pictures are much alike. In Holinshed's *Chronicle of Scotland*, the story of Caradoc is treated at some length,[3] and we meet with at least one of the other characters of the play, the chieftain's sister, Voada. But a different turn is given to her adventures as to the particulars of his. With the possibility of the intervention of some original Welsh

---

[1] On the versions of the Merlin story during this period see Dr. W. E. Mead's *Outlines of the Legend of Merlin, Early English Text Society's Publications*, 1899.

[2] Merivale, *History of the Romans under the Empire*, VI. 34.

[3] See Book V. in which Caradoc is treated as king of Scotland.

source admitted, we must allow much here, as above, to the inventiveness of the playwright.

After 1600 we meet with no play which lays under contribution the sources of ancient mythical British lore until we reach Shakespeare's two great tragedies, *King Lear* and *Macbeth*, and the tragi-comedy, *Cymbeline*, all of which were acted for the first time after the death of Queen Elizabeth and within the first decade of the century. Here, as everywhere, Shakespeare was no innovator, but followed in royal progress in the footsteps of success. During the years that had elapsed since the performance of *Henry V.* a change had come over the English temper and direct appeals to the spirit of nationality were less likely to inspire immediate and popular response. Besides this, other forms of drama had succeeded to the estimation once enjoyed by the Chronicle Play. Shakespeare's use of the material of ancient British history in *King Lear* and *Macbeth* is far removed from the spirit which animated his earlier histories, above which they tower alike for the greater universality of their appeal and in their more consummate art in conception and execution. These great tragedies are inspired by a pure artistic spirit, which, working on the accumulated experience of years, the precious outcome of the comedies and the earlier tragedies, gives to them a place which it is impossible to overestimate among the priceless works of the poet's maturity.

The outward history of *King Lear* is illustrative, in one particular, of the marketable value which everything to which the name of Shakespeare was attached commanded in his own day. The registry in 1605 of the old play on Leir as a tragedy, although it ends happily and was subsequently published as a comedy, is a sufficient proof of the recent performance and popularity of a new play—and that a tragedy—on the story of Lear and his daughters. To these conditions of character and date Shakespeare's *History of King Lear* absolutely corresponds, and such a republication of an old play upon the revived popularity of an old theme is among the commonest proceedings of the time. Although no copy has ever been found to make assurance doubly sure, we may assume that the entry in the Stationers' Register of May, 1594, of *The moste famous Chronicle historye of Leire Kinge of England and his Three Daughters* refers to the earlier play which we have in the edition of 1605, bearing the similar title, *The True Chronicle History of King Leir.* It is the registry of this latter edition which is entered and assigned as *The Tragical Chronicle History of Kinge Leir.* The emphasis of the actual entry of the first quarto of Shakespeare's *King Lear* in 1607 is significant: " a booke called. *Master William Shakespeare his ' historye of Kinge Lear' as yt was played before the kinges maiestie at Whitehall vppon Sainct Stephens night at Christmas Last by his maiesties ser-*

vantes playinge vsually at the 'Globe' on the Banksyde." [1]
There was to be no mistake about this *King Lear.*
Moreover two quartos in the same year by the same
publisher are a sufficient attestation of the popularity
by which the piratical printer of the old play was endeavoring to profit. The Jacobean printer was not
more scrupulous of trifles where the selling of a book
was concerned than some of his successors in the trade.
Indeed there could be no other reason for the anonymous publication of the old play eleven years after
its first appearance.

The relation of *King Lear* to the older play with
the position which the latter holds in the evolution of
its species has already been indicated. The source of
the subordinate story of Gloucester in the episode of
the Paphlagonian king and his sons in Sidney's
Arcadia was long since pointed out. Turns of phrase
have been found in *The Mirour for Magistrates* and in
Camden's *Remaines*, while the softened form of the
name Cordelia has been referred to *The Faery Queene.*
The phraseology of witchcraft and the allusions thereto
of Edgar in his feigned madness have been traced to
a contemporary pamphlet by Dr. Harsnet entitled *A
Declaration of egregious Popish Impostures;* although
the genuine madness of Lear and the babbled wisdom
of the Fool remain sourceless and forever undiscover-
able. Nowhere does the futility of mere scholarship

[1] Arber's *Transcript of the Stationers' Register*, II. 648 and III. 366.

disclose such hopelessness as in a discussion of Shakespearean sources. In the words of one whose own deep learning is only equalled by the absolute sanity with which he recognizes the just limitations of all human research : " But what false impressions are conveyed in the phrases which we have to use to express the process whereby Shakespeare converted the stocks and stones of the old dramas and chronicles into living, breathing men and women ! We say he ' drew his original ' from this source, or he ' found his materials ' in that source. But how much did he ' draw,' or what did he ' find ' ? Granting that he drew from Holinshed, or from the old comedy, or whence you please, where did he find Lear's madness, or the pudder of the elements, or the inspired babblings of the Fool ? Of whatsoever makes his tragedies sub-lime and heaven-high above all other human compo-sitions,—of that we find never a trace. . . . When, after reading one of his tragedies, we turn to what we are pleased to call 'the original of his plot,' I am re-minded of those glittering gems, of which Heine speaks, that we see at night in lovely gardens, and think must have been left there by kings' children at play, but when we look for these jewels by day we see only wretched little worms which crawl painfully away, and which the foot forbears to crush only out of strange pity." [1]

The general impression which the reader—and far

[1] Dr. Furness, *King Lear*, Variorum ed., p. 383.

14

more the auditor—of *King Lear* takes away with him is
that of a broad and vigorously painted canvas, definite
in outline to harshness, structurally logical to the point
of severity, in tone high, and displaying violent contrasts
of color, yet withal consummate in its art and above
stricture in its completeness. *Lear* has been said to
lie between *Hamlet*, which is slow in the development
of the action, and the faster *tempo* of *Macbeth*. " *Lear*
combines length with rapidity,—like the hurricane and
the whirlpool, absorbing while it advances." [1] The
action of *King Lear* is not only speedy, it is direct
and unswerving.   In few of his plays has Shakespeare
so unerringly relieved his story of all superfluities and
knit together the entire structure in a unity so com-
pact and so vital.   As Coleridge remarked of the exposition of the theme of filial impiety in Goneril and
Regan : " Not a sentiment, not an image, which can
give pleasure on its own account, is admitted ; when-
ever those creatures are introduced, and they are
brought forward as little as possible, pure horror
reigns throughout." [2]   There was but one feature of
feminine depravity to add to these monsters and that
Shakespeare contrived to introduce in the passion
which the base born Edmund inspires in both, a passion which arises from likeness of character and from
that craving for sympathetic relations with others for

[1] *Works of S. T. Coleridge*, ed. Shedd, 1884, IV. 133.
[2] *Ibid.*, p. 140.

which human nature yearns even when most loath-
somely perverted.   In this the dramatist heightened
at one stroke the unscrupulous ambition of Edmund
and the depravity of the sisters, contrived in their
mutual jealousy a motive for their taking off, and
united the two plots of the play.   That Edmund
should be made the instigator of the murder of Cordelia, while Edgar, his abused brother, becomes indi-
rectly her avenger is a further example of this interweaving of the two plots.

The harshness of outline and contrast of color which
have been remarked on above are exemplified not only
in the two sisters painted as they are in monotone,
but in the much criticised brutality of the plucking
out of Gloucester's eyes and in the piteous manner of
Cordelia's related death, who, princess though she was,
it will be remembered, was hanged in prison by the
hand of a hired murderer.   Kent has been described
as a character of unmixed virtue, and he indeed stands
out conspicuous in his honest loyalty and forgetful-
ness of self.   Edgar is at times too conscious of his
own sufferings ; and even Cordelia seems not without
the fault of pride in her judgment of her sisters and
wanting in forbearance in her unwillingness—not in-
ability—to humor what she must have known was
after all no more than the whim of her aged and petu-
lant father.[1]   It is the unconscious recognition of all

---

[1] *King Lear*, I. 1, especially lines 99–103.

this, perhaps, that tempers our feeling of horror at Cordelia's pitiable death and makes it endurable ; precisely as we feel that there is something to be said in extenuation of Edmund's crimes against his father, when we recall that father's brutal jest as to Edmund's base birth, uttered in his presence, and the circumstance that in his boyhood, Edmund had been bred abroad a stranger.[1]

On his visit to Oxford in 1605, King James was addressed at St. John's gate by three youths costumed as Sibyls (*tres quasi Sibyllae*), who alluded in fitting Latinity to "the weird sisters" and their prophecies concerning the immortal line of kings sprung from the loins of Banquo, thane of Lochaber. The Sibyls seem in this instance likewise to have typified the three kingdoms and in these rôles extended in the succeeding lines a welcome to the king. The speech contains no more than a passing allusion to a familiar tradition appropriately employed, and it is neither a source, as was once conjectured, nor a suggestion of anything in Shakespeare.[2] On the basis of a random allusion of Kemp's in 1600 and the entry of a "ballad of *Macdobeth*" in 1596, an earlier play on the subject has been by some surmised.[3] Another indication of an earlier play of possibly similar content is to be

---

[1] *Ibid.*, I. 1, 7-23, and line 30; this view was first broached by Coleridge.

[2] *Macbeth*, Variorum ed., p. 377, where this subject is discussed.

[3] Kemp's *Nine Daies Wonder*, ed. Dyce, Camden Society, p. 21.

found in Henslowe's mention of a drama entitled *Malcolm King of Scots* in the year 1602. Be all this as it may, Shakespeare founded his *Tragedie of Macbeth* on Holinshed's *Chronicles of Scotland*, not only using the material which he found there relative to Duncan and Macbeth, but transferring to his characters Holinshed's chronicles of King Duffe and Donwald and other matters.[1] The earliest performance of *Macbeth* is placed by the majority of critics subsequent to *King Lear* and about 1606.

In *Macbeth*, which Hallam preferred to all Shakespeare's tragedies, we have the greatest height to which English epic drama attained. *Romeo and Juliet* is lyrical, and the current of its action is hurried or checked with the alternate promptings of passionate love and passionate hate. *Hamlet* is speculative, its action swirling slowly about in eddies or purling with a seeming quiet where the secret streams are working most deeply. In *Macbeth* all is action, though here, too, the specific story, while losing none of its concreteness, has attained, through the exercise of consummate art, a universal significance. Less weighted with detail and underplot than *Lear*, and likewise less violent, though in no respect less dynamic in its power, *Macbeth* combines with the deepest soundings of the depths of human temptation and crime a winged speed of action and an undeviating directness of purpose incom-

[1] See Holinshed, as above, V. 233–235 and 252–278.

parable among tragedies.   I am loath to refer an effect
so consummate to the accidental cutting down of a
longer play for acting in the provinces as some would
have us suppose,[1] or to believe, despite some acknowledged flaws, that the haphazard interpolations of an
able, but certainly inferior playwright, such as Middleton, could miraculously weld themselves with Shakespeare's work to produce a whole so organic.[2]   Indeed,
the mingling together in *Macbeth* of the material world
with the supernatural is not the least of the many won-
ders of this great tragedy.   Nor outside of that sable
troop of the Eumenides of Æschylus, foul-visaged and
horrible in their dogged perturbed sleep as they lie on the
temple's steps awaiting the coming of Orestes, shall we
find creatures of the supernatural at once so grim, so
awe-inspiring and of such dignity as are the weird sisters.   Our very uncertainty as to the precise character
of their intermeddling in the affairs of men fills us with
a deeper awe, for we know not whether they may be
no more than the embodiment in prophetic form of
Macbeth's innate human depravity or supernatural
compelling forces making for evil, fated at times to
drive even an innocent man to destruction and perdi-
tion.   The power of this sublime tragedy, as of much

[1] The opinion of Mr. Fleay.   See his *Life of Shakespeare*, p. 238.
[2] For this view, which has obtained some consent, see Clark and
Wright's ed. of *Macbeth*, in the *Clarendon Press Series*, by whom it is
held that Middleton interpolated much of this play after Shakespeare's
death.

else in Shakespeare, lies in this subtle suggestiveness,
a quality by means of which questions are raised and
doubts started, the answers to which—if we are to find
answers—must, to a certain degree, remain subjective.
To one Macbeth is "a man of sanguine nervous tem-
perament, of large capacity and ready susceptibility,"
into the slack-water of whose nature, so to speak, a
contact with the supernatural may set the current
towards good or evil.[1] To another Macbeth is a
moral coward, so intense in his egotism that he can
never be touched by the slightest compunction of
conscience for the suffering or the wrong which he
has inflicted on others, although vulnerable to the degree of irritability when the thought of failure, of public odium and consequent retribution crosses his mind.[2]
So, too, as to Lady Macbeth—almost the most wonderful creation among the women of Shakespeare—
was she a woman of heroic mould and of masculine
aspect, as we take Clytemnestra to have been? Or
was there in Lady Macbeth a contrast in reverse, as
between her lord's stalwart limbs and lily-livered heart?
May this clear-brained, tenacious contriver of mid-
night murder have been a woman of slender frame,
and even of delicate beauty, the more violently to contrast that iron will and resolute repression of remorse
which in the end brought down mind and body in uni-

[1] Bucknill, *The Mad Folk of Shakespeare*, 1867, p. 7.
[2] Whateley, *Remarks on Some Characters of Shakespere*, ed. 1839,
p. 79.

versal wreck? In a work of ordinary art, if our understanding is once complete, there is little room for difference of opinion. That men should differ as to the character of Macbeth is as much to be expected as that men should differ in their estimates of Oliver Cromwell or Robespierre. Except that these latter estimates might be obscured by some circumstances extraneous to a simple judgment of personal character and conduct in life, in all a given estimate must depend not only on the object seen, but on the perception, the understanding, the training and the natural bias of the beholder. In this power to awaken, so to say, the resonance of divers capacities and to stir by one ground note very different strings Shakespeare stands alone.

Mr. Fleay is of the opinion that an earlier version of *Cymbeline* than that which we now possess followed closely on *Macbeth* and that our present form of the play was not only rewritten by Shakespeare but also retouched by another hand after Shakespeare's retirement from the stage.[1] All this, however, is matter of pure surmise, and there is nothing to show that *Cymbeline* was acted prior to 1609 or 1610, the years which have been assigned to Forman's contemporary description of the play.[2] In *Cymbeline* Shakespeare returned to Holinshed, but only for the canvas of his work. The picture which he has painted into the

---

[1] *Life of Shakespeare*, p. 246.
[2] *Transactions of the New Shakspere Society*, 1875-6, p. 417.

foreground is one of wifely fidelity and of kin reunited after separation : themes to which he recurs again and again.   Save for two or three scenes in the fifth act in which we breathe for a moment the old martial spirit of the Chronicle History, this beautiful play belongs to a very different class.   In no drama of an age which delighted to ring interminable change upon the everlasting theme of man and woman, has the conjugal relation been so exquisitely drawn and, despite a lapse from purer ideals in a wager inconceivable in the England or perhaps in the Europe of to-day, withal so glorified.

Although a show of adherence to actual historical material might claim for Fletcher's fine *Tragedie of Bonduca* another place, the romantic spirit which rules this play and the freedom of its inventiveness remove it alike from the exclusive category of the historical drama and from those productions the sources of which are wholly in the Latin classics.   Indeed it has been affirmed that Fletcher's immediate source was neither the *Annales* of Tacitus nor the history of Dio Cassius, but that universal quarry Holinshed.[1]   It is impossible to follow the same authority in his belief that *Bonduca* owes suggestions in plot and character to the earlier play, described above, *The Valiant Welshman*.   Both plays treat of the British hero

---

[1] See an article on this play by B. Leonhardt, in *Englische Studien*, XIII. 36–63.

Caractacus ; and his traditional prowess, generosity and magnanimity are seduously preserved in both. But *Bonduca* is confined to the deeds of Caractacus against the Romans, to which it unites unhistorically the story of the fate of Boadicea and her daughters ; while *The Valiant Welshman* gives the life of Caractacus and his kin in so full a detail as to suggest some hitherto undiscovered Welsh origin. There is really no similarity in these two productions for which common sources will not account. On the other hand, the connection of *Bonduca* in subject and treatment with the later romantic treatment of themes from Roman history, such as Fletcher's own *Valentinian* or *The False One*, is obvious.

Bonduca is the work of a consummate dramatist. Not a possibility in the presentation of character or the development of situation is lost from the love-lorn young officer, Junius, and his merry, cynical friend, Petilius, to the unfortunate commander, Pœnius, heroically meeting with self-imposed death the disgrace which his touchy pride has brought upon him ; from the weak and cruel but heroic Bonduca and the two shrilled-voiced furies, her daughters, to the high-minded hero, Caratach, his courteous recognition of a true man's obligations even to his foes, his generous admiration for their military prowess and his touching solicitude for his young charge, the pretty boy prince, Hengo. No production could better exemplify the advance which the English drama had made in technique and finish in the generation which had elapsed since the heyday of the Chronicle Play. In the old drama there was a feeling that everything must be told. *The Valiant Welshman* deals with the doings of four British kings, three queens, and many princes and Roman generals; it introduces bards, enchanters, the Roman goddess, Fortuna, and wanders from Wales to Scotland, ending before the emperor Claudius at Rome. In *Bonduca* all surplusage is ruthlessly cut out, the interest is concentrated by the union of two well-known stories, and place and time are unified so that the entire action is developed in Britain in one neighborhood and within a reasonably short period.[1] Again, for the representation of character the old drama depended on the events of the story. Caradoc is generous because he spares the emperor when he holds him at his mercy; he is the morally unconquered hero because he refuses melodramatically to kneel at Cæsar's behest.[2] In Fletcher's play, on the other hand, character is constantly suggested by invented detail and the total effect thus prepared and strengthened. Such details are Caratach's opening

[1] Leonhardt (p. 49) finds the suggestion of this combination in Holinshed, V. 62, where Voada, the sister of Caratach, is made the wife of Arviragus, king of Britain. Elsewhere (I. 495) Holinshed describes Voadicia or Boadicea as the wife of Arviragus. Warner in his *Albions England* identifies Bonduca with Vaoda. See ed. 1602, p. 82.

[2] *The Valiant Welshman*, II. 3 and V. 5.

rebuke to Bonduca for her unseemly joy at the repulse and misfortunes of her foes, by which the shal-
lowness and lack of generosity in the queen's nature
and the magnanimity of Caratach are equally displayed.[1] Such too is the touching fondness of Caratach for his nephew, Hengo, and the fine scene in
which Petilius relentlessly plays on the remorse of
Pœnius for his lost honor in withholding the aid of
his legion when it was demanded by the general Suetonius : both equally the pure invention of the dramatist.[2] Lastly an enormous advance has been made in
the difficult stage problem, the scenic representation
of war. Instead of the old single encounters, "alarms
and excursions," we observe from a point of vantage
with Suetonius, Pœnius or the British queen the progress of the day, and hear the commands for the drawing up of the legions or the movement of a chariot
charge. In place of exaggerated prowess, ill represented

> With three rusty swords
> And helpe of some foot-and-halfe-foote words,

we have a scene at once congruous and effective. Inadequate realism has given place to a full recognition
of the power and possibilities of suggestion.

Later employment for dramatic purposes of Roman
doings in Britain or of British myth is rare. Of un-

---

[1] *Bonduca*, I. 1.
[2] *Ibid.*, II. 3 III. 5 ; V. 3 and IV. 3.

certain date and subject is a play called *St. George for England* by William Smith, the manuscript of which was destroyed by Warburton's servant. Smith flourished in the reign of King James and was the author of a play entitled *The Hector of Germany*, which is still extant. He is mentioned by both Langbaine and Baker, and there is no reason for confusing him with either Wentworth Smith or with his namesake, the author of *Chloris*, or for doubting his existence as has been done.[1] Of equally uncertain date and character is *The History of Mador, King of Britain*, attributed without reason in the Stationers' Register, 1660, to Francis Beaumont. This production also has perished.

In the year 1633 was published *Fvimvs Troes, The Trve Troianes, Being a Story of the Britaines valour at the Romanes first invasion*. This play, which is described as "publicly represented by the gentlemen students of Magdalene College in Oxford," is the work of Dr. Jasper Fisher. It is an academic experiment in Chronicle History harking back to Seneca, but affected by more popular English models as well. Thus a chorus of Druids closes each act and the Induction is conducted by Mercury, Brennus and Camillus. On the other hand the negotiation and encounters of Cæsar and the Britons are lightened by a love intrigue

---

[1] See Langbaine, *An Account of the English Dramatick Poets*, 1691, 488; *Biographia Dramatica*, ed. 1812, I. 677; and Fleay, *Biographical Chronicle*, II. 251.

and the foolery of a cowardly clown, Rollano. *Fuimus Troes* is well written and with an evident effort after poetic effect; but it is rhetorical and essentially un-dramatic. Fisher is solicitous as to his authorities, and carefully notes, as became an academic author, his debts to Livy, Cæsar and Geoffrey. The latter's *Historia* is his chief source. In 1635 a play entitled *Stonehenge* by John Speed, a son of the antiquarian of that name, was performed, also at Oxford. The title suggests that it may have belonged to the class of chronicle plays, but it is described by Wood and others as a pastoral drama.[1] In the following year a tragi-comedy in two parts entitled *Arviragus and Philicia* by Lodowick Carlell was acted at the Cockpit and before King Charles at Whitehall and Hampton Court. Carlell is described by Langbaine as "an ancient courtier, being gentleman of the bows to King Charles the First."[2] Unfortunately, whatever pleasing visions may be conjured up by the name of Arviragus, the long-lost brother of Imogen, the husband of Boadicea and a valiant champion against the Roman invasions of Britain, they are doomed to disappointment when we learn that this Arviragus is prince of Pickland, a prisoner in a Saxon camp, and that the Guiderius of the play is not his brother, whilst their adventures, in which an heroic Danish princess largely

[1] *Athenæ Oxonienses*, ed. 1815, II. 660.
[2] Langbaine, p. 45.

figures, are of the pseudo-heroic type which filled the prose romances of that day and belong to the dramatic forebears of the Restoration Heroic Drama.[1] Shirley's dramatic curiosity, too, *St. Patrick for Ireland*, which was performed in Dublin about 1638, does not belong here. This strange production conforms to the Chronicle Play solely in its foundation on popular legend and tradition ; its real interest is religious, and it belongs with such other late plays as *The Virgin Martyr* and *Appius and Virginia* in that interesting group of romantic dramas into which a religious *motif* has been infused.

[1] There is an allusion by name to Arviragus in Juvenal, *Satire IV.*, 127, by which it appears at least that this British chieftain was an actual person.

VIII

THE BIOGRAPHICAL CHRONICLE PLAY

WE have traced the growth of the earlier Chronicle Play to its culmination as tragedy in Marlowe's *Edward II.*, in Shakespeare's plays on the two kings Richard, and to its glorification above its species in *King Lear* and *Macbeth.* We have seen how Shakespeare too reverted to the older type of the Chronicle in which comedy and tragedy existed side by side, realized in the trilogy of *Henry IV.* and *Henry V.* possibilities hitherto unthought; and how dramatists of the class of Heywood and Dekker continued the practice of the earlier variety of the historical play affected somewhat by the restraining artistic principles of Shakespeare but straying more commonly into derivative species of folk-lore and pseudo-history. It remains for us to consider the biographical chronicle and the allied plays, the theme of which is travel and adventure, and then to trace to its end the main strand of the epical Chronicle History. Although a biographical character belongs to many of the earlier chronicle histories and this class of plays in its few typical specimens falls within the last ten years of the sixteenth century, it has been deferred to this place because of its affiliations to that interesting group of plays which owe their existence to the reawakened interest in the more immediate historical past which that momentous event, the death of Queen Elizabeth, revived.

In the biographical chronicle the story centers in the career of a single personage. In the remarkable rise of Thomas Cromwell from the son of a Putney blacksmith to all but the highest place in the realm or in the vicissitudes of an adventurer and soldier of fortune such as Sir Thomas Stukeley, the interest excited is personal; and the incidents of the lives of these worthies throw into shadow the sketches of historical and political events in the midst of which they move. The tragic is the more usual kind. In its highest tragic form the biographical chronicle at times rises above personal details and makes the passion in its individual representation and not the man its real theme. *Macbeth* is an excellent illustration of this; for here we have mythical history treated biographically. The presentation of the passion of the protagonist at all times holds the center of the canvas. But the biographical comedy of an historical or supposedly historical personage is by no means unknown, especially as a device to relieve the matter of a serious plot. Thus in Heywood's *If You Know Not Me,* what purport to be the private affairs of Sir Thomas Gresham are set forth as well as his founding of the

15

Royal Exchange, and his life is used as a foil to the political doings of the late queen. *The Pinner of Wakefield,* already considered above, is a good example of the biographical drama wholly and consistently given over to comedy. The reader will recall several instances of such comedies and tragedies among the plays mentioned in the foregoing pages if we are to apply the term generically. These examples need not receive further attention as we are now specifically concerned with those dramas in which the story is told primarily for the hero's sake and neither for the historical events in which he may chance to have figured nor for the artistic possibilities of the theme.

Three plays especially fulfil these conditions. They are *Sir Thomas More, The Life and Death of Lord Cromwell* and *The Famous History of Captain Thomas Stukeley.* All remain, despite surmises, the works of unknown authors; and all were staged during the height of the popularity of the Chronicle Play. *Sir Thomas More* exists in a single manuscript written and apparently revised by several hands.[1] This manuscript is of great interest because it is the official copy submitted by the actors to Edward Tilney, the then Master of the Revels, in his capacity of censor, and because it contains his notes and deletions. Dyce dated *Sir Thomas More* at about 1590; Mr. Fleay as

[1] *MS. Harleian* 7368 in the British Museum; reprinted by Dyce in 1844.

late as 1595.[1] Simpson finds in the scenes which concern the famous "ill May day" of 1517, a reference to the disturbances of 1586, and quotes from a letter in which Recorder Fleetwood wrote to Burghley : " My lord Maior and myselfe . . . dyd examyne certaine apprentices for conspiring an insurrection in this cittie against the Frenche and Dutche . . . all things as like unto Yll May Daye, as could be devised in all manner of cyrcumstances, *mutatis mutandis*." [2]   Other allusions seem to support the earlier date.   The play was certainly performed by the Chamberlain's company, as Simpson pointed out, and it is not impossible that it was revised in 1595 owing to renewed troubles of Londoners with foreigners at that date.[3]

Sir Thomas More is strictly a biographical play, for every scene is directly employed to illustrate the life and character of the hero.   The story follows the career of the great lay chancellor from his shrievalty to his execution, although it skillfully evades the actual cause of his fall and makes him rather the passive sacrifice of an ill-starred fate than the victim of a wantonly tyrannic sovereign.   More's love of the common folk, his faithfulness to promises made even to the humblest, his encouragement of the drama set forth in the

[1] See Dyce's Introduction and Fleay, *Biographical Chronicle*, II. 312.

[2] *Notes and Queries*, Series IV., Vol. VIII., 1 ; and Wright, *Queen Elizabeth and her Times*, II. 308.

[3] *Notes and Queries*, as above, VIII., 1.

included interlude in which the chancellor himself acts
an extemporaneous part, his association with Erasmus
and the Earl of Surrey, the simple beauty of his family
life and his cheerful fortitude at the approach of un-
merited death—all are included in this interesting play.
The grave jocularity of speech which distinguished
Sir Thomas is well preserved in a series of episodes
and situations which are borrowed direct from Halle's
Chronicle and Roper's familiar *Life,* and several anecdotes of the witty Lord Chancellor are bodily conveyed
into the play. A shaggy-haired " ruffian," Faukner,
has raised a disturbance in the street and is brought
before Sir Thomas as a " principall broacher of the
broile."

> *Moore.*   How long have you worne this haire?
> *Fauke.*   I have worne this haire ever since I was borne.
> *Moore.*   You know thats not my question, but how
>   long
>   Hath this shagg fleece hung dangling on thy
>   head ?
> *Fauke.*   How long, my lord ! why, sometimes thus
>   long, sometimes lowere, as the Fates and
>   humors please.
> *Moore.*   So quick, sir, with me, ha ? I see, good fellow,
>   Thou lovest plaine dealing.   Sirra, tell me
>   now,
>   When were you last at barbars ? How longe
>   time
>   Have you vppon your head woorne this
>   shagg haire ?

Fauke. My lord, Jack Faukner tells noe Æsops
       fables : troth, I was not at barbars this
       three yeires ; I have not byn cutt nor will
       not be cutt, vppon a foolish vow, which as
       the Destanies shall derect, I am sworne to
       keepe.

Moore. When comes this vow out ?

Fauke. Why, when the humors are purgd, not theis
       three years.

Moore. Vowes are recorded in the court of Heaven,
       For they are holly acts. Young man, I
         charge thee
       And doe advise thee, start not from that vow :
       And, for I will be sure thou shalt not shreve,
       Besides, because it is an odious sight
       To see a man thus hairie, thou shalt lie
       In Newgate till thy vow and thy three years
       Be full expired.—Away with him ! [1]

Although this play is rambling in construction, a
certain unity is preserved by reason of the uniform
prominence given to the figure of Sir Thomas. Parts
are clearly devised and by no means badly written.
The exposition in which French and Spanish insolence
to citizens of London is represented, is so active and
vigorous and pictured with so strong a contemporary
allusiveness that the stylus of the censor wrote on the
margin : " Leave out . . . the insurrection and the
cause thereof," and bade the players relate Sir

---

[1] *Sir Thomas More*, Shakespeare Society's Publications, 1844, p.
45. This anecdote is related of Cromwell by Foxe, *Book of Martyrs*,
ed. 1641, II. 512.

Thomas's "good service done . . . upon a mutiny against the Lombards, only by a short report and not otherwise at your own perils." These perils the actors seem not to have hesitated to brave, as several scenes remain to attest. One of them contains Sir Thomas's sagacious speech to the rebels whose shout has been for the immediate banishment of all foreigners, "which can not choose but much advantage the poor handicrafts of the city." Sir Thomas replies:

> Graunt them remoued, and graunt that this your noyce
> Hath chidd downe all the maiestie of Ingland;
> Ymagin that you see the wretched straingers,
> Their babyes at their backes and their poor lugage,
> Plodding tooth ports and costes for transportacion,
> And that you sytt as kinges in your desyres,
> Aucthoryty quyte sylenct by your braule,
> And you in ruff of your opynions clothd;
> What had you gott? I'le tell you: you had taught
> How insolence and strong hand shoold prevayle,
> How ordere shoold be quelld; and by this patterne
> Not on of you shoold lyve an aged man,
> For other ruffians, as their fancies wrought,
> With sealf same hand, sealf reasons and sealf right,
> Woold shark on you, and men lyke ravenous fishes
> Woold feed on on another. [1]

Although he acknowledged that no shadow of contemporary evidence can be found for such a supposition, the ingenious Richard Simpson was of opinion

[1] *Sir Thomas More*, p. 27.

that the two passages quoted above—the one in the quality of humor, the other in its "imagery and morality"—are "alike Shakespearean . . . and quite unlike the poetry of Greene, Marlowe, Lodge or Robert Wilson."[1] Simpson did not hesitate to advance boldly to the inference that the longer revisions, which include these passages are not only of Shakespeare's authorship, but probably in his own handwriting, a theory which has obtained no support save from the late Mr. James Spedding, whose suggestion that the manuscript of these scenes be reproduced in *facsimile*, and thus studied, has never been carried out.[2] Be the merits of this theory what they may, it may be remarked that the hendecasyllabic character of the verse of the speech of Sir Thomas is very unlike the versification of Shakespeare's earlier period.

The History of the Life and Death of Thomas, Lord Cromwell, first registered in 1602 and dated by Ulrici 1592, is a typical example of its species and a production of merit.   In the title of the earliest extant edition, that of 1613, occur the words "written by W. S." The play was reprinted in the third folio of Shakespeare. Wherefore Schlegel not only declared his belief that Shakespeare was undoubtedly its author, but gibbeted his own critical acumen forever by affirming it "to

[1] *Notes and Queries*, Series IV., Vol. VIII., 2.

[2] *Ibid.*, Vol. X., 227. The passages in question are from the entrance of More on p. 22 to the bottom of p. 29, and from the beginning of the scene on p. 39 to the top of p. 53.

belong, in my judgment, to his maturest and most excellent works."[1]   Sounder opinion differs as to whether these initials were intended to deceive the unwary purchaser or stood in all innocence for no more than Wentworth Smith, an obscure playwright of whom we know only from Henslowe.[2]   Be this as it may, the play is of early date.   Although unusually free from allusions of a contemporary kind, the frequency of rime, the mannerism by which a character often speaks of himself in the third person, and the non-appearance of King Henry among the *dramatis personæ*, all point to this.   As to source, this play is founded almost wholly on the account of the early life of Cromwell contained in Foxe's *Book of Martyrs*, an account which the historian, the late John Richard Green, characterized as " a mass of fable."   Even the episodes concerning the relations of Cromwell and the Italian merchant Ferabosco, which have been referred to one of the *novelle* of Bandello, might have been found in Foxe detailed with equal minutiæ.[3]   The play, too, partakes to a degree of the Protestant zeal which animates Foxe's extraordinary work.   In it Cromwell had been called " a mighty wall and defense of the Church."   In the play, on Gardiner's

[1] *Dramaturgische Vorlesungen*, ed. Leipzig, 1846, II. 308.
[2] This is the opinion of the most recent editor of *Cromwell*, Mr. T. Evan Jacob.   *Old English Dramas*, 1889, p. 166.
[3] See *Cromwell*, III. 1 and cf. Bandello, *Novelle*, Milan, 1560, II. 140 and Foxe, ed. 1641, II. 498–501 and 508-513.

telling Cromwell that he had "no colour" for his
seizure of the Abbey lands, the latter replies :

> Yes, the abolishing of Antichrist,
> And of his Popish order from our Realm :
> I am no enemy to Religion,
> But what is done, it is for England's good.[1]

With the intervention of the years in which Queen
Mary had exacted bloody reprisals for the sufferings
of those who were faithful to Rome in her father's
time the religious and political tone of England had
changed.   It was now possible for the grandchildren
of the very men who had trembled under Henry's
ruthless Machiavelian instrument of tyranny to believe
Thomas Cromwell the ideal of martyred gentleness
and plain dealing.   In *The Life and Death* Cromwell
stands for the glorification, the very apotheosis of citizen virtue.   It is Cromwell's honorable thrift and capacity in trade, his temperance, piety and staunch
Protestantism which are dwelt on and extolled.   He
befriends the broken debtor and outwits the wrong-
doer.   He is mindful of others' favors to him, forget-
ful of his own.   When humble intimates of his youth
claim the notice of his lordship, he acknowledges them
with gracious candor and bestows largesses on them,
and he kneels in his chancellor's robes to receive the
blessing of his aged blacksmith father.   Except this
last, which seems an invention of the dramatist, all is

---

[1] *Cromwell*, IV. 2 ; and cf. Foxe, as above, p. 503.

a vivid *replica* of Foxe's picture. In the play, however, politics are treated with greater circumspection.
King Henry is felt, as in *Sir Thomas More*, as an un-
seen but inexorable power whose relations to his
victims, though not at all clear, are above scrutiny,
much less criticism. Even Tilney must have approved
an utterance at once so patriotic and so modest as this
which Cromwell applied to Wolsey's enquiry respecting his opinion of foreign lands :

> My Lord, no Court with England may compare,
> Neither for State nor civil government :
> Lust dwells in France, in Italy, and Spain,
> From the poor pesant, to the Princes train,
> In Germany, and Holland, Riot serves,
> And he that most can drink, most he deserves :
> England I praise not : for I here was born,
> But that she laugheth the others unto scorn. [1]

The fall of Cromwell is referred by this unveracious
historian wholly to the jealous personal enmity of
Gardiner, Bishop of Winchester, who hates his enemy
for his "dove-like looks," and subornes two witnesses
to swear to his treason, absolving them for their crime,
after a favorite Protestant gibe, before it has been
committed. In the end the king, won by Cromwell's
reported fortitude and by the memory of his many
virtues, sends a pardon, but unhappily the axe has
already fallen on the neck of this *bourgeois* anticipation
of the impeccable perfections of Sir Charles Grandison.

[1] *Cromwell*, III. 3.

In one of the choruses of *Cromwell*, which are in-
tercalated after the manner of this class of plays to
eke out the broken continuity of the action, the auditors
are naïvely besought to

> Pardon if we omit all Wolsey's life,
> Because our play depends on Cromwells death.[1]

It was several years before the great Cardinal became
the subject of a play.   Henslowe's book contains
several mentions of two plays on Wolsey, the earliest
of which bears date June, 1601.[2]   This play was called
The Life of Cardinal Wolsey and was the production
of Chettle and Samuel Rowley.   It was staged at an
unusual cost as Henslowe's several entries of pay-
ments " for tynsell and taffeney and lynynge and other
thinges" go to show, and was so great a success that
in the following August Chettle was recalled and set
to work with Drayton and Munday on "a hurry order"
to produce another play on the same subject.   This
was called *The Rising* (i. e., *Rise*) *of Cardinal Wolsey*
and probably dealt with the events which led up to the
beginning of Chettle's and Rowley's play.   Both of
these productions have perished, though it is not impossible that in Rowley's *When You See Me, You
Know Me, or the Famous Chronicle History of Henry
VIII.* we may have some of the material of these
plays in a later revised form.

1 *Cromwell*, IV. 1.
2 Henslowe, pp. 189, 203; 221-222.

It is not difficult to make out a list of some length of non-extant plays from the titles of which a biographical character may be reasonably inferred. They fall almost without exception within the last decade of Elizabeth's reign and vary in subject from the celebration of the deeds of warriors such as John of Gaunt and his "conquest of Spain" to political adventurers like Martin Swart, a foreign leader in the revolt of Simnel against Henry VII.; from personages such as Owen Tudor and the Duke of Buckingham who fell victim to Richard III., to Alice Pierce, the mistress of Edward III., and Belin Dun described as "the first thief that was ever hanged in England." Of these plays, that on John of Gaunt was registered in 1594; the others appear by name in Henslowe's *Dairy* within the years 1593–1597. That several of these plays were histories rather than biographies is likely. But that a strong biographical and local interest attached to others seems equally unquestionable. Drayton's *William Longbeard* is doubtless the hero which Lodge describes in his pamphlet of the same title as "the most famous and witty English traitor, born in the city of London," the leader of the London crusade in 1190, and of a city riot—a man whose temper and attitude are indicated by the fact that he wore his beard untrimmed in scorn of the Normans who were shaven. An even more certain local interest must have attached to the play on Whittington, whose ad-

ventures in Morocco and rise to be Mayor of London
could not but have appealed to a city audience.[1]   The
subject, too, of Haughton's *Six Yeomen of the West*,
mentioned two or three times by Henslowe during
1601, is known to us from a later extant edition of
*Thomas of Reading or the Six Worthy Yeomen of the
West*, a prose tale by Thomas Deloney.[2]   A second
part, in which Hathway and Smith assisted, was called
The Six Clothiers of the West.   The story relates the
adventures of six notable cloth merchants of Western
England, chiefly on their journeys up to London.   The
scene is laid in the reign of Henry I., who appears
as a character.   The adventures range from farce of
amorous intrigue to the grewsome tragedy of Thomas
Cole,t he chief clothier, who meets his death, like
Barabas in *The Jew of Malta*, by a fall through a trap
into a boiling caldron.

In *The Famous History of the Life and Death of
Captain Thomas Stukeley, with His Marriage to Alderman Curteis' Daughter, and Valiant Ending of His Life
at the Battle of Alcazar* we have a dramatized version
of the career of one of the most daring and successful
of Elizabethan adventurers.   Born of the restless
Devonshire stock that gave Raleigh, Drake and Gil-

[1] *The History of Richard Whittington, of his lowe birthe, his great
fortune, as yt was plaied by the Prynces Servants* was licensed in 1605.
Hazlitt, *Handbook to Literature*, p. 654.

[2] Reprinted from a later edition in Thoms, *Early English Prose
Romances*, ed. 1858, I. 57.

bert to the service of the queen, Stukeley began life as
a soldier of fortune and political spy and intriguer in
irregular vacillation between the courts of England
and France.   Under disguise of a project to plant a
kingdom in Florida, Stukeley became a buccaneer.
But failing to return a profit adequate to the main-
tenance of the favor of Queen Elizabeth, who was not
improbably his fellow adventurer, he went over to the
services of Spain and the Roman Church and engaged
in the systematic fomenting of rebellion against his
former mistress in Ireland.   Renegade, braggart and
egregious liar that he was, Stukeley contrived to impose upon the courts of Madrid and Rome and to
maintain for years the port and following of an earl
under the pompous style of Duke of Ireland, a title of
his own invention though he contrived to have it in-
sured by a papal grant.   Though Stukeley's promised
ventures against Ireland were always deferred, he
served in several continental campaigns and always
with distinguished bravery.   He met at last an heroic
death in fighting against the Moors.   Such a hero was
precisely the one to allure the active Elizabethan
imagination ; and Stukeley's impudence, his magnificence and his valor, obscuring his less dazzling traits,
became theme for pamphlet, ballad and drama.   He
appears as a character in Peele's *Battle of Alcazar* and
Henslowe affords repeated mentions of a play which
he calls " *Stewtly*," from 1596 onward.   It seems alto-

gether reasonable to identify this play with the one under discussion, and this notwithstanding the adverse opinion of Simpson who edited the play of *Stukeley* and collected much material about the man.[1] This play exhibits less unity than either *Cromwell* or *Sir Thomas More*. The scene shifts from London to Ireland and from Madrid and Lisbon to Morocco ; and except for the hero, the entire *dramatis personae* change with each act. This is in the plan and calls for no comment in itself. Unfortunately, save for the first act, the state in which this play has come down to us is hopelessly confused and corrupt. It seems reasonable to believe that we have here an extreme case of borrowing, patching and interpolation, for it is certain that fragments of at least one earlier play, *The Battle of Alcazar*, mentioned above, appear in the text. We need not, however, follow Simpson in the gratuitous invention of a lost play called *Antonio*, or Fleay in his confident assignment of authorship to Dekker and Peele.[2] The author or mender of *Stukeley* took great liberties with his subject. The first and best act tells of Stukeley's suit to the daughter of Alderman Curteis. Although this marriage actually did take place, the story is wrought as to detail out of the whole cloth. Here Stukeley is made to conform to the type of the young spendthrift of the day and we

---

[1] *The School of Shakspere*, I., pp. 139, 140; and 154 ff.
[2] *Ibid.*, p. 141, and *Biographical Chronicle*, I. 127.

are treated to a clear dramatic sketch of a determined and infatuated girl, overcoming the reluctance of her prudent father to yield a consent to her marriage with a gallant whom he distrusts but can learn little about. Married and his wife's dowery and jewels in his hands, the Stukeley of the play in a capital scene which neither Dekker nor Middleton might have disdained, pays his cringing creditors, equips a company of soldiers for the service of his sovereign and declares to his weeping bride :

> It is not chambering,
> Now I have beauty to be dallying with,
> Nor pampering of myself with belly-cheer
> Now I have got a little worldly pelf,
> That is the end or levels of my thought.
> I must have honour ; honour is the thing
> Stukley doth thirst for, and to climb the mount
> Where she is seated, gold shall be my footstool.[1]

It is this note which, harped on throughout the play, transforms a traitor and a renegade into the popular embodiment of that insolent and untamed spirit which in worthier careers defied Spain and circled the globe.

The dramatized biography of travel and adventure, with which Stukeley allies itself on one side, is for the most part a development of later times, although sporadic examples of plays depicting the adventures of Englishmen on the high seas and in foreign lands are scattered throughout the period of the popularity of the

[1] *The School of Shakspere*, I. 186.

Chronicle Play.   The earliest specimen of a drama of this [class is apparently *The Blacksmith's Daughter*, "containing the trechery of Turks, the honourable bountye of a noble mind, the striuing of vertue in distresse."   This production, which is now lost, is mentioned by Stephen Gosson in his *School of Abuse*, 1579, and seems alone in its kind in these first days of the Elizabethan drama.[1]   Two non-extant plays, certainly of this class, were *Sir John Mandeville*, recorded by Henslowe in 1592, and *The Siege of Dunkirk, with Allyn the Pirate*, 1603.[2]   A typical play is preserved in the shapeless and hastily constructed performance, *The Travailes of The three English Brothers*, which may have been written as early as the year 1607, the patchwork of Day, Wilkins and William Rowley. This play details the adventures of Thomas, Anthony and Robert Shirley, a species of tripartite hero, in Persia, Russia and Italy, and, as might be expected, is more concerned in the search after novelty than in any attempt to adhere to biographical fact.[3]   About the year 1609 popular interest was excited by several robberies on the high seas of a peculiarly daring nature. The stage at once responded with several plays in which piracy figures.   Such is the ranting and melodramatic biography of two notorious pirates, Ward

[1] *Publications of the Shakespeare Society*, 1841, p. 30.
[2] Henslowe, pp. 21 and 231.
[3] Bullen, *The Works of John Day*, 1881, II. 93.

16

and Dansiker, entitled *A Christian turn'd Turke*, which
was written by Robert Daborne, the least of Elizabethan playwrights.[1]   Such, too, is the graceful adaptation of this popular interest of the moment to romantic drama, *Fortune by Land and Sea*, the joint work of
Heywood and William Rowley, and the two parts of
Heywood's breezy and wholesome *Fair Maid of the
West*, in which we breathe the very air of Elizabethan
Plymouth and consort with corsairs and sea-rovers on
shipboard and in strange lands.   The plays on piracy
fall between 1609 and 1612.   *The Travailes of The
three English Brothers* and *A Christian turn'd Turke* are
dramatized directly and slavishly from contemporary
pamphlets.[2]   These plays are of the very stuff of
which the corresponding variety of modern journalism
is made, and they performed for their day precisely the
same function.   Heywood's dramas are of a higher
order.   The nature of a play entitled *A Tragedy of
the Plantation of Virginia*, which was licensed in 1623
on condition that the profaneness be left out, must
remain matter for divination.

The old English spirit burst out anew in the vigorous and well-written underplot of *Dicke of Devonshire*,
a dramatic version of a pamphlet entitled *Three to One.
Being an English-Spanish Combat performed by a
Western Gentleman of Tavistock in Devonshire, with*

---

[1] Reprinted in *Anglia*, XX. 188.
[2] See Dr. Swaen's Introduction, *ibid.*, p. 151, and *The Works of
Day*, as above.

*an English quarterstaff against three Spaniards with
rapiers and poniards at Sherris in Spain.* The
homely narrator and actor of this exploit is one Richard Peeke, who describes his fingers as " fitter for the
pike than the pen " ; and the play, in the parts which
concern him, has preserved much of his soldierly frank-
ness.   It would be a pleasure to agree with Mr. Bullen in adding this fresh bit of effective realism to the
many laurels of Heywood ; but there seems to be no
sufficient reason to accept either this or the several
other surmises as to its authorship.[1]   The author,
whoever he was, retained a lively recollection of the
old and mortal quarrel with Spain and could scarcely
have been a young man at the time of writing the
play.   These lines breathe the very spirit of 1588 and
must have sounded strange in the first years of the
reign of the second Stuart.

Spaines anger never blew hott coales indeed
Till in Queene Elizabeths Raigne when (may I call
    him so)
That glory of his Country and Spaynes terror,
That wonder of the land and the Seas minyon,
Drake of eternall memory, harrowed th' Indyes.

.   .   .   .

[1] See Bullen, *Old English Plays*, II. 1, where the play is reprinted,
and Arber's *English Garner*, I. 621, for the pamphlet.   Ward, *Dramatic Literature*, II. 583n., mentions a paper on *Dick of Devonshire*,
by Mr. D. P. Alford, printed in the *Transactions of the Devonshire
Association*, 1892.

                        Yes, when his Ilands
Nombre de Dios, Cartagena, Hispaniola,
With Cuba and the rest of those faire Sisters,
The mermaydes of those Seas, whose golden strings
Give him his sweetest musicke, when they by Drake
And his brave Ginges were ravishd ; when these red
    apples
Were gather'd and brought hither to be payrd—
Then the Castilian Lyon began to roare.

.   .   .   .   .   .

                    The very name of Drake
Was a Bugbear to fright Children ; Nurses still'd
Their little Spanish Nynnyes when they cryde
" Hush ! the Drake comes."[1]

Let us now return to the main thread of our subject, the epical Chronicle Play, and consider the temporary revival of popular interest in the scenic representation of English history of which the death of
Queen Elizabeth was the immediate cause.   Mention
has already been made of *The Famous History of Sir
Thomas Wyatt with the Coronation of Queen Mary
and the coming in of King Philip* by Thomas Dekker
and John Webster, first printed in 1607.   The commonly received identification of this play with the two
parts of *Lady Jane Grey* mentioned by Henslowe in
the autumn of 1602 may be accepted,[2] although it
seems preferable in view of the general coherence of
the existing version to describe it as a condensation

[1] *Dick of Devonshire*, I. 2.
[2] Henslowe, pp. 242, 243.

or revision rather than as a "cobbled" or a "muti-
lated abridgment" of the earlier plays.[1] We may
also admit the possibility of Mr. Fleay's identification
of *Sir Thomas Wyatt* with *The Overthrow of the Rebels*
for which Henslowe was buying properties in November of the same year.[2] In subject this "history"
comprises Northumberland's conspiracy to pocket the
kingdom for himself by inducing the dying King
Edward to disinherit his two sisters and settle the succession on the Lady Jane Grey to whom Northumberland had married one of his sons ; the rise of the
popular tide of loyalty to the Princess Mary; the
negotiations for her hand carried on by Philip of Spain
and the consequent rebellion of Wyatt and the Kent-
ishmen with their overthrow. *Sir Thomas Wyatt* is
singularly colorless in its political and religious allusions, although an antithesis between Wyatt as the
exponent of the liberal Protestant spirit and Gardiner,
Bishop of Winchester, his foil, is not unhappily suggested.   The side on which the popular sympathy of
the Elizabethan audience was sure to be enlisted is
plain enough in the following passage. The royal
counsel has just received Philip's offer of marriage
made to Queen Mary, and Bishop Winchester declares :

We haue cause
To thanke our God, that such a mightie Prince

[1] See Fleay, *Biographical Chronicle*, II. 269, and Ward, *Dramatic
Literature*, II. 468.

[2] Henslowe, p. 244, and Fleay as above.

> As Philip is, Sonne to the Emperor,
> Heire to wealthy Spaine, and many spacious
> Kingdomes will vouchsafe—

Wia. Vouchsafe! my Lord of Winchester! pray, what?

Win. To grace our mightie Soveraigne with his honour-
    able Title.

Wia. To marrie with our Queene: mean you not so?

Win. I doe, what then?

Wiat. O God! is shee a beggar, a forsaken Maide,
> That she hath neede of grace from forraine princes?
> By Gods dear mother, O, God pardon sweare I,
> Me thinkes she is a faire and louely Prince,
> Her onely beautie (were she of meane birth)
> Able to make the greatest Potentate.
> I the great Emperor of the mightie Cham,
> That hath more Nations vnder his Commaund,
> Then Spanish Philip's like to inherrit townes,
> To come and lay his Scepter at her feet,
> And to intreate her to vouchsafe the grace
> To take him and his Kingdome to her mercy.[1]

The subject of this play was a delicate one; for
Mary, "the Popish persecutor," had been none the
less an anointed sovereign of England. Wyatt's rising
was popularly believed to have been an attempt to an-
ticipate by a few years the coming Protestant rule of
Queen Elizabeth. But in his failure Wyatt became
indistinguishable from other traitors to the crown. It
may be suspected that the furthur exposition of this
contrast between the new and the old *régime* as repre-

---

[1] *Sir Thomas Wyatt, Dekker's Dramatic Works,* 1873, III. 106.

sented in the persons of Wyatt and Gardiner was one of the chief omissions of the revised version of this play. The touching story of Lady Jane and her lover husband, the innocent victims of an ambition not their own, is by no means inadequately told ; though it, like other parts of the play, seems to have suffered by excision. Notwithstanding its merits *The Famous History* must be pronounced much below the standard of the better work of either of its authors.

From many contemporary allusions it appears that in November, 1602, the Swan, which was one of the larger theaters on the Bankside, was engaged for the presentation of a very curious production of an historical cast. This was entitled *Englands Joy*, and is usually described as a species of political pageant or dumb show detailing more or less allegorically the chief events of Elizabeth's reign.[1] The books and plays of the time are full of ironical allusions to it,[2] and the projector of it, one Richard Vennar, went ever after by the nick-name, Englands Joy. Vennar, who appears to have been a grave person, resented this mockery and wrote, in 1614, *An Apology*, dedicated to "the same pur-blinde Multitude, who feede with spectacles to make their meate seeme bigger."[3] It does

---

[1] Collier, *Dramatic Literature*, III. 321. Ward does not mention this production.

[2] See Jonson's *Masque of Augures*, folio, 1640, II. 83 ; and *The Goblins*, Suckling's Works, ed. 1892, II. 51.

[3] Collier, *Bibliographical Account of the Rarest Books*, IV. 193 ; and the same editor's reprint of *An Apology* in his *Illustrations of Old English Literature*, 1866, III. No. 4.

not seem that *Englands Joy* was ever presented. Whether with intent to defraud or from fear on discovering that he had attempted more than he could carry out, Vennar tried to get away from London, after having collected considerable earnest-money on the score of his project. He was caught, however, and brought before the Lord Chief Justice, who, a contemporary letter informs us, "wold make nothing of yt but a jest and merriment."[1] Day doubtless expressed the prevalent opinion as to Vennar when he made one of his characters say : " He drew more Connies [*i. e.*, fools] in a purse-nette than euer were taken at any draught about London."[2] A curious relic of this dramatic venture is preserved in a broadside on which is printed a synopsis of the plot. This was apparently intended for the use of the auditors much as a synoptic programme might be used to-day. According to this broadside eight scenes were to have followed each other representing among other things, the early disunion of England and Scotland, the enmity of Spain, the machinations of the Jesuits, the defeat of the Armada and the recent victories of Lord Mountjoy in Ireland. The strong allegorical bias of the production is patent throughout. At her corona-

[1] *Bibliographical Account*, as above, p. 193, where this letter is quoted entire.

[2] *The Works of John Day*, ed. Bullen, II. 56. See also the allusion of Taylor the Water Poet in his *Cast over the Water to William Fenner*, Spenser Society's reprint of Taylor's folio of 1630, II. 155.

tion Elizabeth is represented, " Her throne attended
with Peace, Plenty and Civill Policy : a sacred prelate
standing at her right hand, betokening the serenity of
the Gospell "; whilst at the conclusion we have a complete reversion back to the old religious drama in
Elizabeth's apotheosis, an event herein anticipated by
some four months.   After being crowned with an imperial crown garnished with the sun, moon and stars,
she is "taken up into Heaven ; when presently appears a [throng] of blessed soules ; and beneath under
the stage, set forth with strange fire-works, divers
blacke and damned soules, wonderfully described in
their several torments." [1]

On the twenty-fourth of March, 1603, Queen Elizabeth died.   Her powers of body and mind had been
failing for many months and the brilliant court, the
stately progresses and princely entertainments had
long since become recollections of the past.   The men
who had stood at her side and made her reign memorable had fallen away one by one, and a new generation of subjects was growing up, ununited to their
queen by the common interests and the common fears
which had stirred their fathers and eagerly expectant
of the new reign at hand.   None the less when expectation became certainty a natural revulsion of feeling
ensued and the thoughts of men reverted to the days

[1] This broadside is reprinted in *The Harleian Miscellany*, ed. 1813,
X. 198.

when England had lowered the pride of Spain and
Elizabeth had stood for the ideal of English national
spirit and progress, material prosperity and the triumph
of the Protestant faith.   In the literature which followed on the death of the queen the drama holds an
interesting place, although the plays which this event
directly inspired are few and of slender literary merit.

In 1851 Collier reprinted two plays by Thomas
Heywood under the general title *If You Know not
Me, You Know No Bodie*.   The first part has the sub-
title, *or The troubles of Queene Elizabeth*, the second,
the added words : " *With the building of the Royall Exchange and the famous Victory of Queen Elizabeth:
Anno 1588.*"   The original dates of publication were
1605 and the year following, and the popularity of
both plays was such that five subsequent editions of
the first part appeared and three of the second, the
last bearing date 1633.[1]   Despite all these reprintings
the first play is fragmentary if not corrupt.   It was
printed (according to a prologue which the author
wrote for its revival at the Cockpit at a date unknown)
from a stolen stenographic report.   And the assurance of this prologue that " the Author now to vindi-
cate that wrong hath tooke the paines, upright upon its
feete to teach it walke " does not seem to have been
fulfilled.[2]   The second part is in better condition and

---

[1] For these and other particulars see Collier's ed. for the Shakespeare Society, *Introduction*.

[2] This prologue was printed by Heywood in his *Pleasant Dialogves
and Dramma's*, 1637.

has probably come down to us substantially as it was presented. Both plays appear to be founded on a pamphlet of Heywood's later published as *Englands Elizabeth*, 1631.

The first part of *If You Know Not Me* opens at the period in the reign of Queen Mary at which the play of *Sir Thomas Wyatt* ends. Wyatt and Lady Jane Grey have suffered execution, and Mary, sure of her crown, is preparing to meet Prince Philip who is reported "safely arrived and landed at Southampton." From this point onward the one consistent theme is the persecution to which the Princess Elizabeth was subjected by the jealousy of her sister and the incessant machinations of Gardiner, Bishop of Winchester; her trials, imprisonments and the petty hardships to which she was exposed at the hands of overzealous servants of the queen. Mary is thrown as much as possible into the background and her religious persecutions are not so much as mentioned. Elizabeth's maidenly demeanor, her virtue, her steadfastness in refusing to plead guilty before Winchester and thus submit to the false charges of unloyalty, the sorrow of her household, the affection which she inspired in common folk and in the very guard set to watch her prison—these are the themes which are expanded and illustrated in a series of dramatized anecdotes, eked out by dumb shows depicting matter such as the departure of Philip, and Mary's consequent despair, the funeral of Winchester and the coronation of Elizabeth. The following brief scene is one of the series of little sketches which joined together go to make up this loosely knit play. It serves in its place as one of several like devices by which Heywood produces what we should call the historical atmosphere.

Enter the Englishman and Spaniard.

Spa. The wall, the wall.

Eng. Sblood. Spaniard, you get no wall here, vnless you would haue your head and the wall knockt together.

Spa. Signor Cavalero Danglatero, I must haue the wall.

Eng. I doe protest, hadst thou not enforst it, I had not regarded it ; but since you will needs haue the wall, Ile take the pains to thrust you into the kennel.

Spa. Oh, base Cavalero, my sword and poynard, well-tried in Toledo, shall giue thee the imbrocado.

Eng. Marry, and welcome, sir. Come on.

They fight : he hurts the Spaniard.

Spa. Holo, Holo ! Thou hast given me the canvissado.

Eng. Come, sir ; will you any more ?

Spa. Signor Cavalero, look behind thee. A blade of Toledo is drawne against thee.

He lookes backe : he [the Spaniard] kills him. [1]

At this moment Philip of Spain enters and, horrified at the baseness of the deed, protests that the great

[1] *1 If You Know Not Me, Heywood's Dramatic Works*, ed. 1874, I. 224.

Turk's empire shall not redeem his cowardly follower from a felon's death ; and he forthwith orders him to execution.   Indeed throughout the play Philip is represented in a remarkably favorable light, as a just and courteous gentleman, zealous to bring about a reconciliation of the royal sisters and in the end successful.

The second part of *If You Know Not Me* is made up of a comedy of London merchant life and a few sketchy and unsatisfactory historical scenes ; the proportion of the two elements is four-fifths comedy and one-fifth "history."   The actual hero of this play is Sir Thomas Gresham, who it will be remembered was glorified at a much earlier date in the Latin play, *Byrsa Basilica.*   In the English play Gresham figures not only in his capacity of a typical London merchant but in his famous rôle of founder of the Royal Exchange.   Indeed this renowned structure, of which the Elizabethans were never weary of boasting, rises before the mind's eye in the play from its foundations to the grasshopper, the sign of the Greshams, which adorned the pinnacle.   This drama is an excellent, if somewhat rambling, specimen of its class ; and is of peculiar interest for the reason that it stands between the biographical drama on the one hand and the comedies of London life with their pictures of purely fictitious events on the other, and in this respect belongs with the earlier merchant scenes of *Cromwell* and the first act of *Sir Thomas Stukeley.*   The historical parts of *2 If You Know Not Me* sketch in outline Parry's attempt on the queen's life, the deliberations of the Duke of Medina and his council before the sailing of the Spanish fleet, the queen's review of her troops at Tilbury and a purely epic account—and that a very bald one—of the defeat of the Armada. The play ends with the royal reception of Sir Francis Drake, and Sir Martin Frobisher who present their captured Spanish standards to the queen and talk very prosily about their victory. With due allowance for an imperfect text in the first part, not obscuring, however, the readiness of diction and cleverness of dramatic device which is found even in the inferior work of Heywood, the historical parts of these dramas might have been written in 1590. In view of the possibilities of the subject and the abilities of such a dramatist as Heywood is at his best, it is impossible not to deplore the throwing away of so unusual an opportunity.

The Whore of Babylon by Thomas Dekker was printed in 1607. In regard to it Mr. Fleay has done much theorizing. He places its performance late in 1605 because of an allusion to the Isle of Gulls which he says can apply only to Day's drama of that title. He imagines an earlier version in Elizabeth's reign because of the allusion to Mary Queen of Scots and the ambiguity of its involved reference to Essex, and he "thinks" *Truths Supplication to Candlelight*, one of the non-extant plays mentioned by Henslowe, its

original title.   To cap all he even finds allusions to it
in contemporary uses in Puritan cant of the phrase con-
stituting the title.[1]   In none of these surmises does it
seem possible to follow Mr. Fleay.   Dekker's play was
doubtless acted soon after the two parts of *If You Know
Not Me* and in emulation of that play.   Heywood's plays
had been acted by the Queen's players ; Dekker's was
performed by the Prince's servants.   Instead of pursuing
the rudely direct method of Heywood and buoying the
historical matter with comedy, Dekker chose allegory
and served his history with a dressing of mysticism
that added little to its palatableness.   Dekker's play
is constructed out of popular current notions concerning Elizabeth's struggles in diplomacy and warfare
with Spain, allegorically expressed under the guise of
an imagined attack of the empress of Babylon and her
creature cardinals and kings on Titania, the fairy queen.
The mission of the Jesuits to England is represented in
Campeius, a thin disguise for Edmund Campion ; and
several scenes detail the plots against the queen's life by
Dr. Lopez and Parry, on whose person to the scandal of
all Christians a plenary indulgence for his attempted
crime was alleged to have been found.   Even the
practice of witchcraft against the queen's health by
means of the maltreatment of a waxen image is carefully detailed, and a species of satirical comedy is developed in the sayings of Plain Dealing who, on

---

[1] *Biographical Chronicle,* I. 132.

leaving the court of Babylon, comes to reside per-
manently in England and is bidden by the queen to
live with his kinsman, Truth. The indebtedness of
the main allegory of this play to Spenser's famous
epic in obvious. There is, however, something so un-
utterably preposterous to our present way of thinking
in the cloaking of Burghley and Leicester under the
names Fideli and Parthenophil, and in King Philip and
Henry VIII. as Satyrane and Oberon, that we find it
difficult to conceive of the possible satisfaction which
such a production may have afforded men to whom
the allegory of *The Faery Queene* had a living significance. Dekker was not without his difficulties. The
great horse of the Spenserian allegory had a pace beyond his menage. At times his steed deserts him and
he stands a sorry figure among his grotesque puppets
who in taking on the outward habiliments of fairies
have forfeited the slightest resemblance to men. The
cant phrase of extreme Puritanism which gives to this
play its forbidding title is indicative of the violent political and religious bias which it exhibits throughout, a
bias which doubtless represents faithfully enough the
popular contemporary attitude of the lower classes of
Englishmen towards Spain and towards Rome. The
nature of Dekker's allegory will be sufficiently indicated in the following passage, which like many others
in this extraordinary production is far from ill written.
The change of allusion from Mary of Scotland to

Essex (indicated in the change of the gender of the pronoun used to denote the embodiment of Elizabeth's enemies in one person) is characteristic of the devious methods of Elizabethan allegory.   Fideli offers Titania a paper :

Titan.   What comes this paper for ?
  Fid.   Your hand.
Titan.   The cause ?
Fidel.   The Moone that from your beames did borrow light,
    Hath from her siluer bow shot pitchy clowds
    T'ecclipse your brightnes : heauen tooke your part,
    And her surpriz'd ; A jurie of bright starres,
    Have her vnworthy found to shine agen :
    Your Fairies therefore on their knees intreat,
    Shee may be puld out from the firmament,
    Where shee was plac'd to glitter.
Titan.   Must we then
    Strike those whom we have lou'd ? albeit the children,
    Whom we have nourisht at our princely breast,
    Set daggers to it, we could be content
    To chide, not beat them, (might we vse our will)
    Our hand was made to saue, but not to kill.
  Flor.   You must not (cause hee's noble) spare his blood.
Titan.   We should not, for hee's noble that is good.[1]

---

[1] *The Dramatic Works of Thomas Dekker*, ed. 1873, II. 246.

IX

PLAYS ON HENRY VIII. AND LATER HISTORICAL DRAMAS

In the discussion of the biographical chronicle above we met with four plays which treated of historical events of the reign of King Henry VIII. Two of these are extant and are concerned with the lives of Sir Thomas More and Thomas Lord Cromwell. Between them and the two non-extant plays of Cardinal Wolsey in 1601 a decade had elapsed. In 1605 a play was printed with the following title : *When You See Me You Know Me. Or the famous Chronicle Historie of King Henrie the Eight, With the Birth and vertuous Life of Edward Prince of Wales . . . by Samvell Rowley servant to the Prince.* This play enjoyed great popularity, if we may judge by the four editions that appeared up to 1632. This title suggests Heywood's *If You Know Not Me You Know Nobody ;* and the parallel becomes complete when we learn that both plays were published by the same publisher and that the title-page of each is ornamented with a woodcut portrait of the sovereign whose reign it concerns. The play of Henry probably preceded that of Elizabeth, as the former was registered in February, 1605, the two parts of *If You Know Not Me,* in the following

July and September. Rowley's play was doubtless in
existence some years before it appeared in print, although no entry which can be identified with it appears
among Henslowe's disbursements for the Admiral's
men, the company that became the Prince of Wales'
upon the accession of King James.

When You See Me You Know Me fulfills all the conditions of a typical chronicle play. In subject it comprises events of the reign of King Henry from the
period just prior to the birth of Prince Edward to the
visit of the German Emperor to the English Court.
It includes the death of the Queen Jane Seymour, the
education of the prince, the plot of Bonner and Gardiner against Queen Katharine Parr with its failure, and
an escapade by night of King Henry in the city of
London in which he beats a notorious bravo at broad-
sword practice and is lodged in prison by the watch
until his courtiers seek him out. A less important
rôle is assigned to Cardinal Wolsey than might be
expected when we recall that in order to introduce him
at all Rowley was compelled to lengthen his life some
fifteen years. The central figures of the play are King
Henry and Will Summers, the famous court fool, and
both are represented with great fidelity to the coarser
outlines of contemporary tradition. Henry's court is
pictured to us as it might have been seen by menials
from below stairs. Rowley's hand is heavy but his
stroke is vigorous and his realism, though startling at

times, is tempered by a natural flow of homely humor.
We may agree with Professor Ward when he says
that "The author succeeds to perfection in depicting
King Henry's Court as a bear-garden, where high
policy, religious controversy, births, deaths, marriages,
and the unsavory witticisms of Will Summers freely
jostle one another; and a full justification is thus furnished of the uncomplimentary combination of epithets
by which the *Prologue* to Shakspere's *Henry VIII.*
seems to characterize Samuel Rowley's play." [1]   While
Rowley might have found most of his material in
Holinshed, his vivid and circumstantial pictures of
everyday life in the king's antechamber, the small
talk of attendants and the impertinences of the fools
suggest some additional source at present unknown.
Anecdotes of Summers are found scattered through
the lighter literature of the time, but most of these apparent sources date from a time subsequent to the
play.   Popular tradition as to Bluff King Harry must
have remained strong throughout the century and it is
doubtless to such unwritten sources that we owe much
in this case.   The daily and domestic life of princes
had a charm to the lowly subject in those days as in
ours.   A scene of this play which represents King
Henry in one of his periodical fits of rage has a quality
so realistic that it is difficult to escape the conviction
that it must have been measurably true to life.

[1] *Dramatic Literature*, II. 549.

Wolsey has presumed to enter the royal presence after the King had charged his courtiers that no one disturb him. The courtiers fall back as they hear their angry lord approaching with the crestfallen intruder who is being roundly abused for his temerity. Will Summers and Patch, the Cardinal's fool, cower in a distant corner, perhaps have crept behind the arras with which the stage, as the presence-chamber, was hung. Will whispers to his trembling fellow: " Lie close, cousin Patch ! " To which the latter replies : " I'll not come near him, cousin ; he's almost killed me with his countenance." The king demanding that the presence-chamber be cleared, Brandon, one of his attendants, in passing out whispers to Summers :

> Now Will, or never ! Make the king but smile,
> And with thy mirthful toys allay his spleen
> .   .   .   .
> And by mine honour, I'll reward thee well.

Left alone with the angry king who is now seated, Will turns to look for his fellow, Patch :

Will.   Where art thou, cousin ? Alas, poor fool, he's
         crept under the table : up, cousin, fear nothing,
         the storm's past, I warrant thee.
Patch. [*Sticking out his head cautiously.*] Is the king
         gone, cousin ?
Will.   No, no, yonder he sits : we are all friends now,
         the lords are gone to dinner, and thou and I
         must wait at the king's table.

Patch.   Not I, by'r lady, I would not wait upon such a
lord for all the livings in the land : I thought he
would have killed my lord cardinal, he looked
so terribly.

Will.   Foh, he did but jest with him.

After some whispered argument and assurance Will,
who is not quite so certain as his words would imply,
persuades poor Patch to become his cat's paw and approach the king to "frighten" him.   We can imagine
the unhappy fool, half trembling, half impudent, slipping up to the side of the frowning monarch and fal-
tering :

Patch.   Bo !

King.   Mother of God, what's that ?

Patch.   Bo !

King.   Out ass, and tumble at my feet,
For thus I'll spurn thee up and down the house.

Patch.   Help, cousin, help.

Will.   No cousin, now he's conjuring ; I dare not come
near him.

King.   Who set this natural here to trouble me ?

Enter Compton.

Who's that stands laughing there ?   The fool ! Ha,
ha !   Where's Compton ?   Mother o'God, I
have found his drift : 'tis the craftiest old villain
in Christendom.   Mark, good Sir William, because the fool durst not come near himself, seeing our anger, he sent this silly ass, that we
might wreak our royal spleen on him, whilst he
stands laughing to behold the jest : by th' blessed

Lady, Compton, I'll not leave the fool to gain
a million, he contents me so. Come hither,
Will.

Will. I'd know whether ye have done knocking first :
my cousin Patch looks pitifully. Ye had best
be friends with us, I can tell you : we'll scare
you out of your skin else.

King. Alas, poor Patch : hold, sirrah, there's an angel
to buy you points.
But wherefore came ye ?

.   .   .   .

Will. To make thee leave thy melancholy and turn
merry man again : thou hast made all the court
in such a pitiful case as passes [understanding].
The lords has attended here this four days and
none dares speak to thee, but thou art ready to
chop off their heads for't : and now I, seeing
what a fretting fury thou continuedst in, and
every one said 'twould kill thee if thou kepst
it, pulled e'en up my heart and vowed to loose
my head, but I'd make thee leave it.

King. Well, William, I am beholding to ye. Ye shall
have a new coat and cap for this.

Will. Nay, then I shall have two new coats and caps,
for Charles Brandon promised me one before
to perform this enterprise.

King. He shall keep his word, Will. Go call him in,
Call in the lords, tell them our spleen is calmed.[1]

The relation of this play of Rowley's to the Shakespearean play on Henry VIII. is a subject attended with

---

[1] *When You See Me You Know Me*, ed. by the late Professor Elze,
Dessau, 1874, p. 20.

some doubt. It seems beyond question that the prologue of *Henry VIII.* refers to *When You See Me You
Know Me* in the words :

> Onely they
> That come to heare a Merry, Bawdy Play,
> A noyse of Targets : Or to see a Fellow
> In a long Motley Coate, guarded with Yellow,
> Will be deceyu'd.

The "noyse of Targets" is the king's fray with
Black Will, the "long Motley Coate" is Summers'
customary dress as fool. It is not unlikely that the
allusion of the epilogue of *Henry VIII.* to the disappointment of the auditors in not hearing the city
abused may refer to Summers' witticism in which
he appears before the king dressed for a journey,
and asked where he is going, replies to London
for the latest news of the happenings at court.[1] So
specific a reference could be significant only in relation to a play at that time holding the boards for the
first time or in revival. We must then either suppose
that Shakespeare's play dates earlier by some years
than is usually admitted, or regard these allusions as
applicable to a revival of *When You See Me* about
1612 or 1613. There is nothing to oppose either
supposition. It is of course not impossible that the
revival of Rowley's play was due, as was frequently
the case, to the staging of *Henry VIII.* at this date ;

[1] *Ibid.*, pp. 29 and 8.

in which case the prologue with its reiteration of the words, *true* and *truth*, as applied to the story, is a re-joinder to the challenge of Rowley's title : *When You See Me You Know Me.*[1]   It remains none the less re-markable that Shakespeare, whose latest chronicle play, if we except this, was staged in 1599, should have re-turned at the very end of his career to the writing of a species of drama now completely out of the popular fashion ; just as it is noteworthy that he should have contributed no play (again if we except the present one) to the group which responded to the popular re-vival of interest in the lately deceased queen.   There is an obvious temptation to suppose that an earlier version of *Henry VIII.*, linking on to the series of plays treating the reigns of Henry and Elizabeth, may have been written by Shakespeare ; and to surmise that this version was intended to be an immediate corrective and reproof of what must have seemed to a lover of the dignity and majesty of royalty like Shakespeare an unworthy misrepresentation of history on the part of Rowley.[2]

Be all this as it may, it is certain that *The Famous History of the Life of King Henry the Eight*, as we have it in the folio of 1623, when it was printed for

---

[1] See the *Prologue* to *Henry VIII.*

[2] See Elze's article *Zu Heinrich VIII.* in the *Shakespeare Jahrbuch*, IX. 55, for an opinion that this play was written in 1603, but set aside because of Elizabeth's death and revived on the performance of Rowley's *When You See Me* after revision by Fletcher.

the first time, dates 1612 or 1613. Three witnesses
attest the burning of the Globe theatre in June of the
latter year, during the performance of a play " representing some principal pieces of the reign of Henry
the Eight, which was set forth with many extraordinary circumstances of pomp and majesty."   And one
of them, Sir Henry Wotton, called the play a new one
and gave it the title *All is True*.[1]   Notwithstanding a
contemporary allusion to a fool in this play—which
may well have been used of such characters in general
or in confusion with Rowley's Will Summers—the
theater, the company and the date all point to this as
the play of Shakespeare's folio.[2]   The prologue, as we
have already seen, suggests the alternative title, which
may have been given the play at a first production or
on a revival in reference to Rowley's title, although,
having served its temporary purpose, it was afterwards
suppressed on publication in the folio.

Henry VIII. has been criticised for its want of unity
and design.   It has been especially objected that " the
greater part of the fifth act, in which the interest ought
to be gathered to a head, is occupied with matters in
which we have not been prepared to take any interest
by what went before, and on which no interest is reflected by what comes after."[3]   Judged apart from

[1] *Reliquiæ Wottonianæ*, 1675, pp. 425–426.

[2] For this allusion and an adverse opinion as to its reference to
Shakespeare's play, see Halliwell-Phillipps, *Outlines of the Life of
Shakespeare*, ed. 1881, p. 187.

[3] The opinion of W. Hertzberg, quoted by Professor Dowden,
Shakspere Primer, p. 154.

the circumstances of its age and the character of the
class of dramas to which it belongs, the justice of
these strictures is not to be denied. But to the Englishman of the day the great events of the reign of
Henry were the great events of this play : the divorce
of Queen Katharine, the fall of Wolsey, the separation from Rome, the rise of Cranmer and Protestantism, the coronation of Queen Anne Bullen and the
birth of Elizabeth. The pathos of the situation of
Queen Katharine had made a deep impression on
England which even the hated faith and nationality of
that unhappy wife could not materially impair. But
Anne Bullen was less remembered as Katharine's successful rival and the cause of her sorrows than as the
mother of the queen that had made England glorious.
A conviction of the innocence of Anne must have
been a canon of the historical faith of every Elizabethan Protestant ; for thus alone could he refute the
calumnies of Rome. In such a view of the unity of
the subject, the rise of Cranmer becomes as important
a topic as the fall of Wolsey, and no more fitting
close for the drama could be conceived than the
christening of that infant who was destined to fulfill the
promise of Protestantism and national greatness. But
even granting all this, there still remains about this
play an inequality which caused Dr. Johnson to observe that " the genius of Shakespeare comes in and
goes out with Katharine " ; while in the very same

year that Johnson wrote this, attention was called to the peculiar character of the blank verse of this play which differs materially in parts from that of Shakespeare.[1]   In this verse there is a tendency to insert an extra syllable after the accent, not only at the end of the line but before a pause within it.   Besides this, there is a more frequent pause at the conclusion of a line than was usual in Shakespeare's later verse. These qualities with some minor ones which need not delay us here, are the recognized " notes " of the versification of John Fletcher, and from their marked peculiarity and persistence in his works and their absence in the work of other dramatists afford a sound criterion of authorship.   In short it is now generally, though by no means universally, accepted that *Henry VIII.* is the joint production of Shakespeare and Fletcher with perhaps the aid of Massinger.[2]   It is surmised that either Fletcher revised and rewrote in part an existing and completed play of Shakespeare's, or that he finished one which Shakespeare had already planned and written in part.   When we recall that Shakespeare retired to Stratford on his well-earned competency about 1611, and that Fletcher's career as

[1] *General Observations on Shakespeare's plays, Works of Johnson.* American ed., 1825, I. 379, and Roderick, *Remarks on Shakespeare,* Edwards, *Canons of Criticism,* ed. 1758, p. 225.

[2] See a *résumé* of this subject in Dowden, *Shakspere—his Mind and Art,* p. 414, and Mr. Sidney Lee's *Life of Shakespeare,* p. 262.   Boyle was of opinion that our present version " contains only fragments of the original play by Shakespeare." *Englische Studien,* X. 393.

a dramatic writer could scarcely have begun much
before 1607, it becomes more likely that Fletcher
dusted with dross the gold of Shakespeare than that
Shakespeare gilded Fletcher's less noble metal.

The famous passage put into the mouth of the fallen
Cardinal and beginning : " Farewell ? A long farewell,
to all my Greatnesse " is certainly of Fletcher's composition.[1]   As Professor Dowden says : " When one
has perceived this, one perceives also that it was an
error ever to suppose it written in Shakspere's manner." [2]   Indeed the interests of the master-dramatist, as
the evening of life drew down upon him, were not in
the warfare of faction, the succession of princes or the
pomp and pageantry of fading greatness. We may
agree with the eminent critic just quoted that to Shakespeare the one absorbing interest of this story of
Henry's reign was " the presence of a noble sufferer,—
one who was grievously wronged, and who by a plain
loyalty to what is faithful and true, by a disinterested-
ness of soul, and enduring magnanimity, passes out of
all passion and personal resentment into the reality of
things, in which much indeed of pain remains, but no
ignoble wrath or shallow bitterness of heart." [3]

Henry VIII. is the latest play that can possibly be
referred to the original impulse which produced the
Chronicle History.   As we advance in the days of King

[1] *Henry VIII.*, III. 2, 351–372.
[2] *Shakspere Primer*, p. 156.
[3] *Shakspere—his Mind and Art*, p. 414.

James the drama which treats of English history becomes rarer and rarer and the few plays that were
written on such themes fall under the romantic spell
or revert back to classical and Senecan imitations.
We may pass two Latin plays, the titles of which suggest their general kinship to the historical drama.
Alvredus sive Alfredus by William Drury was acted
three times by students of the English college at Douay
in the year 1619. Drury was Professor of Poetry and
Rhetoric there and his play, which with a comedy entitled *Mors* was published in the next year, treats of
the life of King Alfred and his deliverance of his
people. *Sanctus Edwardus Confessor* is described by
Halliwell-Phillipps as "an academic play on the story
of Edward the Confessor most probably represented
before King James at one of the Universities." [1] We
may also omit further mention of the lost *Tragedy of
Richard the Third or the English Prophet*, the work of
Samuel Rowley and licensed for the Palgrave's players
in July, 1623; and touch with mere notice another
lost play, *The History of Henry I.*, by Robert Davenport, which was licensed for the King's Company in
the following year. This latter play has been identified with *Henry I. and Henry II.*, registered as the
work of Shakespeare and Davenport in 1653, though
apparently never brought to the press. [2] In this same

---

[1] *Dictionary of Plays*, 1860, p. 219. This play is extant among the
Heber MSS., *Bibliotheca Heberiana*, 1834–36, XI. 113.

[2] Bullen, *Old English Plays*, New Series, III. xi.

years 1624, Sir Henry Herbert licensed for the Palgrave's company an inferior chronicle play entitled
The Life of the Duchess of Suffolk by Thomas Drue.
In granting his license Herbert noted that this play
was "full of dangerous matter" and that it "was much
reformed by me :   I had two pounds for my pains." [1]
The Duchess of Suffolk has not been reprinted since its
appearance in 1631.   Langbaine attributed it incor-
rectly to Heywood but referred its sources correctly
enough to Foxe's *Book of Martyrs* and Clarke's *Mar-
tyrology*.[2]   *The Duchess of Suffolk* in its strong Protestant bias, its crudity of form and construction, and its
general conformity with the earlier Chronicle Play offers
an interesting example of something often repeated in
the history of literature : namely, the indirect or mediate
effect which a literary movement of the past may ex-
ert on writers far removed from actual contact with it.
Of Drue little is known except that he was associated
in the writing of at least one play, *The Woman's Mistake*, with Davenport.   Drue lays the plot of his chronicle play in the days of Queen Mary.   Lady Suffolk,
like the Duchess of Malfi, has married one of her
servants, and for this and for her faith is deprived of
her household and hunted into exile by Bishop Bonner who is absurdly represented as personally aiding
his creatures in their search for the fugitives.   Some

[1] Quoted by Collier, *Dramatic Poetry*, I. 446.
[2] Laingbaine, as above, p. 262.

comedy is furnished by a tyler who inadvertently helps Dr. Sands to escape a hue and cry, and by a servant of the Duchess, named Fox, who devises clumsy tricks, such as a feigned funeral, in his mistress's behoof. Latimer, Ridley, Cranmer and Erasmus are lugged in though nothing to the plot, the first three for their martyrdom, Erasmus to afford the author an opportunity to air his Latinity, such as it is. With Fletcher drawing to the close of a brilliant career and Shirley just beginning his, with plays like *The Changeling* of Middleton and Rowley, and Massinger's *Bondman* and *The Great Duke of Florence* holding the stage, such a production as *The Duchess of Suffolk* is almost inconceivable. Except for a little pathos, picked out by Charles Lamb with the unerring instinct for true literature that was his and quoted in his *Specimens of English Dramatic Poets*,[1] and the increased ease in versification which the veriest poetaster could scarcely have escaped acquiring in an age of such metrical facility, this play exhibits no advance on the rudest specimens of the biographical chronicle. Considering all this, Collier's conjecture that this play was rewritten on a play of Haughton's called *The English Fugitives* mentioned by Henslowe under date of April, 1600, seems not unreasonable.[2]

Although not printed until 1655, Mr. Bullen, the

---

[1] Ed. 1893, II. 247.
[2] See Collier's note, Henslowe, p. 168.

editor of this poet's dramatic works, refers the writing of Robert Davenport's one extant historical drama, *King John and Matilda*, to the year 1624.[1] Of Davenport, who was a writer of other poetry as well as of dramas, we know next to nothing. A paper in that excellent old garner of criticism *The Retrospective Review* justly appraised this play as early as 1821 ; and Charles Lamb included a passage from it in his *Specimens* and discovered " much passion and poetry in it." [2] Though observed without discerning its extent by Genest,[3] it is not generally known that Davenport owes his theme almost wholly to the last four acts of Munday's and Chettle's *The Death of Robert Earl of Huntington*. From this source Davenport borrowed not only this latter story but also the underplot of the cruel torture by a brutal jailor of Lady Bruce and her young son and their agonizing deaths by starvation. Davenport has retained the distinguishing traits of most of the personages of the older play. This is especially true of Matilda's father, Fitzwater, "this mad, merry, feeling, insensible-seeming lord," as Lamb calls him, and the scheming, pitiless and sensual John whom only the honesty of Fitzwater and the steadfastness of his heroic daughter dare withstand. But Davenport has developed the characters of *The Death* as he developed the plot to a degree of excel-

[1] *Old English Plays*, New Series, Vol. III.
[2] *Specimens*, as above, II. 244.
[3] *Some Account of the English Stage since 1660*, ed. 1832, X. 72

18

lence far beyond the attainment of Munday and Chettle. This is especially discernible in the definition of out- line which the latter dramatist gives to the intrigues of John, his treatment of the scene in which Matilda appears as a nun with the abbess on the walls of the Abbey of Dunmowe and his suppression of the gross temptations of Matilda by the abbess and a monk, "two damned spirits in religious weeds." *The Death* too offers little more than a hint of the terrible details of Brand's cruelty to Lady Bruce and her son, of which Mr. Bullen very justly remarks: "It is hardly fair for a playwright to work on our feelings in this ruthless manner." [1]

King John and Matilda is a tragedy of genuine merit and exemplifies in its treatment the long step which had been taken by Shakespeare, Fletcher and others from the use of drama to illustrate a succession of historical events to the employment of historical material for the dramatic delineation of human passion. Despite the subtile portraiture of the most ignoble of English kings, the touching story of Prince Arthur and the lyricism of the grief of Constance, Shake- speare's *King John* is a typical chronicle play. The subject-matter concerns the public life of that king, his relation to France, to Rome and to his rebellious barons at home ; the sequence of events is chronolog- ical. What little unity there is centers in the royal

[1] Bullen, *Old English Plays*, New Series, III., p. x.

malefactor and in his loyal attendant, " Cordelions
Base sonne," whose humorous, honest, and clear-sighted
view of the wrongs and intricacies about him serves
the twofold function of comedy and chorus, and
affords at once a contrast to the somber tone of the
rest of the play and a normal standard by which to
judge among the contending parties. The epic quality
of the Chronicle Drama, already so often adverted to,
is characteristic of this play of Shakespeare to a remarkable degree. There is substantially no action in
the second act in which the French and English
armies meet before the walls of Angiers and bandy
taunts, negotiate and parley, while, during the long
conversations of other parts of the play, the action
halts or is narrated rather than presented on the stage.
In *King John and Matilda* all this is changed. It is
the character of John as a man, not as a king, which
is the central theme ; his unlawful pursuit of the steadfast and resourceful Matilda. Davenport does not lose
sight of the fact that his protagonist is a king and he
presents us with vividness, though only in the background, that portion of the reign of John in which was
concentrated England's deepest degradation : the re-
moval of the papal interdict and John's acceptance of
his crown at the hands of Cardinal Pandulph as vassal
of Rome. In a word, though dealing with historical
material, this play is primarily concerned with the portrayal of passion. Without raising any question of

comparative literary or poetical excellence—a matter
which does not concern us here—Davenport's tragedy
is far less epical than Shakespeare's and must be pronounced unhesitatingly more dramatic.

After the accession of King Charles plays founded
on English history became more and more rare.
With a drama almost evenly divided between romantic
tragi-comedy and the several grades of the comedy
of manners there was no place for productions so different in their appeal.   A few scattered titles of plays
no longer extant may be enumerated.   These are
Duke Humphrey, The History of King Stephen and
The History of Mador King of Britain.   All are entries
made for H. Mosley in 1660.   The first two are therein
ascribed to Shakespeare, the last, with all but equal
absurdity, to Beaumont.   "A play called *Salisbury
Plain*" is also mentioned as entered on the Stationers'
Register in 1653 and is described as a comedy by Halliwell-Phillipps.[1]   It will be remembered that the Gemot
of Salisbury Plain in 1086 was that at which the
Saxon chiefs finally took the oath of allegiance to
William the Conqueror.   All of these plays are dated
roughly by Mr. Fleay as "*Tempore* Charles I."[2]
The last two entries of Sir Henry Herbert's register of
licenses record two plays by a playwright named John
Kirke, from whose pen only one drama, *The Seven
Champions of Christendon*, has come down to us.

[1] *Dictionary of Plays*, 219.
[2] *Biographical Chronicle*, II. 335.

The entry was made in June, 1642, and relates that one of the plays was entitled *The Irish Rebellion*. This was acted about 1623. The other, Herbert reports : "I burnt for the ribaldry and offence that was in it."

The long succession of the English Chronicle Drama comes to an end with John Ford's interesting and successful effort to revive this kind of play, *The Chronicle Historie of Perkin Warbeck*, acted at the Phœnix about 1633. This wholly admirable drama was first printed in 1634. The date of its earliest performance is unknown, but it was doubtless not long prior to this. In his prologue Ford expresses the general attitude of his day towards this all but forgotten species of drama :

> Studyes haue, of this Nature, been of late
> So out of fashion, so vnfollow'd ; that
> It is become more Iustice, to reviue
> The antick follyes of the Times, than striue
> To countenance wise Industrie.

He blames contemporary drama not so much for "want of art" as for "want of truth," and animadverting to another tendency of his time, declares that

> Hee shew's a Historie, couch't in a Play :
> A Historie of noble mention, knowne,
> Famous, and true : most noble, 'cause our owne :
> Not forg'd from Italie, from Fraunce, from Spaine,
> But Chronicled at Home ; as rich a strayne
> Of braue Attempts, as ever fertile Rage
> In Action, could beget to grace the Stage.

Although Ford with this ideal of truth before him has followed his acknowledged authority, Bacon's *Life of Henry VII.*, with fidelity,[1] he has thoroughly appreciated the dramatic possibilities of his subject and contrived a play of consummate constructive excellence clothed in effective characterization and written with grace and uniform artistic restraint. The impostor, Perkin, is drawn with genuine skill. His very unreality, of which Professor Ward complains,[2] is a necessary element of the dramatist's problem, which demanded that he produce in the spectator the same doubt as to the truth of the pretentions of Warbeck which rendered explainable his temporary success. Hence, though followed by a paltry retinue of some half dozen broken tradesmen who cut a sorry figure at the court of Edinburgh, the reputed Duke of York is of handsome person, engaging and courtly bearing and manners whereby he wins the chivalrous King James to his cause and gains and holds to the end the love of James's beautiful and high-spirited kinswoman, Katharine Gordon. On the other hand neither Perkin's virtues nor his graces impose on the keen-sighted but honorable old Earl of Huntley, and at the turning point of the play, it is Perkin's humane but "effeminately dolent" expostulation against the Scottish king's order to devastate England, which opens that mon-

[1] Cf. Gehler, *Das Verhaeltnis von Fords Perkin Warbeck zu Bacons Henry VII.*, 1895.

[2] *Dramatic Literature*, III. 85.

arch's eyes to the real nature of the man whose cause
he has espoused.[1] In the end the tragic fortitude of
Perkin, who accepts death rather than acknowledge
himself an impostor, is artfully contrived to leave us
alike unconvinced of his genuine royalty and yet
compassionate of an imposture which from inveteracy
has become a delusion. Warbeck with his petty following is brought guarded before King Henry who,
curiously regarding the defeated claimant for his
throne, addresses their captor :

> Dawbney,
> We obserue no wonder ; I behold ('tis true)
> An ornament of nature, fine and pollisht,
> A handsome youth indeede, but not admire him.
> How came he to thy hands?
>
> . . . . . .
>
> *Dawb.*   Gracious Lord,
> They voluntarily resign'd themselues
> Without compulsion.
> *K. H.*   So ? 'twas very well ;
> T'was very very well—turne now thine eyes
> (Young man) vpon thy selfe, and hy past ac-
>   tions.
> What revells in combustion through our King-
>   dome,
> A frenzie of aspiring youth hath daunc'd,
> Till wanting breath, thy feete of pride haue slipt
> To breake thy necke.
> *Warb.*   But not my heart ; my heart
> Will mount, till every drop of bloud be frozen
> By deaths perpetuail Winter : If the Sunne

[1] *Perkin Warbeck*, III. 4.

> Of Maiestie be darkened, let the Sunne
> Of Life be hid from mee, in an eclipse
> Lasting and vniversall.

And Warbeck continues, reminding the king of his own small following when he landed at Milford Haven. Dawbney breaks in :

>   Whither speeds his boldnesse ?
> Checke his rude tongue (great Sir !)

K. H.   O let him range :
> The player's on the stage still, 'tis his part ;
> A' does but act.
> .   .   .   .

> The lesson prompted, and well conn'd, was moulded
> Into familiar Dialogue, oft rehearsed,
> Till learnt by heart, 'tis now, receiv'd for truth.
> .   .   .   .

>   Sirra, shift
> Your anticke Pageantrie, and now appeare
> In your owne nature, or y'oule taste the daunger
> Of fooling out of season.

Warb.   I expect
> No lesse, than what severitie calls Iustice,
> And Politicians safetie ; let such begge,
> As feed on almes : but if there can be mercie
> In a protested enemie, then may it
> Descend to these poor creatures, whose engagements
> To th' bettering of their fortunes, haue incur'd
> A losse of all ; to them, if any charitie

>   Flowe from some noble Orator, in death
>   I owe the fee if thankfulnesse.
> *K. H.*   So braue ! [1]

In the words of Henry whose prudence and far-
reaching diplomacy are set forth in this play with less
shadow and suspicion than Bacon suggests :

>   The custom, sure, of being styled a King
>   Hath fasten'd in his thought that he is such.

Altogether, it cannot but be regretted that the demands of an age which from long surfeit of delicacies
had come only to regard spiced meats and a flavor
somewhat high, should have seduced so strong and
fundamentally healthful a genius as that of John Ford
from the historical drama in which he was fitted to
occupy a place beside Marlowe and Shakespeare.

In 1637 a play called *The Valiant Scot* was printed
as "by J. W. Gent." The dedication to the Marquess
of Hamilton was signed "by the Publisher and Pro-
moter of the Copy to the Press, Mr. William Bowyer."[2]
"The subject of the play," says Ward, "is the career
and catastrophe of Sir William Wallace, dealt with in
the artless fashion of a Chronicle History, but with
the addition of a romantic effect or two suggested by
later theatrical reminiscences." [3] According to an epitome of its contents given by Genest it follows closely
the Scottish tradition of the life of Wallace and ap-

[1] *Ibid.*, V. 2.
[2] Langbaine, p. 523.
[3] *Dramatic Literature*, III. 159.

pears to have been, as acted, a play of considerable bustle and vivacity.[1]   Although possibly beyond the range of our period this long tale of the English Chronicle Drama may be concluded with the mention of *Colas Furie or Lyrenda's Miserie*, by one Henry Birkhead, printed in 1645.   This extraordinary hodgepodge of bombast and bathos is an attempt to place the contemporary events of the Irish rebellion of 1641 on the stage under the thin disguise of feigned names.   The play is preceded by much dedicatory nonsense by unknown writers, the friends of the author, in which he is compared to Jonson and Shakespeare. Birkhead is innocent of the most rudimentary conception of verse and is content to dole out ten syllables to each line, come what may.   The songs—for Birkhead even attempts to sing—are beyond the fondest brayings of Bottom in the period of his transformation. Indeed this unlucky dramatist furnishes us his own inglorious epitaph in the words of one of his characters : " Here's needless fustian."   On the border of our period, if not beyond it, is the anonymous blending of the two parts of *Henry IV*. into one play and a production entitled *Edmund Ironside : the English King or a trew chronicle History called War hath made all Friends*.   The former was first printed for the Shakespeare Society in 1845 ; the latter remains in manuscript in the British Museum.[2]   Halliwell-

[1] Genest, as above, X. 107.
[2] *Egerton MS.* 1994.

Phillipps states that it was written about 1647 ;[1] an Mr. Bullen curtly dismisses it with the words: "tedious business."[2] Neither of these productions need detain us.

The representation of the popular drama on the Elizabethan stage is a subject worthy of careful attention. A word as to certain salient characteristics of the Chronicle Play as acted, however, must here suffice. The construction of the Elizabethan stage was utilized by the historical drama to the full. The stage of the period provided after its original, the inn yard, a balcony which was raised some few feet above the general stage. In the chronicle plays this balcony commonly represented the walls of a besieged city. Parley was held from it, scaling-ladders raised against it, the routed enemy leaped from it, as did Prince Arthur in his attempted escape. In *1 Henry VI.* this balcony represents one of the turrets of inspection which the besieging English had reared against Orleans ; and Salisbury is slain in it by a cannon-shot from the stage, which in this instance is taken to be the rampart of the beleaguered town. The balcony was also employed to indicate an inner room or the dais. Thus, in *Richard III.*, when the citizens are brought in to behold the Duke of Gloucester's godliness and reluctance to take the cares of state upon him, Rich-

[1] *Dictionary of Plays*, p. 82.
[2] *Old English Plays*, II. 420.

ard is represented as entering "aloft, betweene two Bishops." Under the balcony were two doors which were variously used. The stage, though devoid of what we now call scenes, was hung with arras or hangings spread on wooden frames. It was behind such an arras that Falstaff was discovered by Prince Henry "asleep, and snorting like a Horse." The use of a hanging as a means of changing scene is to be found in *Sir Thomas More* where an arras is "drawne" after the first scene, which is evidently that of a street, "and behinde it (as in sessions) sit the L. Maior, . . the prisoner at the barre." Properties were simple. The state of the Chancellor in this same play is indicated by "a table, being couered with a greene carpet, a state cushion on it and the Pursse and Mace lying thereon." A scaffold with ascending ladder or stairs ordinarily appears in scenes representing executions. The cottage of George a Greene is mentioned in the play of that title and a castle in *John a Kent;* while in the last-named play it is directed that a spirit rise from under the stage, whither the witches of *Macbeth* may have disappeared, and that another spirit come "out of a tree, if possible it may be." The difficulty of representing warfare, tumult and masses of people on the stage was recognized not only by the playwrights but by their critics and satirists as well. This difficulty was met in part by noise and bustle, by the rattle of arms, the clash of swords, the beating of drums and blowing of trumpets. Even ordnance and chambers—the contemporary terms for cannon—were frequently discharged to increase the verisimilitude of victory or battle. A memorable example of the danger of this practice is mentioned above in the burning of the Globe theater in 1613. On that occasion a wadding used in charging a cannon on the stage ignited the thatched roof, and the building which was wholly of wood was speedily in ruins. Although in the representation of battle we commonly have "enter the two kings with their powers at severall doors" or "march over bravelie first the English Hoste," the device in action was to center interest in the single encounter, in which these plays abound, and by "beating in" and reëntry to signify a varied and running fight. Sometimes the aid of tableaux was invoked to represent scenes of war : "Enter two battailes strongly fighting" ; or we have "alarmes and excursions," in which the activity of the entrances and exits doubtless made up for the small number of the actors engaged. Effects of sound, "alarm afarre off," "a sound of battle as afarre" are also common stage directions.

The Elizabethan "dumb shew" was seldom a stationary tableau. It usually partook more or less of the nature of a pantomime. The action might be allegorically illustrated as in the well-known dumb shows of *Gorboduc*. A show of this kind in *The Misfortunes of Arthur* introduces nymphs with sheaves,

olive branches and cornucopia to represent Peace, and
one "with black, long shagged haire downe to his
shoulders appairled with an Irish Iacket and shirt,
hauing an Irish dagger by his side and a dart in his
hand" to signify "Reuenge and Furie." Not infrequently the show was so devised as to carry on the
action. Thus in *1 If You Know Not Me* such a show
enters, attended by six torches, and representing the
court of Philip and Mary. The king and queen
"conferre, he takes leaue, and exit. Nobles bring
him to the door and returne ; she falls in a swound ;
they comfort her." In *The Death of Robert Earl of
Huntington* there are many elaborate shows of this
kind, in one of which the story of King John and his
nephew is thus told in pantomime. John is represented seated on his throne, "enter Constance, leading
young Arthur : both offer to take the crown, but with
his foot he [John] overturneth them ; to them cometh
Insurrection . . . and leads the child again to the chair ;
but he only layeth his hand on his sword, and with his
foot overthroweth the child, whom they take up as
dead ; and, Insurrection flying, they mournfully bear in
the body." In later times when the splendid scenic
devices of the masque reacted on the popular stage,
some of these shows were extremely elaborate and
sumptuous. The shows of *Henry VIII.* are indicated
at length in the stage directions and are reported to
have been of great magnificence and cost. Indeed it

would not be difficult to establish the existence of a
series of fashions in these particulars from the allegorical dumb show, the employment of ghost and
dream, the use of the play within the play, to the
later tableaux pantomime.   But the subject concerns
the drama at large rather than the Chronicle Play.

It requires an effort of mind to conceive Munday's
Sherwood Forest, although he is continually prating
about it.   In *As You Like It* we breathe without any
effort the free air of the Forest of Arden.   That fair
Temple Garden wherein was plucked the red and the
white rose which divided England against herself and
sent thousands of her sons to untimely graves ; that
other garden in which the queen of Richard II. overheard the gardener's shrewd homily on state-craft,
couched in vegetable terms ; the " mole-hill " on which
pious Henry sat and bewailed in impotent grief the
woes of his unhappy country while nature smiled
around him—how are these things the better for the
scene-painter's art ?   *Locrine* begins with thunder and
the entrance of Até ; and the birth of Merlin is heralded
by the appearance of Lucina and the three Fates,
which a scenic fitting unknown to the Elizabethan
stage might enhance and which stage carpentry might
improve.   But could painter's art make more real the
enchanted moonlit copses and thyme-scented glades of
the wood near Athens, or more veritable " the mire and
puddle " of the dungeon-sink which the piteous words

of King Edward carry to the mind's eye ? Such art
can dispense with carpentry. The best Elizabethan
plays lost little in the contemporary paucity and pov-
erty of scenic device.

In the foregoing pages we have traced the origin,
development and decline of the English Chronicle
Play. We found in the play of St. George a link
which seemed to connect the national drama with the
miracle plays and saints' plays, while *Kinge Johan*
offered a corresponding point of contact with the
political morality to which it is allied from its polemical
intent and use of abstract figures, despite its concern
with alleged historical personages and events. The
national spirit first glimmered in the dramatized ballads of Robin Hood, in the few but unmistakable
pageants in which historical personages are represented
and in the imitated action of the *Hock Tuesday Play*
which was commemorative of an actual historical
occurrence.

That the earliest English tragedy, *Gorboduc*, should
have drawn on a subject derived from English mythological lore is a circumstance to which an undue significance may be readily attached. That famous play
with its direct follower, *The Misfortunes of Arthur*,
and the Latin *Richardus Tertius* are purely Senecan
dramas, which departing from the usual classical subjects of their type have strayed into English fields.

But the choice of such subjects, however accidental, had great effect on what was to come. *Locrine,* though hardly a successful combination of Senecan dignity and terror with popular comedy and horse-play, is none the less the link between the Senecan ideal and that of the early popular stage. It is, how-ever, in productions such as *The Famous Victories of King Henry the Fift,* and *The Troublesome Raigne of John* that we find the first genuine chronicle plays and their vogue at the moment when Elizabeth by the irrevocable step of the trial and execution of Mary Queen of Scots had placed herself at the head of a united nation in open defiance to the power of Spain and of Rome, is as interesting as it is significant. From this point on the Chronicle Play held the stage against the romantic drama, the comedy of manners and the older tragedy of Senecan or classic type, never once losing its hold on the popular imagination until King James was firmly seated on his throne and new and changed ideals had succeeded to those of the earlier reign. The main stock of the Chronicle Play which reached its height in Shakespeare's trilogy of *Henry IV.* and *V.* continued from first to last to dis-play an epic quality, to mingle serious political events with the relieving comedy of daily life and to straggle in a mere succession of scenes devoid for the most part of abstract unity. It strayed into regions of folk-lore and pseudo-history and after an interval returned to

19

mythological themes.   It indulged, with a large class of plays not based on English subjects, in disguises and in the supernatural and, in rare instances, reverted to the satirical and to the didactic.   But out of this confusion was developed the superior unity of the biographical chronicle and a tragic type of high artistic quality which passed beyond the local and national limitations of plays like *Edward II.* and *Richard III.* and became in *Lear* and *Macbeth* a world drama of universal appeal.   The final absorption of the historical drama was romantic : the absorption of all other species of the serious drama of the age.   In the romantic drama the trend is ever towards greater novelty of subject and greater novelty of treatment ; and this it was which led the historical drama away from English topics to those of strange countries in which the fancy might wander and the playwright might feel himself untrammeled by the narrowing claims of consistency.

These pages have been written in vain if they have not made patent the intensely English nature of the Chronicle Play.   To say that the Chronicle Play would have developed in the reign of Queen Elizabeth as it did, despite the classics of the universities and the Italian culture of the court would be to say too much. And yet it is significant that with few exceptions these plays were written to supply a popular demand of the moment and won their success on the boards of the

public theaters.   A chronicle play from the hand of
John Lyly is inconceivable.   In the hands of Jonson, if
we may judge from the fragment of *Mortimer his Fall*,
it would have been transformed into a classical tragedy
like his *Cataline*, as in Fletcher's hands it was actually
transformed into the romantic tragi-comedy, *Bonduca*.
That Shakespeare should have been the most successful writer of chronicle plays was in the nature of
things, because he was the truest realist of his age.
That competitors like Heywood and Samuel Rowley
should at times in the opinion of their contemporaries
have rivalled his popularity is explainable by the
homely truth of their representations of the life about
them.   On the other hand it is the ideal element in
the chronicle histories of Shakespeare, it is their sheer
poetry, which has preserved them a perennial joy to
us.   Merely realistic art has ever within it the element
of decay.   The comments of the archæologist must
be invoked to embalm what otherwise would fall away
into indistinguishable dust.   And when the archæologist has done his work he has but preserved a corpse.
Not so is it with the art which the poet has touched.
The ideal has entered into it, and in so doing has im-
bued it with the indestructibility of spirit.   This is
why we read the chronicle plays of Munday and
Dekker with an interest and curiosity which rises to
real pleasure in many of the scenes of Greene and
Heywood.   This is why, if we except a solitary play
of Ford and of Marlowe, we find enduring delight in
the chronicle plays of Shakespeare alone.

TABLE OF EXTANT PLAYS IN SUBJECT WHOLLY OR PARTLY FROM ENGLISH HISTORY.

Italics denote Latin Plays, all of which save Byrsa Basilica are Senecan. The King of Scots is non-extant, but is included because of its historical position. Marginal figures denote approximate dates of acting.

	HISTORICAL MORALITIES.	HISTORIES AND BIOGRAPHIES.	SENECAN DERIVATIVES.
1538	Kynge Johan.		
1562			Gorboduc.
1566	Albyon Knight.		
1567		(King of Scots).	
1570		*Byrsa Basilica.*	
1579			*Richardus Tertius.*
1580		Victories of Henry V.	
1586			*Ricardus Tertius.*
"			Locrine.

	PSEUDO-HISTORY AND FOLK-LORE.		
1587		Jack Straw.	Misfortunes of Arthur.
1589	James IV.	1, 2 Raigne of John.	
"	Fair Em.		
"	George a Greene.		
1590		1, 2 Contention.	
"		Edward I.	
"		Edward II.	
"		Edward III.	
"		Sir Thomas More.	
"		1 Henry VI.	
1591	Friar Bacon.	True Tragedy of Richard III.	
"		Woodstock.	
1592		2, 3 Henry VI.	

			MYTHICAL HISTORIES.
1592			Nobody and Somebody.
"		Cromwell.	Knack to Know.
1593		Richard III.	
1594		Richard II.	
"	John a Kent.	1, 2 Edward IV.	King Leir.

	Pseudo-Histories and Folk-Lore.	Histories and Biographies.	Mythical Histories.
1595		King John.	Valiant Welshman.
1596	Old Fortunatus.	Stukeley.	Mayor of Queenborough.
1597		1, 2 Henry IV.	Birth of Merlin.
1598	1, 2 Huntington.	Oldcastle.	
1599		Henry V.	
"	Look About You.		
"	Shoemakers' Holiday.		
1600	Blind Beggar of Bednal.		*Fatum Vortigerni.*
1601	Satiromastix.		
1602		Mortimer (Senecan).	
"		Sir Thomas Wyatt.	
1604		When You See Me.	
"	Lovesick King.	1, 2 If You Know Not Me.	
"	Maid of Bristow.	Whore of Babylon.	
1605			King Lear.
1606		Battle of Hexham.	Macbeth.

	Travels and Adventure.		
1607	Travels of Three Brothers.		
1609	Fortune by Land and Sea.		Cymbeline.
1610	Christian Turned Turk.		
1612	Maid of the West.		
1613		Henry VIII.	
1616			Bonduca.
1619	Sad Shepherd (Folk-Lore).		*Alfredus.*
1620	Warwick (Folk-Lore).		*Sanctus Edwardus.*
"	Serule and Astrea (German).		
1624		Duchess of Suffolk.	
"		John and Matilda.	
1625	Dick of Devonshire.		Fuimus Troes.
1633	Royal King.	Perkin Warbeck.	
1636	Alphonsus of Germany.		
"	Arviragus and Philicia.		
1637		Valiant Scot.	
1644		Henry IV.	
1645		Cola's Fury.	
1647		Edmund Ironside.	

A LIST OF PLAYS ON ENGLISH HISTOR-
ICAL SUBJECTS.

Non-extant plays are printed in Italics. *The first date is that of
probable acting ; the second that of earliest publication. L. stands for*
Latin ; *H., for* Henslowe's Dairy ; *S. R., for the* Register of the Stationers' Company ; *Sh. for Shakespeare.*

Albyon Knight, 1566. Sh. Soc. Papers, 1844.
Alucius, A History of, 1579. Revels' Accounts, Sh. Soc.
     1842. 154.
Alice Pierce, 1597, H. 105.
All is True, 1613. Henry VIII. See Reliquiæ Wottonianæ,
     1675.
Allyn the Pirate, 1603. See *The Siege of Dunkirk.*
Alphonsus of Germany, 1636? Chapman ? 1654 ; ed. Elze,
     1867.
Aluredus sive Alfredus, L. 1619, Drury, 1620.
Arthur, The Life and Death of King, 1598, Hathway. H.
     122.
Arthur, The Misfortunes of, 1587, Hughes and others, 1587.
     Ed. Grumbine, Litt. Forschungen, XIV.
Arviragus and Philicia, 1636, Carlell, 1639. Genest X.

Battle of Alcazar, The, 1589, Peele, 1594. Bullen's Peele,
     1888.
Battle of Hexham, The, 1606? Barnes, MS. extant in 1807.
Beauchamps, The Bold, 1599, Heywood? See Dyce, Beau-
     mont and Fletcher, I. 274.
Bear a Brain, 1599, H. 155.
Beggar, 1 Blind, of Bednal Green, 1600, Day, Chettle, 1659 ;
     Bullen's Day, 1881
Beggar, 2 Blind, of Bednal Green, 1601, Day, Haughton.
     H. 180.

Beggar, 3 Blind, of Bednal Green, 1601, Day, Haughton. H. 188.

Belin Dun, 1594, S. R. 1594. See *Chronicle of Henry I.*

Birth of Merlin, The, 1597, William Rowley, 1662; ed. Warnke and Proeschoeldt, 1887.

Blacksmith's Daughter, The, 1579. Gosson, School of Abuse.

Bonduca, 1616, Fletcher. Folio 1647.

Brute, The Conquest of, 1598, Chettle, Day. H. 131.

Brute Greenshield, 1598. H. 147.

Buckingham, 1593. H. 31.

Byrsa Basilica, L. 1570, Rickets. Tanner MS. 207. See Sh. Jahrbuch XXXIV.

Canute, 1597. H. 91.

Caradoc the Great, The Chronicle History of. See The Valiant Welshman.

Chester Tragedy. See *Randall Earl of Chester.*

Child hath lost his Father, The. See The Birth of Merlin.

Chinon of England, The History of, 1596. H. 62. S. R. 1596.

Christian Turned Turk, A, 1610. Daborne, 1612. Anglia XX.

Cola's Fury, Birkhead, 1645; 1646.

Conan Prince of Cornwall, 1598, Dekker, Drayton. H. 136.

Conquest of Portugal, The. See *The Life of the Humorous Earl of Gloucester.*

Conquest of Spain, The. See *John of Gaunt.*

Contention, 1. The first part of the, betwixt York and Lancaster, 1590. Quarto, 1594; facsimile, 1889.

Contention, 2. The True Tragedy, with the Whole, between Lancaster and York, 1590. Quarto, 1595; facsimile, 1891.

Cromwell, The Life and Death of Lord, 1592. Ed. 1602: "Written by W. S." Sh. Folio, 1663–64. Ed. Jacob, 1889.

Cutwell. See *The Irish Knight.*

Cymbeline, The Tragedy of, 1609, Sh. Folio, 1623.

Dick of Devonshire, 1625. Bullen, Old English Plays, II.

Edmund Ironside, 1647,   Egerton MS. 1994.

Edward I., The Famous Chronicle of King, 1590, Peele, 1593.
Bullen's Peele, 1888.

Edward I. See *Longshanks.*

Edward II.. The Troublesome Reign of, 1590, Marlowe, 1594.

Edward III., The Reign of King, 1590 ; 1596.   Temple Dramatists, 1897.

Edward IV., 1 King, 1594, Heywood, 1600.   Ed. 1874, I.

Edward IV., 2 King, 1594, Heywood, 1600.   See Part 1.

Edwardus Confessor, Sanctus, L. 1620.   Heber MS. 1091,
Bibliotheca Heberiana XI.

Elizabeth, The Troubles of Queen. See 1 If You Know Not Me.

Elizabeth, The Victory of Queen. See 2 If You Know Not Me.

Elydure, The Chronicle History of, See Nobody and Somebody.

England's Joy, 1602, Vennar.   Harl. Miscellany, ed. 1813. X.

English Fugitives, The, 1600, Haughton.   H. 168.   See the
Duchess of Suffolk.

English Prophet, The. See *Richard III.*

Fair Em the Miller's Daughter of Manchester, 1589. Wilson ?
1631.   Ed. Warnke and Proeschoeldt, 1883.

Fair Maid of Bristow, The, 1604 ; 1605.   Ed. Quinn, 1902.

Fair Maid of the West, The, 1, 2, 1612, Heywood, 1631.
Ed. 1874, III.

Fatum Vortigerni, L. 1590–1605, MS. Lansdowne 723.   Sh.
Jahrbuch XXXIV.

Ferrex and Porrex.   See Gorboduc.

Ferrex and Porrex, 1599, Haughton.   H. 166.

Fortune by Land and Sea, 1609, Heywood and W. Rowley,
1655.   Ed. 1874, VI.

Friar Bacon and Friar Bungay, 1591, Greene, 1594, Grosart's
Greene, XIII.

Fuimus Troes, 1625, Fisher, 1633.   Dodsley XII.

Gentle Craft, The.   See The Shoemakers' Holiday.

George a Greene, A Comedy of, 1589, Greene, 1599, Grosart's
Greene, XIV.

Gloucester, The Life of the Humorous Earl of, Wadeson. H. 183.

Godwin and his Three Sons, Earl, 1598, Drayton, Dekker, Chettle, Wilson. H. 121.

Godwin, The Second Part of, 1598, Drayton, Dekker, Chettle, Wilson. H. 123.

Gorboduc, 1562, Sackville, Norton, 1565, Ed. L. Toulmin Smith, 1883.

Guy Earl of Warwick, The Life and Death of, S. R. 1620, Day, Dekker, 1661.

Hardicanute, 1597. H. 91.

Harford, The Earl of, 1602. H. 226.

Harry of Cornwall, 1592. H. 21.

Hengist King of Kent, 1597. H. 89. Earlier title of the Mayor of Queenborough.

Henry I., The Famous Chronicle of. S. R. 1597 ; H. 35, 88.

Henry I., The History of. Licensed 1624, Davenport.

Henry I. and Henry II. S. R. 1653. ''Shakespeare and Davenport.'' Warburton MS.

Henry I. and the Prince of Wales, The Famous Wars of, 1598. Drayton, Dekker, Chettle. H. 120.

Henry IV., 1 The History of, 1597. Sh. 1598.

Henry IV., 2 The Second Part of, 1598. Sh., 1600.

Henry IV., MS., 1644 ; Sh. Soc. 1845.

Henry V., 1595. H. 61.

Henry V., The Chronicle History of, 1599. Sh., 1600.

Henry V., The Famous Victories of, 1580, Tarlton ? 1598. Facsimile Reprint, 1887.

Henry VI., The First Part of, 1590, Greene, Peele, Marlowe, Sh. Folio 1623.

Henry VI., The Second Part of, 1591–92, Revision by Sh. Folio 1623.

Henry VI., The Third Part of, 1591–92. Revision by Sh. Folio 1623.

Henry Richmond, The Second Part of, 1599. H. 159.

Henry VIII., The Famous Chronicle History of. See When You See Me.

Henry VIII., The Famous History of the Life of King, 1612–
    13. Sh. and Fletcher. Folio, 1623.
Humphrey, Duke, S. R. 1660.
Huntington, 1 The Downfall of Robert Earl of, 1598. Mun-
    day, Chettle, 1601. Dodsley VIII.
Huntington, 2 The Death of Robert Earl of, 1598. Munday,
    Chettle, 1601. Dodsley VIII.

If You Know Not Me, 1. 1604, Heywood, 1605. Sh. Soc.
    1851.
If You Know Not Me, 2. 1604, Heywood, 1606. Sh. Soc.
    1851.
Irish Knight, The, 1577. Revels' Accounts, 114. Sh. Soc.
    1842.
Irish Rebellion, The, 1642. Kirke.

Jack Straw, The Life and Death of, 1587. Dodsley V.
Jack Straw and Wat Tyler, The Life and Death of, S. R.
    1638, Kirke. See Genest, X.
James IV. The Scottish History of, 1589, Greene, 1598. Ed.
    Grosart, XIII.
Jane Grey, 1 Lady, 1602, Dekker, Heywood, Smith, Webster.
    H. 242. Earlier version of Sir Thomas Wyatt.
Jane Grey, 2 Lady, 1602, Dekker. H. 243.
John, 1 The Troublesome Reign of, 1588; 1591, facsimile,
    1888.
John, 2 The Troublesome Reign of, 1588–89. See Part 1.
John, The Life and Death of King, 1595. Sh. Folio, 1623.
John a Kent and John a Cumber, 1594, Munday. Sh. Soc.
    1851.
John and Matilda, King, 1624, Davenport, 1655. Bullen's
    Old Plays, n. s., I.
John of Gaunt, The Conquest of Spain by, 1601. Hathway,
    Rankins. H. 185. S. R. 1594.

King of Scots, The Tragedy of the, 1567. Harl. MS. 146.
Knack to Know a Knave, A, 1592; 1594. Dodsley VI.

Koeniges Sohn aufs Engelandt, Eine Comoedia von eines,
1620 ; 1630.   Cohn, Sh. in Germany, cviii.

Lear, Master William Shakespeare, his History of King, 1605 ;
1608.
Leir, The Tragical Chronicle History of King, S. R., 1605.
See the True Chronicle History of King Leir.
Leir, The True Chronicle History of King, 1594 ; 1605.   Haz-
litt's Sh. Library, Part II., Vol. II.
Locrine, The Tragedy of, 1586, Peele, 1595.   Tyrrell, Doubt-
ful Plays of Sh., n. d.
Longshanks, 1595.   H. 55.   S. R. 1600.
Look About You, 1599, Wadeson, 1600.   Dodsley VII.
Lovesick King, The, 1604, Brewer, 1655.
Lud, King, 1594.   H. 32.
Lyrenda's Mysery.   See Cola's Fury.

Macbeth, The Tragedy of, 1606.   Sh. Folio 1623.
Mador, The History of, S. R., 1660.
Malcolm, King of Scots, 1602.   H. 219.
Mandeville, Sir John, 1592.   H. 21.
Martin Swarte, 1597.   H. 89.
Marshall Osric, 1602.   H. 85.
Mary, The Coronation of Queen, See Sir Thomas Wyatt.
Mayor of Queenborough, The, 1596, Middleton, 1661.   Bul-
len's Middleton II.
More, Sir Thomas, 1590–96.   Ed. Dyce, Sh. Soc., 1844.
Mortimer His Fall, 1602, Jonson.   H. 226.   See fragment
in folio 1640.
Mulmutius Dunwallow, 1596, Rankins.   H. 135.

Nobody and Somebody, 1592, [1606.]   School of Sh. I.
Northern Man, The.   See *Too Good to be True*.

Oldcastle, 1 The Life of Sir John, 1598, Munday, Drayton,
Wilson, Hathway, 1600.   H. 158.   Sh. fol. 1663–64.
Oldcastle, 2 The Second Part of Sir John, 1599, Drayton.
H. 158.

Old Fortunatus, 1596, Dekker, 1600.   Ed. 1873, I.
Overthrow of the Rebels, The, 1602.   H. 244.
Owen Tudor, 1600, Hathway, Wilson.   H. 163.

Perkin Warbeck, The Chronicle History of, 1633.   Ford, 1634.
    Ed. Pickburn, 1896.
Philip of Spain, 1602.   H. 225.
Philip, The Coming of King.   See Sir Thomas Wyatt.
Piers of Exton, Sir, 1598, Wilson, Dekker, Drayton, Chettle.
    H. 121.
Piers of Winchester, 1598, Dekker, Drayton, Wilson.   H. 129.
Pinner of Wakefield, The.   See George a Greene.
Plantation of Virginia, A Tragedy of the.   Licensed 1623.

Randall, Earl of Chester, 1602, Middleton.   H. 227.
Richard Cordelion's Funeral, 1598, Wilson Drayton, Chettle,
    Munday.   H. 124.
Richard, Duke of York, The True Tragedy of.   See 2 Con-
    tention.
Richard the Confessor, 1593.   H. 31.   Fleay II. 298.
Richard II., A Tragedy on.   Mentioned by Forman, 1611.
Richard II., A Tragedy of King.   See Woodstock.
Richard II., The Deposing of, 1601, Sh.'s Richard II.
Richard II., The Tragedy of King, 1594, Sh., 1597.
Ricardus Tertius, L., 1586, Lacey.   MS.   See Retrospective
    Rev. XII.
Richardus Tertius Tragedia, L., 1579, Legge.   Ed. Sh. Soc.,
    1844.
Richard III., The Tragedy of, 1593, Sh. 1597.
Richard III., The Tragedy of, or the English Prophet,
    Licensed 1623.   Samuel Rowley.
Richard III., 1 The True Tragedy of, 1591.   Ed. Sh. Soc.,
    1844.
Richard Crookback, 1602, Jonson.   H. 223.
Robert II. King of Scots, 1599, Jonson, Dekker, Chettle.   H.
    156.

Robin Hood.   See Huntington.
Robin Hood, A Tale of.   See The Sad Shepherd.
Robin Hood, The New Play of.   Pr. [1550.]
Robin Hood and Little John.   A Pastoral Comedy of, S. R.
    1594.
Robin Hood's Pennyworths, 1600, Haughton.   H. 174.
Royal Exchange, The Building of the.   See If You Know Not
    Me, 2.
Royal King and Loyal Subject, 1633, Heywood, 1637.   Sh.
    Soc., 1850.   Ed. 1874, VI.

Sad Shepherd, The, 1619, Jonson.   Folio 1640.
St. George for England, 1615–1623, William Smith.   War-
    burton MS.
St. Patrick for Ireland, 1658, Shirley.   1640.   Ed. Dyce, IV.
Salisbury Plain, S. R., 1653.
Satiromastix, 1601, Dekker, 1602.   Ed. 1873, I.
Serule and Astrea.   See Eine Comoedia von eines Koeniges
    Sohn aufs Engelandt.
Shoemakers' Holiday, The, 1599, Dekker, 1600.
Shore's Wife, 1599, Chettle, Day.   H. 214.
Siege of Dunkirk, The, 1602.   H. 231.
Siege of Edinburgh Castle, The, Davidson, 1573.   Andrew
    Melville's *Diary.*
Siege of London, The, 1594.   H. 46.
Six Clothiers of the West, 1601, Haughton, Hathway, Smith.
    H. 203.
Six Yeomen of the West, 1601, Haughton, Day.   H. 188.
Spencers, The, 1599, Chettle, Porter.   H. 146.
Stephen, The History of King, S. R., 1660.
Stewtley, 1596.   See Sir Thomas Stukeley, H. 77.
Strowd, Thomas.   See *2* and *3 Blind Beggar of Bednal
    Green.*
Stukeley, The History of Captain Thomas, 1596, 1605.   School
    of Sh. I.
Suffolk, The Life of the Duchess of.   Licensed 1624, Drue,
    1631.

INDEX.

20

INDEX

INDEX   299

JACOB, T. E., 216
JACOBS, JOSEPH, 171
Jahrbuch der deutschen Shake-speare-Gesellschaft, see *Shake-speare*
JAMES (a Scottish King), 155; JAMES I., 1, 34, 37, 38, 52, 110, 196, 205, 254, 273; JAMES IV., 56, 167, 262; *Scottish Historie of*, 30, 53, 56, 72, 166–169
Jamy, 130, 133
Jesuits, 232, 239
Jew of Malta, 221
Joan Go-too-t, 184, 189; Joan of Arc, 53, 127
JOHN, KING, vii, 17, 47–49, 52, 257–259, 270; as prince, 158, 160, 163, 164; *Kynge Johan*, 16, 19, 28; *Troublesome Raigne of*, 40–50, 53, 57, 60, 63, 273; *Life and Death of*, 47, 258, 260; *and Matilda*, 257–260; JOHN, PRINCE (son of Henry IV.), 117; JOHN OF GAUNT, 52, 111, 220
John a Kent and John a Cumber, 136, 164, 165, 268
John, Little, 157
John of Wrotham, Sir, 129, 132, 133
JOHNSON, DR. SAMUEL and *Works*, 251, 252
Jolly Pinder of Wakefield, 157
JONSON, BEN, 77, 135, 141, 142, 162, 163, 170, 231, 266, 275; *Study of*, 163
Journalism, 226
Junius, 202
Justice, 19
JUVENAL, 207

KATHARINE, queen of Henry V., 37, 42; queen of Henry VIII., 14, 243, 251; Gordon, 262
KELLER, W., 99, 102
KEMP, THOMAS, 17, 196
Kenilworth, 15
Kendall, Earl of, 153, 154
Kent, villeins' revolt in, 45
Kent, Earl of (in *Lear*), 177; Edmund, Earl of, 69, 71, 72
Kind-Harts Dreame, 138
King Edward I., etc., see *Edward I.*, etc.
King of Scots, Tragedy of the, 40, 155
King's Company, 254
KIRK, JOHN, 260
KIRKMAN, FRANCIS, 183
Knack to Know a Knave, 17–19, 28
Knack to Know an Honest Man, 18
Koeniges Sohn aufs Engellandt, 169
KOEPPEL, E., 171
Kritische Schriften, 168, 170, 184
KYD, THOMAS, 56, 57
Kynge Johan, 16, 19, 28

LACEY, HENRY, 21, 23
LAMB, CHARLES, viii, 151, 256, 257
LAMBARDE, WILLIAM, 110
LANCASTER, House of, 7, 64, 75–78, 88, 139, 144, 271; EDMUND, EARL OF, 66; JOHN OF GAUNT, DUKE OF, 52, 99, 111, 220
LANEHAM, ROBERT, 15, 16
LANGBAINE, WILLIAM, 205, 206, 255, 265
LANGTON, STEPHEN, 17
Lansdowne MS. 723, 185
LaPoole, 104–108